LEADING ISSUES IN
INDIAN ECONOMY

LEADING ISSUES IN
INDIAN ECONOMY

Edited by

MANORANJAN SHARMA

ATLANTIC®
PUBLISHERS & DISTRIBUTORS

Published by

ATLANTIC®

PUBLISHERS & DISTRIBUTORS
B-2, Vishal Enclave, Opp. Rajouri Garden,
New Delhi-110027
Phones : 25413460, 25429987, 25466842

Sales Office
7/22, Ansari Road, Darya Ganj,
New Delhi–110002
Phones : 23273880, 23275880, 23280451
Fax : 91-11-23285873
web : www.atlanticbooks.com
e-mail : info@atlanticbooks.com

ISBN 81-269-0479-8

Printed in India
at Nice Printing Press, Delhi

PREFACE

In recent years, the process and pattern of India's economic development have undergone a profound change, a paradigm shift. While there is a fair degree of consensus that because of the far-reaching measures initiated in the wake of liberalisation the economy today is on a much sounder and stronger footing, the transformation of the Indian economy has evoked considerable debate. Some of the main strands of this debate relate to software companies like Infosys, Wipro, Tata Consultancy Services and a host of pharmaceutical and bio-technology companies becoming truly globally competitive, buoyant foreign exchange reserves, transformed Indian banks, surging business process outsourcing and strengthening of international economic relations between countries across a diverse spectrum. Simultaneously, in the aftermath of 9/11 and altered geo-political-economic realities, there has been a heightened consciousness of the key role of India—now and even more in the future. Clearly, India now has its own place in the sun. These are impressive achievements, particularly against the background of colonial subjugation and economic stagnation of nearly two centuries, the adoption of a 'mixed-economy' framework after achieving independence and the long shadow of the sluggish economic growth.

Things have perceptibly improved with the trend growth rate accelerating from 3.5 per cent in 1979 to 6.3 per cent today. But every-thing is not hunky-dory. At this defining moment of history, we should not be swayed by the hype and need to have a sense of balance and proportion for a realistic objective assessment of the tectonic forces at work.

There are persisting problems of fiscal deficit, inflation,

omnipresent corruption and still considerable, though greatly reduced, bureaucratic red tape. Hence, there is a need to ensure that the attainment of a higher growth trajectory does not remain a flash in the pan and becomes sustainable over the long haul by synchronised and concerted measures with a sense of urgency. There is also a manifest need to foster creativity, incubation and innovation and provide an enabling environment for patenting inventions on an increasingly larger scale. A renewed accent on infrastructure and labour market reforms, particularly a clearly delineated exit policy, is solely needed. And finally, development simply cannot bypass large sections of the population, particularly the poor, the deprived and the destitute — euphemistically called 'below the poverty line' — estimated at about 300 million. Solutions to the problems of extensive disguised unemployment, large and growing unemployment, extremely skewed distribution of income and wealth brook no delay. These are the challenges before us.

To be sure, the attainment of the Millennium Development Goals (MDGs), particularly against the revolution of rising expectations, necessitates significantly enhanced expenditure on the social dimension — education, health, drinking water and sanitation. Creation of what Amartya Sen called 'social safety nets' for the vulnerable sections of population requires massive investment — public and private, domestic and foreign — leading to higher growth and catalyzing employment. But in view of the past unhappy experience and myriad problems associated with financing, the litmus test of policy pronouncements lies in implementation of 'economic reforms with a human face'. Consequently, for persons at the 'bottom of the pyramid', what is more important is the plugging of widespread leakages and loopholes in the system. Unless such real and worrisome faultlines are repaired and there is a sharper focus on outcomes and not just on outlays, economic development will not be meaningful in the true sense of the term. Consequently, we immediately need to explore development options by addressing such issues. New game requires new rules and new strategies for equitable allocation of resources and attention to quality of economic growth. For, as Albert Einstein cogently argued, "we need a substantially new manner of thinking if mankind is to survive". There may not be immediate, easy answers since bringing about qualitative improvement and ensuring 'inclusive' growth is a dynamic process that must essentially be viewed in the context of long-term issue of significantly improving the quality of life and economic opportunities. More specifically, well-defined policy and procedures need include political will and determination to implement response actions for new initiatives, cooperation and coordinated action reflecting sectoral and regional differences and supplementing the role of markets by government orientation of actions to realise growth with distributive equity.

I express my deep gratitude to all contributors, who have worked hard to present their papers. The papers included in this volume cover a wide range of issues across the development spectrum including the globalization process, impact of financial sector reforms, integration of financial markets, rural finance, rural non-farm sector, fiscal reforms, etc. These papers should, by no means, be taken as exhaustive. They together, however, provide a perspective for future enquiry by providing meaningful information, critical examination and reflection on various themes of considerable contemporary significance to the Indian economy. It is hoped that the book would be useful to a wide cross section of the reading public, including scholars and academicians, the government, international institutions, business communities and planners and policy makers. I am grateful to Sri M.B.N. Rao, Chairman and Managing Director, Sri B. Swaminathan, Executive Director and Sri Gokuldas, General Manager, Canara Bank, Bangalore for their blessings and good wishes, which have been a source of strength and inspiration to me. I am also thankful to my friends and colleagues working in the Economic Research Section of Canara Bank for acting as a sounding board and providing help and assistance at all times.

I acknowledge the guidance received from my family members, for whom academic excellence is a way of life. I would particularly like to mention the role of my father, Professor D.D. Sharma (PhD) (Edinburgh), former Pro Vice-Chancellor, Lucknow University and my mother, late Dayamoyee Sharma, for instilling in me a passion for academic pursuits. I am thankful to my parents-in-law, Professor J.C. Choudhary and Mrs. Usha Choudhary for their constant encouragement and advice. I am deeply thankful to wife, Archana Choudhary, IRS for her support to me in all my professional and academic endeavours. I am also thankful to my children Utkarsh and Upasana who by their playful pranks made it possible for me to finish this work in a much longer time than would otherwise have been needed.

Manoranjan Sharma

CONTENTS

INTRODUCTION

The deregulation of the Indian economy, which started in the 1980s, received an impetus in 1991. While the balance of payments crisis may have provided the immediate trigger, there were structural and deeper long-term reasons underlying a paradigm shift of the economy in 1991. The post-independent economic history can easily be broken into three periods — 1951-79, 1980-91 and 1992-2004. Against the background of stagnation in 1900-50, India's GDP grew by a modest 3.5 per cent in 1951-79 — a growth rate which can be considered sluggish by any yardstick. During 1980-91, the country achieved a GDP growth little in excess of 5 per cent. But the economy's post-reforms (1992-2004) growth rate, with partial dismantling of license-quota-permit raj, has been good at about 6 per cent. Thus this period, which marks a decisive break with the past trend of macroeconomic growth, saw India exploring new avenues that led to the global superhighway. Significantly, data recently released by the IMF show that India recorded a whopping 46 per cent-plus growth in per capita income during 1992-2002, whereas the growth was negative in most countries — the US (-4.3 per cent), China (-6.6 per cent), Malaysia (-12.7 per cent), Singapore (-24.2 per cent), Indonesia (-36 per cent), Korea (-50.3 per cent), Taiwan (-50.6 per cent), Hong Kong (-51.4 per cent) and Thailand (-61.8 per cent). Explanatory factors for the increase in per capita income indicate "convergence" of appropriate policies — free flow of capital to the poorer countries, imitation of technological changes of the richer countries by the poorer ones, and positive cascading effects of information and communication technology (ICT) — which slash transaction costs and increase output for firms across sectors.

Against this backdrop, the debate about a resurgent India moved to central focus. This is as good as far it goes. But does it go far enough? Certainly not if the following dissonance is considered: A GDP growth of 8 per cent in 2003-04 implied a simple average of only 5.8 per cent between 1999-2000 and 2003-04 *vis-à-vis* 6.7 per cent in 1993-94 and 1997-98. Apart from the reliability of data about the rapid growth in services, there are also the issues of banks continuing to park their funds in government securities, the sustainability of the rise in the Index of Industrial Production (IIP), moderate rise in core infrastructure industries, uncertain merchandise growth and the fear of spiralling inflation. Further, high fiscal deficit and low domestic investment continue to cause concern and consternation.

Cross-cutting Strategic Themes

Post-independent India has also taken impressive strides in the spheres of economy, industry, banking, science and technology. Despite the milestones reached by India in these areas, there continue to be several grey areas, e.g., patents, functioning of several institutions, including R&D laboratories, set up by the CSIRs, etc. Given India's enormous resource endowment in terms of talent, skills and other resources, India has the potential of being in the forefront of technological revolution now sweeping across the world. The realisation of this potential is, however, contingent on putting in place an effective policy and operational frame to attain the avowed goals of development.

While India has to traverse some way before it can become a global manufacturing hub, low interest rates, surging demand and enhanced productivity-propelled corporate profitability and growth. The many arrows that point upwards include the recent $10 billion exports of information technology software; sale of components by Indian firms to 15 of the world's major automobile manufacturers; emergence of the Indian pharmaceutical industry as the fourth-largest in the world in terms of volume of production with a growth rate of 10 per cent a year; India becoming one of the three countries, apart from the US and Japan, to build supercomputers; and one of the six countries to launch communication satellites.

The second half of the 1990s and the initial years of new millennium were characterised by sweeping changes in scale of operation, adoption of technology, restructuring of marketing chains, introduction of IT and labour restructuring. Across sectors, over 91 per cent of the companies above Rs 500 crore in size effected changes relating to reduction of labour force and restructuring of the workforce to boost productivity. The restructuring includes focus on cost control, outsourcing, diversification, striking strategic alliances and re-engineering. Restructuring should ideally be vision driven and must encompass the whole organization to create a competitively superior company. The approach to restructuring of Indian firms evokes mixed feelings because of past experience, the fear of failure of radically new steps and governmental regulations. While restructuring domestic companies should develop a roadmap, detailing the investments required in certain areas and mobilization of resources through in-depth organizational analysis, strategic analysis, structured changes and attitudinal rehash.

Emerging Contours

Year 2004 was characterized by consolidation of the gains of economic reforms. Inflation through a mix of fiscal and monetary measures was reined in to 6.5 per cent by the end of the year. GDP growth in 2004-05 has been robust, capital inflows steady and the Indian stock market breached the psychological barrier of 6600 points of the sensitive index at the end of 2004 as the investors' confidence remained very high. Despite a large trade imbalance of 17 billion dollars in April-November, 2004, because of high oil prices and large non-oil imports reflecting industrial uptrend, India's balance of payments position is comfortable. Most development indicators seem to be positive with foreign exchange reserves rising from an abysmally low of 5 billion dollars in 1991 to above 130 billion dollars, the country's manufacturing acquiring a measure of international competitiveness, the onward march of the Indian financial system, likely acceleration in IT sector growth and enhanced trade and investment cooperation between India and ASEAN (Association of South East Asian Nations) countries.

Real GDP growth projection (RBI) at over 6.5-7.0 per cent during 2004-05 is based on the expectations of normal monsoon, sustenance in industrial sector, exceptionally good performance of services sector and external sector, projected inflation at around 6.5 per cent, money supply (M3) growth at 14 per cent and a robust 19 per cent increase in non-food credit. The services sector is expected to gain further momentum from the commodity producing sectors, particularly in the trade, transport and communication segments and in "new economy" activities.

Choices and Challenges

Management challenges confronting the Indian economy relate primarily to improving international competitiveness, professionalism and organizational effectiveness both in private and public sectors, greater openness in trade, especially in the post-WTO regime and enhancing resilience by laying long-term focus on planning and strengthening core competence based on competitive advantage.

There is a compelling need to make the economy more competitive, open and efficient through adoption of appropriate macroeconomic policies and financial standards. The government can play an enabling role in spurring growth through macroeconomic stability (with adequate safeguards), higher investment in physical infrastructure with adequate private initiative, scaling up social infrastructure (productive efficiency of human capital) and arresting fiscal deterioration. Recent global developments have significant implications for Indian corporations and policy makers. But structural factors, such as, steady southward movement of interest rates, industrial resurgence across key segments like steel, automobiles, pharmaceuticals and a range of engineering goods, infrastructural improvement, demographic change, ascendancy of the professional middle-class and emergence of the new entrepreneurial class substantiate the belief that the economy is resilient enough to withstand the adverse impact of exogenous shocks including oil price rises or interest rates changes or sharp variations in movements of major currencies.

While professionalism and organisational effectiveness — aspects intrinsic to the firm — would have to be the buzz words for success in the present differentiated system which represents social realities through its heterogeneity and variability, the role of the government continues to be important in reducing uncertainty and risk to the investors and savers and in enhancing the investments in physical infrastructure. At this defining moment of history, it thus becomes necessary for us to take advantage of a virtuous circle of higher growth, higher external capital inflows and higher domestic incomes and savings as an instrument of attaining and sustaining a higher growth trajectory. The Tenth Five-Year Plan (2002-07) foresees an annual growth rate of 8 per cent of real GDP during the plan period. To achieve this potential growth target, plan strategies entail high industrial growth of about 10 per cent per annum, further strengthening of disinvestment measures, policy reforms to boost foreign direct investment, measures to improve infrastructure and incentives to boost to services segments growth, especially IT and IT-enabled services and sunrise segments like biotech.

Theoretical Underpinning

The theoretical underpinning of the resurgence of the Indian economy is provided by the report, *The Path to 2050* (October 2003), by Dominic Wilson and Roopa Purushothaman of Goldman Sachs. The report argues that by 2050, BRIC (Brazil, Russia, India and China) would have a combined economic weighting larger than the current six largest economies (the US, Japan, Germany, the UK, France and Italy). Among the BRIC economies, India has the potential to grow even faster than China over the next 30 years and by 2010 India's growth rate should exceed that of China. The basis for this projection about India is driven largely by what is called the 'demographic dividend' India is likely to reap over the coming decades because of the sharp surge in its working population. In a similar vein, Roger Bootle (*Money for Nothing: Real Wealth, Financial Fantasies and the Economy of the Future,* Nicholas Brealey Publishing) contended that the opening up of India and China, in conjunction with the potential for gains from developments such as biotechnology, would usher in "the greatest increase in prosperity in our history." Faster economic growth, increased openness to trade, reduction in fiscal deficit, changes in exchange rate regime together with changes in social norms, culture, beliefs and fabrics of social interactions are indications of the resurgence and renaissance of India — an India that seems to have come of age.

Globalisation and its Impact on Developing Countries

Globalisation usually implies openness in trade, investment and free cross-country flow of capital. It is widely felt that India is well on the way to rapid globalization and transformation of the socio-economic milieu. But with a minuscule 0.7 per cent share in world trade, annual FDI inflow at 0.3/0.4 per cent of global FDI and low level of foreign institutional investment, India is not globalized — certainly not in a true and meaningful sense. However, 'globalization' has other connotations also like 'shrinkage' in distance due to technological changes and closer integration of product and financial markets worldwide. In this world of obliteration of geographical frontiers and emergence of a "global village", there has also been a greater awareness of the inexorable process of financial integration. Simply put, financial integration is a process of unification of various parts and sub-parts of financial markets. It occurs through elimination of domestic and international controls on trade in assets, goods or services. Integration of markets leads to price convergence as also convergence of various interest rates and minimum arbitrage profits among different markets. The 'services' revolution, currently on, offers advantages to India in terms of professional and knowledge-based services.

The Foreign Trade Policy (FTP) (2004-09) marks a departure from the earlier EXIM policies, through comprehensively addressing issues in India's foreign trade, goals and strategies by taking a holistic view of the overall development of India's foreign trade in a medium-term perspective and in the light of post-WTO developments. The two-pronged objectives of the policy envisage doubling India's percentage share of global merchandise trade by 2009 and enabling employment generation, especially in semi-urban and rural areas. In order to achieve these objectives, the new foreign trade policy stressed unshackling of controls, creating an atmosphere of trust and transparency, simplifying procedures and bringing down transaction costs, adopting the fundamental principle that duties and levies should not be imposed and identifying and nurturing different special focus areas to facilitate development of India as a global hub for manufacturing, trading and services. Sectors with significant export prospects coupled with potential for employment generation in semi-urban and rural areas have been identified as thrust sectors and accordingly, specific sectoral strategies have been chalked out. Threshold limit for designated 'Towns of Export Excellence' has been brought down from Rs. 1000 crore to Rs. 250 crore in these thrust sectors. Special initiatives for agriculture, handicrafts, handlooms, gems & jewellery and leather and footwear sectors have been announced. Foreign trade policy of India, while specifically targeting India's trade share as percentage of global trade to 1.5 per cent by 2009, emphasised foreign trade as a mode for furthering overall economic development, especially in rural and semi-urban areas. It is expected that these measures will usher in a new era of foreign trade for India in a multilateral trade setting under WTO.

The emerging international financial architecture encompassing the issues of capital account liberalisation, market determined exchange rates, short-term debt and foreign exchange reserves needs to be discussed from the standpoint of developing countries in a proper historical and comparative perspective. The collapse of the Bretton Wood's model because of its inherent weaknesses has made it necessary to forge an equal partnership between developed and developing countries. Towards this end, it is necessary to provide greater representation to developing countries on the boards of the IMF and the IBRD with a larger voting power in view of the dramatically altered present-day ground realities.

Of late, the growth of the global economy has been remarkably synchronised and broad-based led by buoyant growth in emerging Asia, particularly China and India and a robust turnaround in the US. Incipient recovery in the Euro area, upbeat economic activity in Japan and resurgent growth in many emerging market economies (EMEs) make the realisability of a higher growth trajectory of the global economy a distinct possibility. The determinants of global growth and the policy requirements for sustaining the present momentum, both at regional and multilateral levels, need to be evaluated in conformity with this tentative rejigging of the economic balance of power.

An important concern for the developing countries is that insufficient human and financial resources and weak institutional capacities restrict the ability of many developing countries to exploit the opportunities open to them under the WTO system, particularly in respect of its dispute settlement mechanism as well as the ability to comply fully with multilateral obligations. The nature of capital inflows into developing countries underwent a sea change in the past three decades and capital inflows did not necessarily generate growth in these countries. There were several shortcomings regarding the size, stability and sustainability of capital flows to developing countries. There was a marked increase in the instability of private capital flows to developing countries and an important part of the capital inflow constituted an unreliable source of development finance.

Fiscal Deficit

Fiscal deficit is regarded as the best available summary indicator of the macroeconomic impact of the budget because excessive government borrowing tends to crowd out private investment, increase inflationary potential, weaken the balance of payments, render bringing of financial sector reforms more difficult and impose a serious burden on future generations. Reduction in fiscal deficit has thus emerged as an important policy objective of the Government. With a view to bringing down the revenue and fiscal deficit of the Central Government and cap its borrowings, the Government of India adopted the Fiscal Responsibility and Budget Management (FRBM) Bill. The major targets of the FRBM Act included elimination of revenue deficit by March 31, 2008, reduction of fiscal deficit to 2 per cent of GDP by end of fiscal year 2008-09, and restricting the total liabilities of the Central government to 50 per cent of the estimated GDP at the end of a period of ten years. In view of the gravity of the situation, it is necessary, as cogently argued by Professor A.K. Singh, to slash the level of fiscal and revenue deficits to sustainable levels, get the growth of unproductive revenue expenditure curbed, public expenditure restructured by reducing revenue expenditure and increasing capital expenditure, and the ratio of government revenues, both tax and non-tax, to GDP increased by widening and diversifying the services tax basket.

While the Tenth Plan estimated fiscal deficit of the Centre and the States at 8.8 per cent and the Eleventh Finance Commission had pegged it at 6.5 per cent by 2004-05, it was perilously close to 10 per cent in 2002-03. As the former RBI Governor and Chairman of the 12th Finance Commission, Dr C. Rangarajan, pointed out, "failure to step up expenditure on necessary items (such as physical and social infrastructure) or failure to achieve fiscal consolidation will dampen the growth momentum."

The Road Ahead

The shift towards a market-oriented economy by the Government and other regulatory authorities has significant implications for the structural changes in the economy. There are many daunting challenges hampering the ushering in of a "new deal". In the ultimate analysis, the crux of the issue lies in a revival of investment (particularly in manufacturing), a transformation of agriculture, check on deficits of the Central and State governments, privatisation, change in labour laws, availability of efficient and sufficient infrastructure at reasonable cost, rise in per capita income, reduced regional disparities and the social dimension of growth — a sharper focus on employment, health, education, housing and gender equality. So, where do we go from here? What policy options and instruments do we have at this defining moment of history? There is a need to support the ongoing transition in the rural sectors in the region by facilitating financial support and technical assistance for rural, environment and social development by examining the synergistic and interdependent relationship between development of rural communities and broad-based socio-economic 'inclusive' development.

The relationship between finance and development has evoked wide interest in the annals of economic history down through the ages. It has been increasingly realized that a strong and resilient financial system and the orderly evolution of financial markets is central to sustained economic development. On the basis of a close examination of the East

Asian crisis of 1997, the nature of the financial markets and emerging policy prescriptions, it could reasonably be maintained that financial reforms and liberalisation of markets are only means to an end and not ends in themselves. In the ultimate analysis, the success of the development strategy rests on a sustained and rising income for all the people and removal of poverty and deprivation within a reasonable time frame.

Agricultural Growth and Diversification

Indian agriculture performed reasonably well in the post-Green Revolution period with total agricultural output (at 1990-93 prices) increasing at a compound annual growth rate of about 2.7 per cent. Since the mid-1960s, yield contributed 85 per cent of incremental agricultural output. During the Ninth Plan, the agricultural gross domestic product (GDP) grew, however, by a measly 1.81 per cent *vis-à-vis* the target of 4.5 per cent per annum and the foodgrains production grew by a lower rate of 1.2 per cent per annum, which failed to offset even the 2 per cent rise in population. Further, about 600 million of India's billion-plus population depends on the farm sector, which generates a quarter of gross domestic product. The farm sector is also a crucial driver of other parts of Asia's fourth-biggest economy through important forward and backward linkages. This is why *The Approach Paper to the Tenth Plan* stressed the need for the agriculture sector to grow by 4 per cent for stepping up the overall GDP growth rate to 8 per cent per annum. Hence, notwithstanding the rapid growth in the service sector in the recent past, it is important to ensure that the quest for higher GDP growth does not render us oblivious to the distributive aspect of growth. In view of the agriculture sector's still sizeable contribution to the national economy, source of livelihood to the teeming millions and its implications for the fragile state of food security, agriculture continues to be the pivot around which socio-economic privileges and deprivations revolve. The growth and transformation of agriculture requires, *inter alia*, spread of insurance against crop losses, development of commodity-derivatives market to minimise the impact of price uncertainties and facilities for meeting the entire needs of the rural economy, measures to enhance productivity, spread the effects of seed-fertiliser technology to other parts, structural changes in the composition of foodgrains production and reduction in the extent of vulnerability to variations in agricultural output by increasing and stabilising agricultural production. An important element of the resuscitation path could be the pursuit of a regionally differentiated strategy taking into account the agronomic, climatic and environmental conditions to realise the full potential of all regions. Measures announced in the Union Budget, 2004-05, such as a nation-wide water-harvesting scheme, restoration of water bodies and restructured Accelerated Irrigation Benefit Programme (AIBP) are contextually significant in keeping the agricultural economy on track. In the Agriculture Summit 2005 organized by the Agriculture Ministry and the Federation of Indian Chambers of Commerce & Industry (FICCI), the Prime Minister Dr. Manmohan Singh stressed on a Second Green Revolution based on the application of new technologies and modern business practices.

The production of foodgrains has been characterised by pronounced peaks and troughs around a rising trend. While troughs are inevitable in the short-run because of uncertain weather, the development strategy justifiably attempts to iron-out troughs in the long run. Gross capital formation in agriculture underwent a sharp decline mainly on account of a steady erosion in the share of public investment with deleterious impact on Indian agriculture. The increase in private sector capital formation has been concentrated in areas with uninterrupted availability of water, power and other inputs together with large subsidy. Irrigation coverage remains distinctly lower than the potential in terms of the gross cropped area. Insufficient village electrification has adversely affected the expansion of irrigation coverage, the growth of processing industries and cold storage facilities. A sustainable growth of the Indian economy, therefore, depends not just on agricultural rebound but also a step-up in public investment in agriculture and rural infrastructure to boost productivity, growth and poverty alleviation. Diversification of agriculture with an accent on demand-driven products with value addition and agro-processing industry acquires a sense of immediacy in the present circumstances.

Food price stabilization is essential in developing countries to provide food security and incentives for farmers. But some of the means used are inefficient and others lend themselves to capture by interest groups. Two changes suggest a possible new solution. First, trade at the margin in agriculture should rise with new agreements under WTO. Second, the currency crises of the nineties have shown the superiority of a managed float for developing country exchange rates. If the exchange rate has to be managed, one way to do so is to vary the nominal exchange rate to partially neutralize variations in world food prices. This, combined with more liberal agricultural trade, can help to stabilize agricultural prices, lower the dependence on the other more distortionary policies, and provide a possible resolution for political deadlocks that make it difficult to remove subsidies. The benefits for macroeconomic policy come from inflation stabilization, more degrees of freedom, and exchange rate behaviour that reduces currency risk. An incisive analysis of Indian experience in the 1990s by Professor Ashima Goyal suggests that the rule would have been beneficial.

Rural Development

In view of the criticality of rural non-farm sector (RNFS) in accelerating 'growth' and bringing about 'equity' through creation of gainful employment and economic inter-linkages between agriculture and the non-farm sector, RNFS has become a potent force in transforming socio-economic life. Though credit is an essential input to foster the growth of RNFS, in the ultimate analysis, RNFS has to improve its productivity and efficiency by adopting modern technology to produce competitive goods and services.

With increasing accent on mechanisation for higher productivity and production gradually decreasing the labour force, the Planning Commission's Task Force on Employment Opportunities stressed the need for a long-term strategy for absorbing the rural labour force in the non-agricultural sector, e.g., rural infrastructure like roads, market places and irrigation and water management. The Tenth Plan (2002-07), by introducing a paradigm shift envisaged agriculture and allied activities as growth engines for rural development by promotion of non-farm activities for value-addition and sustainability in a healthy competitive environment so that rural areas could be provided urban amenities at rural rates. In drawing up RNFS development plans, we have necessarily to identify key aspects, such as, identification and diversification, holistic versus piecemeal, bottom up versus top down, demand driven versus supply driven, group approach versus individual approach, subsidised input cost versus full recovery, vertical and horizontal linkages between RNFS and large industries, effective management, participatory planning and institutional restructuring for successful implementation. Against this backdrop, the issues of productivity, value addition, marketing, credit, infrastructure, resource and technology dissemination, resource management, etc., need to be examined in an ambiance of liberalization, structural reform and globalisation for the RNFS to successfully meet the relentless onslaughts of the market forces.

Distributive Equity

Systematic redressal of the felt needs on a priority basis encompass several thematic groups. The rural policy reforms, agri-business development and strengthening rural finance, restructuring services including irrigation, agricultural research and extension, environmental management and biodiversity conservation, a sound and credible regulatory system and social development constitute some of the key elements of the vision to meaningfully refashion the development strategy. Decisive action on what Professor Amartya Sen (*India: Economic Development and Social Opportunity*) called "the central issue" of "expand(ing) the social opportunities open to the people" is needed to transform the socio-economic milieu. This is a tall order, particularly when, as demonstrated by the recent FAO (Food and Agriculture Organisation) report entitled *State of Food Insecurity in the World, 2003*, over a fifth of India's population still suffers from chronic hunger. What is even more galling is that the incidence of hunger over three reference periods — 1990-92, 1995-97 and 1999-2001 — registered an initial decline from 214.5 million to 194.7 million, before a near total reversal increased the number of the undernourished to 213.7 million. Without quibbling over the details of various surveys, it can safely be maintained that the grim employment scenario reveals a rapid erosion of opportunities, a decline in self-employment and the growing "casualisation" of labour. All this necessitates discernible improvement of the thrust on compelling socio-economic issues, such as basic employment, education, health, women's empowerment and so on, to improve the quality of life of the teeming population. Midcourse corrections needed to reach a new renaissance require coordinated and concerted action with a sense of urgency to meet the challenges of the present and the expectations of the future.

Manoranjan Sharma

1

Financial Sector Reforms in India: Policies and Performance Analysis*

RAKESH MOHAN**

I. Introduction

As the economy grows and becomes more sophisticated, the banking sector has to develop *pari pasu* in a manner that it supports and stimulates such growth. With increasing global integration, the Indian banking system and financial system has as a whole had to be strengthened so as to be able to compete. India has had more than a decade of financial sector reforms during which there has been substantial transformation and liberalisation of the whole financial system. It is, therefore, an appropriate time to take stock and assess the efficacy of our approach. It is useful to evaluate how the financial system has performed in an objective quantitative manner. This is important because India's path of reforms has been different from most other emerging market economies: it has been a measured, gradual, cautious, and steady process, devoid of many flourishes that could be observed in other countries.

Until the beginning of the 1990s, the state of the financial

* Expanded version of lectures by Dr. Rakesh Mohan, Deputy Governor, Reserve Bank of India at the International Monetary Fund, Washington D.C. on September 2, 2004 and at a seminar "Global Banking: Paradigm Shift" organised by the Federation of Indian Chambers of Commerce and Industries, Bangalore on September 16, 2004. He would like to acknowledge the assistance of Sujan Hajra and Partha Ray in the preparation of this paper.

** Reproduced from October 2004 issue of Reserve Bank of India Bulletin.

sector in India could be described as a classic example of "financial repression" *a la* MacKinnon and Shaw. The sector was characterised, *inter alia*, by administered interest rates, large pre-emption of resources by the authorities and extensive micro-regulations directing the major portion of the flow of funds to and from financial intermediaries. While the true health of financial intermediaries, most of them public sector entities, was masked by relatively opaque accounting norms and limited disclosure, there were general concerns about their viability. Insurance companies — both life and non-life — were all publicly owned and offered very little product choice. In the securities market, new equity issues were governed by a plethora of complex regulations and extensive restrictions. There was very little transparency and depth in the secondary market trading of such securities. Interest rates on government securities, the predominant segment of fixed-income securities, were decided through administered fiat. The market for such securities was a captive one where the players were mainly financial intermediaries, who had to invest in government securities to fulfil high statutory reserve requirements. There was little depth in the foreign exchange market as most such transactions were governed by inflexible and low limits and also prior approval requirements.

Compartmentalisation of activities of different types of financial intermediaries eliminated the scope for competition among existing financial intermediaries. In addition, strong entry barriers thwarted competition from new entrants. The end result was low levels of competition, efficiency and productivity in the financial sector, on the one hand, and severe credit constraints for the productive entities, on the other, especially for those in the private sector. The other major drawback of this regime was the scant attention that was placed on the financial health of the intermediaries. Their capitalisation levels were low. The lack of commercial considerations in credit planning and weak recovery culture resulted in large accumulation of non-performing loans. This had no impact on the confidence of depositors, however, because of government ownership of banks and financial intermediaries.

The predominance of Government securities in the fixed-income securities market of India mainly reflects the captive nature of this market as most financial intermediaries need to invest a sizable portion of funds mobilised by them in such securities. While such norms were originally devised as a prudential measure, during certain periods, such statutory norms pre-empted increasing proportions of financial resources from intermediaries to finance high Government borrowings. The interest rate on Government debt was administered and the rate of interest charged by the Reserve Bank of India (RBI) for financing Government deficit was concessional. On top of this, there were limited external capital flows. Such a closed-economy set-up kept debt markets underdeveloped and devoid of any competitive forces. In addition, there was hardly any secondary market for Government securities, and such transactions were highly opaque and operated through over-the-telephone deals. The provision of fiscal accommodation through *ad hoc* treasury bills led to high levels of monetisation of fiscal deficit during the major part of the 1980s.

The phase of nationalisation and 'social control' of financial intermediaries, however, was not without considerable positive implications as well. The sharp increase in rural branches of banks increased deposit and savings growth considerably. There was a marked rise in credit flow towards economically important but hitherto neglected activities, most notably agriculture and small-scale industries. The urban-bias and marked preference of banks to lend to the industrial sector, especially large industrial houses, was contained. The implicit guarantee emanating from public ownership created an impression of infallibility of these institutions and the expectation was self-fulfilling — there was no major episode of failure of financial intermediaries in this period.

Starting from such a position, it is widely recognised that the Indian financial sector over the last decade has been transformed into a reasonably sophisticated, diverse and resilient system. However, this transformation has been the culmination of extensive, well-sequenced and coordinated policy measures aimed at making the Indian financial sector efficient, competitive and stable.

The main objectives, therefore, of the financial sector reform process in India initiated in the early 1990s have been to:

- Remove financial repression that existed earlier;
- Create an efficient, productive and profitable financial sector industry;
- Enable price discovery, particularly, by the market determination of interest rates that then helps in efficient allocation of resources;
- Provide operational and functional autonomy to institutions;
- Prepare the financial system for increasing international competition;
- Open the external sector in a calibrated fashion;
- Promote the maintenance of financial stability even in the face of domestic and external shocks.

Since there is a rich array of literature analysing the anthology of the reform process *per se,* the story of policy reforms in the India financial sector since the early 1990s is quite well-known.[1] What is less probed, however, is the outcome. In fact, from the vantage point of 2004, one of the successes of the Indian financial sector reform has been the maintenance of financial stability and avoidance of any major financial crisis during the reform period — a period that has been turbulent for the financial sector in most emerging market countries. The domain of analysis of the paper is, however, somewhat limited. Specifically, this paper limits itself to the impact analysis of financial sector reforms in the areas where the Reserve Bank of India has had a dominant role. These include the banking sector, foreign exchange and government securities markets and also the conduct of monetary policy.

The rest of the paper is organised as follows. Section II provides the rationale of financial sector reforms in India. While policy reforms in the financial sector are dealt with in section III, section IV is devoted to reforms in the monetary policy framework. Against this brief chronicle of the financial sector reforms process, I shall look into the outcomes of the financial sector reform process in section V in some detail. Instead of presenting any concluding observations, I shall raise some issues in the last section.

II. Financial Sector Reforms: The Approach

The initiation of financial reforms in the country during the early 1990s was to a large extent conditioned by the analysis and recommendations of various Committees/Working Groups set-up to address specific issues. The process has been marked by 'gradualism' with measures being undertaken after extensive consultations with experts and market participants. From the beginning of financial reforms, India has resolved to attain standards of international best practices but to fine tune the process keeping in view the underlying institutional and operational considerations (Reddy, 2002a). Reform measures introduced across sectors as well as within each sector were planned in such a way so as to reinforce each other. Attempts were made to simultaneously strengthen the institutional framework while enhancing the scope for commercial decision-making and market forces in an increasingly competitive framework. At the same time, the process did not lose sight of the social responsibilities of the financial sector. However, for fulfilling such objectives, rather than using administrative fiat or coercion, attempts were made to provide operational flexibility and incentives so that the desired ends are attended through broad interplay of market forces.

The major aim of the reforms in the early phase of reforms, known as first generation of reforms, was to create an efficient, productive and profitable financial service industry operating within the environment of operating flexibility and functional autonomy. While these reforms were being implemented, the world economy also witnessed significant changes, 'coinciding with the movement towards global integration of financial services' [Government of India (GoI), 1998]. The focus of the second phase of financial sector reforms starting from the second-half of the 1990s, therefore, has been the strengthening of the financial system and introduction of structural improvements.

Two brief points need to be mentioned here. *First,* financial reforms in the early 1990s were preceded by measures aimed at lessening the extent of financial repression. However, unlike in the latter period, the earlier efforts were not part of a well-thought out and comprehensive agenda for extensive reforms. *Second,* financial sector reform in India was an important component of the comprehensive economic reform process initiated in the early 1990s. Whereas economic reforms in India were also initiated following an external sector crisis, unlike many other emerging market economies where economic reforms were driven by crisis followed by a boom-bust pattern of policy liberalisation, in India, reforms followed a consensus driven pattern of sequenced liberalisation across the sectors (Ahluwalia, 2002). That is why despite several changes in government there has not been any reversal of direction in the financial sector reform process over the last 15 years.

As pointed out by Governor Reddy (Reddy, 2002a), the approach towards financial sector reforms in India is based on *panchasutra* or five principles:

1. Cautious and appropriate sequencing of reform measures.
2. Introduction of norms that are mutually reinforcing.
3. Introduction of complementary reforms across sectors (most importantly, monetary, fiscal and external sector).
4. Development of financial institutions.
5. Development of financial markets.

An important salient feature of the move towards globalisation of the Indian financial system has been the intent of the authorities to more towards international best practices. This is illustrated by the appointment of several advisory groups designed to benchmark Indian practices with international standards in several crucial areas of importance like monetary policy, banking supervision, data dissemination, corporate governance and the like. Towards this end, a Standing Committee on International Financial Standards and Codes (Chairman: Dr. Y.V. Reddy) was constituted and the recommendations contained therein have either been implemented or are in the process of implementation.

Having delineated the broad philosophy, let me now turn to specifics of reform. I will paint the story of Indian reform with a broad brush so as to provide a context of the impact analysis that follows.

III. Policy Reforms in the Financial Sector

Banking Reforms

Commercial banking constitutes the largest segment of the Indian financial system. Despite the general approach of the financial sector reform process to establish regulatory convergence among institutions involved in broadly similar activities, given the large systemic implications of the commercial banks, many of the regulatory and supervisory norms were initiated first for commercial banks and were later extended to other types of financial intermediaries.

After the nationalisation of major banks in two waves, starting in 1969, the Indian banking system became predominantly government owned by the early 1990s. Banking sector reform essentially consisted of a two pronged approach. While nudging the Indian banking system to better health through the introduction of international best practices in prudential regulation and supervision early in the reform cycle, the idea was to increase competition in the system gradually. The implementation periods for such norms were, however, chosen to suit the Indian situation. Special emphasis was placed on building up the risk management capabilities of the Indian banks. Measures were also initiated to ensure flexibility, operational autonomy and competition in the banking sector. Active steps have been taken to improve the institutional arrangements including the legal framework and technological system within which the financial institutions and markets operate. Keeping in view the crucial role of effective supervision in the creation of an efficient and stable banking system, the supervisory system has been revamped. Stylised features of the banking sector reforms have been given in Box I.

Unlike in other emerging market countries, many of which had the presence of government owned banks and financial institutions, banking reform has not involved large scale privatisation of such banks. The approach, instead, first involved recapitalisation of banks from government resources to bring them up to appropriate capitalisation standards. In the second phase, instead of privatisation, increase in capitalisation has been done through diversification of ownership to private

Box I: Reforms in the Banking Sector

A. Prudential Measures

- Introduction and phased implementation of inter-national best practices and norms on risk-weighted capital adequacy requirement, accounting, income recognition, provisioning and exposure.
- Measures to strengthen risk management through recognition of different components of risk, assignment of risk-weights to various asset classes, norms on connected lending, risk concentration, application of marked-to-market principle for investment portfolio and limits on deployment of fund in sensitive activities.

B. Competition Enhancing Measures

- Granting of operational autonomy to public sector banks, reduction of public ownership in public sector banks by allowing them to raise capital from equity market up to 49 per cent of paid-up capital.
- Transparent norms for entry of Indian private sector, foreign and joint-venture banks and insurance companies, permission for foreign investment in the financial sector in the form of Foreign Direct Investment (FDI) as well as portfolio investment, permission to banks to diversify product portfolio and business activities.

C. Measures Enhancing Role of Market Forces

- Sharp reduction in pre-emption through reserve requirement, market determined pricing for government securities, disbanding of administered interest rates with a few exceptions and enhanced transparency and disclosure norms to facilitate market discipline.
- Introduction of pure inter-bank call money market, auction-based repos-reverse repos for short-term liquidity management, facilitation of improved payments and settlement mechanism.

D. Institutional and Legal Measures

- Settling up of *Lok Adalats* (people's courts), debt recovery tribunals, asset reconstruction companies, settlement advisory committees, corporate debt restructuring mechanism, etc. for quicker recovery/restructuring. Promulgation of Securitisation and Reconstruction of Financial Assets and Enforcement of Securities Interest (SARFAESI), Act and its subsequent amendment to ensure creditor rights.
- Setting up of Credit Information Bureau for information sharing on defaulters as also other borrowers.
- Setting up of Clearing Corporation of India Limited (CCIL) to act as central counter party for facilitating payments and settlement system relating to fixed income securities and money market instruments.

E. Supervisory Measures

- Establishment of the Board for Financial Supervision as the apex supervisory authority for commercial banks, financial institutions and non-banking financial companies.
- Introduction of CAMELS supervisory rating system, move towards risk-based supervision, consolidated supervision of financial conglomerates, strengthening of off-site surveillance through control returns.
- Recasting of the role of statutory auditors, increased internal control through strengthening of internal audit.
- Strengthening corporate governance, enhanced due diligence on important shareholders, fit and proper tests for directors.

F. Technology Related Measures

- Setting up of INFINET as the communication backbone for the financial sector, introduction of Negotiated Dealing System (NDS) for screen-based trading in government securities and Real Time Gross Settlement (RTGS) System.

investors up to a limit of 49 per cent, thereby keeping majority ownership and control with the government. With such widening of ownership most of these banks have been publicly listed; this was designed to introduce greater market discipline in bank management, and greater transparency through enhanced disclosure norms. The phased introduction of new private sector banks, and expansion in the number of foreign bank branches, provided for new competition. Meanwhile, increasingly tight capital adequacy, prudential and supervision norms were applied equally to all banks, regardless of ownership.

Debt Market Reforms

Major reforms have been carried out in the government securities (G-Sec) debt market. In fact, it is probably correct to say that a functioning G-Sec debt market was really initiated in the 1990s. The system had to essentially move from a strategy of pre-emption of resources from banks at administered interest rates and through monetisation to a more market oriented system. Prescription of a "statutory liquidity ratio" (SLR), *i.e.,* the ratio at which banks are required to invest in approved securities, though originally devised as a prudential measure, was used as the main instrument of pre-emption of bank resources in the pre-reform period. The high SLR requirement created a captive market for government securities, which were issued at low administered interest rates. After the initiation of reforms, this ratio has been reduced in phases to the statutory minimum level of 25 per cent. Over the past few years numerous steps have been taken to broaden and deepen the Government securities market and to raise the levels of transparency. Automatic monetisation of the Government's deficit has been phased out and the market borrowings of the Central Government are presently undertaken through a system of auctions at market-related rates. Major facets of the reforms in the government securities are provided in Box II.

The key lesson learned through this debt market reform process is that setting up such a market is not easy and needs a great deal of proactive work by the relevant authorities. An appropriate institutional framework has to be created for

Box II: Reforms in the Government Securities Market

Institutional Measures

- Administered interest rates on government securities were replaced by an auction system for price discovery.
- Automatic monetisation of fiscal deficit through the issue of *ad hoc* Treasury Bills was phased out.
- Primary Dealers (PD) were introduced as market makers in the government securities market.
- For ensuring transparency in the trading of government securities, Delivery *versus* Payment (DvP) settlement system was introduced.
- Repurchase agreement (repo) was introduced as a tool of short-term liquidity adjustment. Subsequently, the Liquidity Adjustment Facility (LAF) was introduced. LAF operates through repo and reverse repo auctions to set up a corridor for short-term interest rate. LAF has emerged as the tool for both liquidity management and also signalling device for interest rates in the overnight market.
- Market Stabilisation Scheme (MSS) has been introduced, which has expanded the instruments available to the Reserve Bank for managing the surplus liquidity in the system.

Increase in Instruments in the Government Securities Market

- 91-day Treasury bill was introduced for managing liquidity and benchmarking. Zero Coupon Bonds, Floating Rate Bonds, Capital Indexed Bonds were issued and exchange traded interest rate futures were introduced. OTC interest rate derivatives like IRS/FRAs were introduced.

Enabling Measures

- Foreign Institutional Investors (FIIs) were allowed to invest in government securities subject to certain limits.
- Introduction of automated screen-based trading in government securities through Negotiated Dealing System (NDS). Setting up of risk—free payments and settlement system in government securities through Clearing Corporation of India Limited (CCIL). Phased introduction of Real Time Gross Settlement System (RTGS).
- Introduction of trading of government securities on stock exchanges for promoting retailing in such securities, permitting non-banks to participate in repo market.

such a market to be built and operated in a sustained manner. Legislative provisions, technology development, market infrastructure such as settlement systems, trading systems, and the like have all to be developed.

Foreign Exchange Market Reforms

The Indian forex exchange market had been heavily controlled since the 1950s, along with increasing trade controls designed to foster import substitution. Consequently, both the current and capital accounts were closed and foreign exchange was made available by the Reserve Bank of India through a complex licensing system. The task facing India in the early 1990s was therefore to gradually move from total control to a functioning foreign exchange market. The move towards a market-based exchange rate regime in 1993 and the subsequent adoption of current account convertibility were the key measures in reforming the Indian foreign exchange market. Reforms in the foreign exchange market focused on market development with prudential safeguards without destabilising the market (Reddy, 2002a). Authorised Dealers of foreign exchange have been allowed to carry on a large range of activities. Banks have been given large autonomy to undertake foreign exchange operations. In order to deepen the foreign exchange market, a large number of products have been introduced and entry of newer players has been allowed in the market. Highlights of reforms in the foreign exchange market have been given in Box III.

The Indian approach to opening the external sector and developing the foreign exchange market in a phased manner from current account convertibility to the ongoing process of capital account opening is perhaps the most striking success relative to other emerging market economies. There have been no accidents in this process, the exchange rate has been market determined and flexible and the process has been carefully calibrated. The capital account is effectively convertible for non-residents, but has some way to go for residents. The Indian approach has perhaps gained greater international respectability after the enthusiasm for rapid capital account opening has been dimmed since the Asian crisis.

Box III: Reforms in the Foreign Exchange Market

Exchange Rate Regime

- Evolution of exchange rate regime from a single-currency fixed-exchange rate system to fixing the value of rupee against a basket of currencies and further to market-determined floating exchange rate regime.
- Adoption of convertibility of rupee for current account transactions with acceptance of Article VIII of the Articles of Agreement of the IMF. *De facto* full capital account convertibility for non-residents and calibrated liberalisation of transactions undertaken for capital account purposes in the case of residents.

Institutional Framework

- Replacement of the earlier Foreign Exchange Regulation Act (FERA), 1973 by the market friendly Foreign Exchange Management Act, 1999. Delegation of considerable powers by RBI to Authorised Dealers to release foreign exchange for a variety of purposes.

Increase in Instruments in the Foreign Exchange Market

- Development of rupee-foreign currency swap market.
- Introduction of additional hedging instruments, such as, foreign currency-rupee options. Authorised dealers permitted to use innovative products like cross-currency options, interest rate and currency swaps, caps/collars and forward rate agreements (FRAs) in the international forex market.

Liberalisation Measures

- Authorised dealers permitted to initiate trading positions, borrow and invest in overseas market subject to certain specifications and ratification by respective Banks' Boards. Banks are also permitted to fix interest rates on non-resident deposits, subject to certain specifications, use derivative products for asset-liability management and fix overnight open position limits and gap limits in the foreign exchange market, subject to ratification by RBI.
- Permission to various participants in the foreign exchange market, including exporters, Indians investing abroad, FIIs, to avail forward cover and enter into swap transactions without any limit subject to genuine underlying exposure.
- FIIs and NRIs permitted to trade in exchange-traded derivative contracts subject to certain conditions.
- Foreign exchange earners permitted to maintain foreign currency accounts. Residents are permitted to open such accounts within the general limit of US $ 25,000 per year.

Reforms in Other Segments of the Financial Sector

Measures aimed at establishing prudential regulation and supervision and also competition and efficiency enhancing measures have also been introduced for non-bank financial intermediaries as well. Towards this end, non-banking financial companies (NBFCs), especially those involved in public deposit taking activities, have been brought under the regulation of RBI. Development Finance Institutions (DFIs), specialised term-lending institutions, NBFCs, Urban Cooperative Banks and Primary Dealers have all been brought under the supervision of the Board for Financial Supervision (BFS). With the aim of regulatory convergence for entities involved in similar activities, prudential regulation and supervision norms were also introduced in phases for DFIs, NBFCs and cooperative banks.

The insurance business remained within the confines of public ownership until the late 1990s. Subsequent to the passage of the Insurance Regulation and Development Act in 1999, several changes were initiated, including allowing newer players/joint ventures to undertake insurance business on risk-sharing/commission basis. The Insurance Regulatory and Development Agency (IRDA) has been established to regulate and supervise the insurance sector.

With the objective of improving market efficiency, increasing transparency, integration of national markets and prevention of unfair practices regarding trading, a package of reforms comprising measures to liberalise, regulate and develop capital market was introduced. An important step has been the establishment of the Securities and Exchange Board of India (SEBI) as the regulator for equity markets. Since 1992, reform measures in the equity market have focused mainly on regulatory effectiveness, enhancing competitive conditions, reducing information asymmetries, developing modern technological infrastructure, mitigating transaction costs and controlling of speculation in the securities market. Another important development under the reform process has been the opening up of mutual funds to the private sector in 1992, which ended the monopoly of Unit Trust of India (UTI), a public sector entity. These steps have been buttressed by measures to promote market integrity.

The Indian capital market was opened up for foreign institutional investors (FIIs) in 1992. The Indian corporate sector has been allowed to tap international capital markets through American Depository Receipts (ADRs), Global Depository Receipts (GDRs), Foreign Currency Convertible Bonds (FCCBs) and External Commercial Borrowings (ECBs). Similarly, Overseas Corporate Bodies (OCBs) and non-resident Indians (NRIs) have been allowed to invest in Indian companies. FIIs have been permitted in all types of securities including Government securities and they enjoy full capital convertibility. Mutual funds have been allowed to open offshore funds to invest in equities abroad.

IV. Reform in the Monetary Policy Framework

What has been the change in monetary policy in the wake of these changes in different market segments as well as sectors? The transition of economic policies in general, and financial sector policies in particular, from a control oriented regime to a liberalised but regulated regime has also been reflected in changes in the nature of monetary management. While the basic objectives of monetary policy, namely price stability and ensuring adequate credit flow to support growth, have remained unchanged, the underlying operating environment for monetary policy has undergone a significant transformation. An increasing concern is the maintenance of financial stability. The basic emphasis of monetary policy since the initiation of reforms has been to reduce market segmentation in the financial sector through increase in the linkage between various segments of the financial market including money, government securities and forex market. Major features of the reforms in the monetary policy framework have been provided in Box IV.

The key policy development that has enabled a more independent monetary policy environment was the discontinuation of automatic monetisation of the government's fiscal deficit through an agreement between the Government and the Reserve Bank of India in 1997. The enactment of the Fiscal Responsibility and Budget Management Act has strengthened this further : from 2006, the Reserve Bank will no longer be permitted to subscribe to government securities

Box IV: Reforms in the Monetary Policy Framework

Objectives

- Twin objectives of "maintaining price stability" and "ensuring availability of adequate credit to productive sectors of the economy to support growth" continue to govern the stance of monetary policy, though the relative emphasis on these objectives has varied depending on the importance of maintaining an appropriate balance.
- Reflecting development of financial market and liberalisation, use of broad money as an intermediate target has been de-emphasised and a multiple indicator approach has been adopted.
- Emphasis has been put on development of multiple instruments to transmit liquidity and interest rate signals in the short-term in a flexible and bi-directional manner.
- Increase of the linkage between various segments of the financial market including money, government security and forex markets.

Instruments

- Move from direct instruments (such as, administered interest rates, reserve requirements, selective credit control) to indirect instruments (such as, open market operations, purchase and repurchase of government securities) for the conduct of monetary policy.
- Introduction of Liquidity Adjustment Facility (LAF), which operates through repo and reverse repo auctions to set up a corridor for short-term interest rate. LAF has emerged as the tool for both liquidity management and also as a signalling devise for interest rate in the overnight market.
- Use of open market operations to deal with overall market liquidity situation especially those emanating from capital flows.
- Introduction of Market Stabilisation Scheme (MSS) as an additional instrument to deal with capital inflows without affecting short-term liquidity management role of LAF.

Developmental Measures

- Discontinuation of automatic monetisation through an agreement between the Government and the Central Bank. Rationalisation of Treasury Bill market. Introduction of delivery versus payment system and deepening of inter-bank repo market.
- Introduction of Primary Dealers in the government securities market to play the role of market maker.
- Amendment of Securities Contracts Regulation Act to create the regulatory framework.
- Deepening of government securities market by making the interest rates on such securities market related. Introduction of auction of government securities. Development of a risk-free credible yield curve in the government securities market as a benchmark for related markets.
- Development of pure inter-bank call money market. Non-bank participants to participate in other money market instruments.
- Introduction of automated screen-based trading in government securities through Negotiated Dealing System (NDS). Setting up of risk-free payments and system in government securities through Clearing Corporation of India Limited (CCIL). Phased introduction of Real Time Gross Settlement (RTGS) System.
- Deepening of forex market and increased autonomy of Authorised Dealers.

in the primary market. The development of the monetary policy framework has also involved a great deal of institutional initiatives to enable efficient functioning of the money market: development of appropriate trading, payments and settlement systems along with technological infrastructure.

Against this discussion of what has been done, let me now turn to what the process has led to in the Indian financial sector.

V. Performance of the financial sector under the reform process

Banking Sector

Banking sector reform has established a competitive system driven by market forces. The process, however, has not resulted in disregard of social objectives such as maintenance of the wide reach of the banking system or channelisation of credit towards disadvantaged but socially important sectors. At the same time, the reform period experienced strong balance sheet growth of the banks in an environment of operational flexibility. A key achievement of the banking sector reform has been the sharp improvement in the financial health of banks, reflected in significant improvement in capital adequacy and improved asset quality. This has been achieved despite convergence of the prudential norms with the international best practices.[2] There have also been substantial improvements in the competitiveness of the Indian banking sector reflected in the changing composition of assets and liabilities of the banking sector across bank groups. In line with increased competitiveness, there has been improvement in efficiency of the banking system reflected *inter alia* in the reduction in interest spread, operating expenditure and cost of intermediation in general. Contemporaneously there have been improvements in other areas as well including technological deepening and flexible human resource management. A more detailed discussion on the performance analysis of the banking sector under the reform process is given below.

Social Objectives and Balance Sheet Management

The Indian banking system has acquired a wide reach, judged in terms of expansion of branches and the growth of credit and deposits (Tables 1 and 2). The expansion of branch network peaked in the phase of social banking during the 1970s and 1980s. Despite the slowdown in branch expansion since the 1990s, the population per bank branch, however, has not changed much since the 1980s, and has remained at around 15,000. It is often asserted that the Indian banking sector is saddled with too many branches, adding to its high-intermediation costs. In fact, at about 8-10,000, the population per branch in developed countries is lower than that in India. Therefore, the reform process has maintained the gains in terms of the outreach of bank branches achieved in the phase of social banking.

TABLE 1: Progress of Commercial Banking in India

Indicators	June 1969	June 1980	March 1991	March 1995	March 2000	March 2001
1. No. of Commercial Banks	73	154	272	284	298	292
2. No. of Bank Offices	8,262	34,594	60,570	64,234	67,868	68,561
Of which:						
Rural and semi-urban bank offices	5,172	23,227	46,550	46,602	47,693	47,496
3. Population per Office ('000s)	64	16	14	15	15	16
4. Per capita Deposit (Rs.)	88	738	2.368	4,242	8,542	12,253
5. Per capita Credit (Rs.)	68	457	1.434	2.320	4,555	7,275
6. Priority Sector Advances @ (per cent)	15.0	37.0	39.2	33.7	35.4	33.7*
7. Deposits (per cent of National Income)	15.5	36.0	48.1	48.0	53.5	51.8

@ : Share of Priority Sector Advances in Total Non-food Credit of Scheduled Commercial Bank.

* : As at end-March 2002.

Source : Reserve Bank of India.

Despite a decline, direct lending to disadvantaged segments of the economy under the priority sector advances remained high during the reform period. The decline in priority sector lending since the initiation of reforms in fact reflects greater flexibility provided to banks to meet such targets. Currently, in the event a bank fails to meet the priority sector lending target through direct lending, the bank can invest the shortfall amount with the apex organisations dealing with flow of funds towards agriculture and small-scale industries. While adherence

TABLE 2: Select Balance Sheet Indicators of Commercial Banks Operating in India

(Per cent)

Years	As a Ratio of Total Assets/Liabilities			
	Deposits	Total investments	Non-SLR Investment	Loans and Advances
1991-92	77.7	28.9	..	46.8
	(17.1)	(28.4)	..	(13.7)
1992-93	78.4	30.5	..	45.0
	(13.9)	(19.0)	..	(8.6)
1993-94	80.3	35.4	5.0	38.7
	(15.5)	(31.1)	..	-(3.0)
1994-95	78.9	33.6	4.6	40.5
	(16.3)	(12.2)	(9.4)	(24.0)
1995-96	76.4	31.0	3.5	42.1
	(12.7)	(7.4)	-(11.71)	(20.9)
1996-97	79.9	33.3	5.0	41.0
	(17.5)	(20.6)	(60.2)	(9.2)
1997-98	81.0	34.2	7.1	40.8
	(19.8)	(21.5)	(69.3)	(17.6)
1998-99	81.1	35.7	8.6	38.8
	(19.7)	(24.9)	(45.3)	(13.9)
1999-00	81.1	37.3	9.1	40.2
	(16.3)	(21.3)	(22.4)	(20.3)
2000-01	81.5	38.0	8.9	40.6
	(17.7)	(19.3)	(14.2)	(18.5)
2001-02	78.5	38.2	8.7	42.0
	(14.3)	(19.4)	(16.5)	(22.7)
2002-03	79.8	40.8	8.1	43.6
	(12.4)	(18.1)	(3.3)	(14.7)
2003-04*	80.5	41.7	7.2	45.0
	(17.5)	(19.7)	(2.9)	(15.3)

* Based on supervisory returns.
.. : Not available.
SLR : Statutory Liquidity Ratio.
Note : Figures in brackets are annual growth rates.
Source : Reserve Bank of India.

of banks to the norms on direct lending towards the priority sector still remains desirable, the current arrangement reflects how the reform process has provided operational flexibility to banks even while meeting social objectives.

The discernible increase in the proportion of bank deposits to national income is reflective of the enhanced deepening of the Indian financial system during the period. Simultaneously, there have been considerable increases in per capita deposits and credit. This also implies an increase in the average business per bank branch, which is likely to have improved the viability of individual bank branches including those in the rural and semi-urban centres.

In the post-reform period, banks have consistently maintained high rates of growth in their assets and liabilities. This is particularly credible given the low inflationary situation that prevailed in this period compared to the earlier periods, most notably in the 1980s. On the liability side, there has not been much compositional change since the initiation of reforms whereby deposits continue to account for about 80 per cent of the total liabilities. On the asset side, however, there is a definite increase in the share of investments. While the share of loans and advances did decline in the 1990s, it has recovered in recent years.

Despite the large decline in SLR in the 1990s,[3] the sharp increase in investments by banks is reflective of their attempt to evolve treasury operations into profit centres. The reduction in cash reserve ratio and improved inter-office adjustments in a substantially computerised and networked environment, *inter alia*, did free up substantial amounts of bank resources, which enabled banks to concentrate on investment operations with greater vigour.

Interestingly, despite the reduced regulatory requirement to invest in government and other securities approved for SLR investment, the major increase in investment operations by Indian banks since the mid 1990s has been on account of their investment in government securities. This reflects the sustenance of high fiscal deficits of both central and state governments, particularly after the Pay Commission award leading to increase in the government salary bill in 1997. Furthermore, subdued industrial growth since 1997 also led to lower credit demand, providing banks further incentive to place their resources in risk-free government securities. It is also possible that, in a declining interest rate scenario in the presence of a developing debt market, this was a rational profit maximising strategy. Banks' investment in non-SLR securities as a proportion of total assets has in fact declined since 1999-2000. While in the 1990s, greater orientation towards investment activities and aversion to credit risk exposure may have deterred banks from undertaking their 'core function' of providing loans and advances, banks seem to have struck a greater balance between investment and loans and advances in recent years. Improved atmosphere for recovery created in the recent years coupled with greater awareness about market risks associated with large holding of securities portfolio seem to have induced banks to put greater efforts in extending loans.

Capital Position and Asset Quality

A set of micro-prudential measures have been stipulated since the onset of reforms aimed at imparting strength to the banking system as well as ensuring safety and soundness in order to fix 'the true position of bank's balance sheet and... to arrest its deterioration' (Rangarajan, 1998). With regard to prudential requirements, norms for income recognition and asset classification (IRAC), introduced in 1992, have been strengthened over the years in line with international best practices. A strategy to attain CRAR of 8 per cent in a phased manner was put in place and subsequently the level was raised to 9 per cent with effect from 1999-2000.

The overall capital position of commercial sector banks has witnessed a marked improvement during the reform period (Table 3). Illustratively, as at end-March 2003, 91 out of the 93 commercial banks operating in India maintained CRAR at or above 9 per cent. The corresponding figure for 1995-96 was 54 out of 92 banks.[4]

Improved capitalisation of public sector banks was initially brought through substantial infusion of funds by government to recapitalise these banks. On a cumulative basis, infusion of funds by government into the public sector banks since the initiation of reforms for the purpose of recapitalisation amounted to less than 1 per cent of India's GDP, a figure much lower than that for some other countries. Subsequently, in order to reduce pressure on the budget and to introduce

TABLE 3: Distribution of Commercial Banks According to Risk-weighted Capital Adequacy

(Number of banks)

Year	Below 4 per cent	Between 4-9 per cent*	Between 9-10 per cent@	Above 10 per cent	Total
1995-96	8	9	33	42	92
1996-97	5	1	30	64	100
1997-98	3	2	27	71	103
1998-99	4	2	23	76	105
1999-00	3	2	12	84	101
2000-01	3	2	11	84	100
2001-02	1	2	7	81	91
2002-03	2	0	4	87	93

* : Relates to 4-8 per cent before 1999-2000.

@ : Relates to 8-10 per cent before 1999-2000.

Note : According to supervisory returns, only 2 banks failed to maintain statutory minimum CRAR of 9 per cent as at end-March 2004. Out of these two, one is scheduled to achieve the minimum CRAR level by September 2004 and other has since been placed under moratorium and merged with another bank.

Source : Reserve Bank of India.

market discipline, public sector banks have been allowed to raise funds through issue of equity in the market subject to the maintenance of 51 per cent public ownership. 20 out of the 27 public sector banks have raised capital from the market (Table 4). In order to improve their price-earning ratios, many public sector banks have also returned part of government's equity subscription. Another important factor in the improvement in capital position of banks operating in India stemmed from deployment of retained earnings out of increased profits.

The reform period also witnessed considerable improvements in the asset quality of banks. Non-performing loans (NPLs) as ratios of both total advances and assets declined substantially and consistently since the mid-1990s. Moreover, for the first time since the initiation of reforms, in 2002-03, the absolute amount of NPLs in both gross and net terms witnessed declines (Table 5). This improved recovery

TABLE 4: Ownership Structure of Public Sector Banks

(As at end-March 2004, Per cent)

	Government/ RBI Share	Share of Others
Nationalised Banks		
Vijaya Bank	53.9	46.1
Corporation Bank	57.2	42.8
Union Bank of India	60.9	39.2
Indian Overseas Bank	61 .2	38.8
Andhra Bank	62.5	37.5
Oriental Bank of Commerce	66.5	33.5
Bank of Baroda	66.8	33.2
Bank of India	69.5	30.5
Dena Bank	71.0	29.0
Allahabad Bank	71.2	28.8
Canara Bank	73.2	26.8
Syndicate Bank	73.5	26.5
UCO Bank	75.0	25.0
Bank of Maharashtra	76.8	23.2
Punjab National Bank	80.0	20.0
Central Bank of India	100.0	0.0
Indian Bank	100.0	0.0
Punjab & Sind Bank	100.0	0.0
United Bank of India	100.0	0.0
State Bank Group		
State Bank of India	59.7	40.3
State Bank of Bikaner & Jaipur	75.0	25.0
State Bank of Travancore	75.0	25.0
State Bank of Mysore	92.3	7.7
State Bank of Indore	98.1	2.0
State Bank of Hyderabad	100.0	0.0
State Bank of Patiala	100.0	0.0
State Bank of Saurashtra	100.0	0.0

Source : Reserve Bank of India.

performance raises a few interesting issues. First, from the pattern of NPLs over the years, it can be argued that to a large extent the NPL problems faced by Indian banks are legacy problems emanating from credit decisions taken before the full implementation of the banking sector reforms. Second, there has been a distinct improvement in the credit appraisal process in the Indian banking system under the reform process

TABLE 5: NPL of Scheduled Commercial Banks

(Per cent)

	Gross NPL/ advances	Gross NPL/ Assets	Net NPL/ advances	Net NPL/ Assets
Scheduled commercial banks				
1996-97	15.7	7.0	8.1	3.3
1997-98	14.4	6.4	7.3	3.0
1998-99	14.7	6.2	7.6	2.9
1999-00	12.7	5.5	6.8	2.7
2000-01	11.4	4.9	6.2	2.5
2001-02	10.4	4.6	5.5	2.3
2002-03	8.8	4.0	4.4	1.9
2003-04*	7.3	..	3.0	..
Public sector banks				
1996-97	17.8	7.8	9.2	3.6
1997-98	16.0	7.0	8.2	3.3
1998-99	15.9	6.7	8.1	3.1
1999-00	14.0	6.0	7.4	2.9
2000-01	12.4	5.3	6.7	2.7
2001-02	11.1	4.9	5.8	2.4
2002-03	9.4	4.2	4.5	1.9
Old private sector banks				
1996-97	10.7	5.2	6.6	3.1
1997-98	10.9	5.1	6.5	2.9
1998-99	13.1	5.8	9.0	3.6
1999-00	10.8	5.2	7.1	3.3
2000-01	10.9	5.1	7.3	3.3
2001-02	11.0	5.2	7.1	3.2
2002-03	8.9	4.3	5.5	2.6
New private sector banks				
1996-97	2.6	1.3	2.0	1.0
1997-98	3.5	1.5	2.6	1.1
1998-99	6.2	2.3	4.5	1.6
1999-00	4.1	1.6	2.9	1.1
2000-01	5.1	2.1	3.1	1.2
2001-02	8.9	3.9	4.9	2.1
2002-03	7.6	3.8	4.6	2.2
Foreign banks in India				
1996-97	4.3	2.1	1.9	0.9
1997-98	6.4	3.0	2.2	1.0
1998-99	7.6	3.1	2.9	1.1
1999-00	7.0	3.2	2.4	1.0
2000-01	6.8	3.0	1.8	0.8
2001-02	5.4	2.4	1.9	0.8
2002-03	5.2	2.4	1.8	0.8

NPL : Non-performing loans.
* : Based on supervisory returns.
.. : Not available.
Note : Bank group specific details for 2003-04 are not available.
Source : Reserve Bank of India.

whereby incremental NPLs have been low despite the fact that Indian industry has gone through a relatively low-growth phase since the mid-1990s. Finally, in recent years, the recovery performance of public sector banks has been better than private sector banks both old and new — in terms of net NPL (*i.e.* net of provisioning). Foreign banks, however, exhibited the best recovery performance and lowest NPL levels among the all bank-groups. This raises a question mark on the applicability of the argument that links performance of banks with ownership pattern in the context of Indian banking.

Another interesting point that merits mention is that despite India's transition to a 90-day NPL recognition norm (from 180-day norm) since 2004, both gross and net NPLs as a percentage of total advances declined between end-March 2003 and end-March 2004. This reflects the success of new initiatives for resolution of NPLs including promulgation of the SARFAESI[5] Act in containing NPLs. Greater provisioning and write-off of NPLs in the face of greater profitability also helped keeping the NPLs low during 2003-04.

Competition and Efficiency

One of the major objectives of banking sector reforms has been to enhance efficiency and productivity through enhanced competition. Such policies have led to considerable and consistent reduction in the shares of public sector banks in the total income, expenditure and assets of the commercial banking system (Table 6). Shares of Indian private sector banks, especially new private sector banks established in the 1990s, in the total income and assets of the banking system have improved considerably since the mid-1990s. A number of new private sector banks have emerged as dynamic components of the Indian banking system, reducing not only the market share of public sector banks but also those of foreign banks. The reduction in the asset share of foreign banks, however, is partially due to their increased focus on off-balance sheet non-fund based business.

Notwithstanding such transformation, the position of public sector banks in the Indian banking system continues to be predominant as these banks account for nearly three-fourths of assets and income. It is important to note that public

TABLE 6: Bank Group-wise Shares: Select Indicators

(Per cent)

	1995-96	2000-01	2002-03
Public Sector Banks			
Income	82.5	78.4	74.5
Expenditure	84.2	78.9	74.8
Total Assets	84.4	79.5	75.7
Net Profit	-39.1	67.4	64.8
Gross Profit	74.3	69.9	76.6
Private Sector Banks			
Income	8.2	12.6	18.5
Expenditure	7.4	12.3	18.6
Total Assets	7.7	12.6	17.5
Net Profit	59.3	17.8	15.6
Gross Profit	10.1	14.4	18.7
Foreign Banks			
Income	9.4	9.1	7.0
Expenditure	8.3	8.8	6.6
Total Assets	7.9	7.9	6.9
Net Profit	79.8	14.8	19.6
Gross Profit	15.6	15.7	4.7

Source : Reserve Bank of India.

sector banks have responded to the new challenges of competition, which is reflected in the increase in share of these banks in the overall profit of the banking sector. From the position of net loss in the mid-1990s, in recent years the share of public sector banks in the profit of the commercial banking system has become broadly commensurate with their share of assets, indicating a broad convergence of profitability across various bank groups. This is yet another example that, with operational flexibility, public sector banks are competing effectively with private sector and foreign banks. The market discipline imposed by the listing of most public sector banks has also probably contributed to this improved performance. Public sector bank managements are now probably more attuned to the market consequences of their activities.

Since the mid-1990s, profitability levels of commercial banks have hovered in the range of 0.7-0.8 per cent, except during certain exceptional years (Table 7). Clearly this is an improvement over the profitability prior to the initiation of the reform process. Moreover, there is a general improvement in the profitability situation in the recent years across bank groups. Since the mid-1990s, consistent with soft interest rate policies, both interest income and interest expenditure of banks as proportions of total assets have declined. However, interest expenditure declined faster than interest income, resulting in an increase in net interest income (Table 7).

TABLE 7: Earnings and Expenses of Scheduled Commercial Banks

(Rs. billion)

Year	Total Assets	Total Earning	Interest Earnings	Total Expenses	Interest Expenses	Establishment Expenses	Net Interest Earnings
1951	12	1	0	0	0	0	0
		(3.8)	(3.1)	(2.6)	(0.9)	(1.3)	(2.2)
1969	68	4	4	4	2	1	2
		(6.2)	(5.3)	(5.5)	(2.8)	(2.1)	(2.5)
1980	582	42	38	42	27	1.0	10
		(7.3)	(6.4)	(7.2)	(4.7)	(1.7)	(18)
1991	3,275	304	275	297	190	76	86
		(9.3)	(8.4)	(9.1)	(5.8)	(2.3)	(2.6)
2000	11,055	1,149	992	1,077	690	276	301
		(10.4)	(9.0)	0.7)	(6.2)	(2.5)	(2.7)
2002	15,355	1,510	1,270	1,395	875	337	395
		(9.8)	(8.3)	(9.1)	(5.7)	(2.2)	(2.6)
2003	16,989	1,724	1,407	1,553	936	3,809	471
		(10.2)	(8.3)	(9.1)	(5.5)	(2.2)	(2.8)

Note : Figures in brackets are ratios to total assets.
Source : Reserve Bank of India.

Reflecting the greater emphasis on income and expenditure management, there has been a general reduction in the operating expenditure as a proportion of total assets (Table 7). This is also reflective of efficiency gain of the Indian banking under the reform process. This has been achieved in spite of large expenditures incurred by Indian banks in installation and upgradation of information technology. Moreover, in order to address manpower redundancies, public sector banks also incurred large expenditures under voluntary pre-mature retirement of nearly 12 per cent of their total staff strength. The process, however, resulted in reduced operating expenditure in the medium-term.

Another reflection of greater competition and efficiency of the Indian banking system can be captured from the considerable reduction in interest spread over the reform period. Once again, this reduction has been across the bank-groups. In fact, the spread is the highest for foreign banks and lowest for new private sector banks (Table 8).

TABLE 8: Important Parameters for Indian Banking Sector

(Per cent)

Bank Group	1996-97	2001-02	2002-03
Operating Expenses/Total Assets			
Scheduled Commercial Banks	2.9	2.2	2.2
Public Sector Banks	2.9	2.3	2.3
Old Private Sector Banks	2.5	2.1	2.0
New Private Sector Banks	1.9	1.1	2.0
Foreign Banks	3.0	3.0	2.8
Spread/Total Assets			
Scheduled Commercial Banks	3.2	2.6	2.8
Public Sector Banks	3.2	2.7	2.9
Old Private Sector Banks	2.9	2.4	2.5
New Private Sector Banks	2.9	1.2	1.7
Foreign Banks	4.1	3.2	3.4
Net Profit/Total Assets			
Scheduled Commercial Banks	0.7	0.8	1.0
Public Sector Banks	0.6	0.7	1.0
Old Private Sector Banks	0.9	1.1	1.2
New Private Sector Banks	1.7	0.4	0.9
Foreign Banks	1.2	1.3	1.6

Note : Spread = interest income – interest expenditure.
Source: Reserve Bank of India.

A major impact of the reform process on the Indian banking has been in terms of change in business strategy of the banks. When banking sector reforms were introduced, over 90 per cent of the income of commercial banks in India was in the form of interest income, this proportion has gone down substantially to about 80 per cent in recent years. This reflects greater diversification of banks into non-fund based business and also emergence of treasury and foreign exchange business as profit centres for Indian banks.

Inflexibility of the Indian labour market is often identified as one of the weak points of the Indian reform process. It is, however, important to note that as a part of financial sector reforms, 26 out of the 27 public sector financial intermediaries have been successful in restructuring their workforce, which involved downsizing of the labour force by 12 per cent. Such steps have resulted in decline in staff cost and increase in business per employee.

This brief quantitative review of the performance of the Indian banking sector documents the very significant improvements that have occurred over the decade of reforms. The performance parameters of Indian banks are now approaching international standards and they are among the better performers in the emerging market group (Table 9). As both domestic and international competition intensifies, it will be essential for Indian banks to further improve their efficiency and also deploy better their resources as fiscal dominance declines.

Debt Market

In nominal terms, fiscal deficit of the central government has increased substantially since the early 1990s and as a proportion of GDP it has hovered around 6 per cent. However, more importantly, the dependence of government on market borrowings has increased sharply in this period. The outstanding stocks of both Centre and State Government debt each increased by about 10 times since the initiation of reforms (Table 10). From around 20 per cent in the early 1990s, share of net market borrowing in financing fiscal deficit of the Central Government has increased to 80 per cent in recent years (Table 11).

Despite such rapid increase in market borrowing and continued dominance of financial intermediaries, especially banks, in the government securities market, there has been substantial reduction in the yield as well as cost of borrowing of the Government (Tables 12 and 13). While a major part of such reductions are in line with the high liquidity phase of the global financial market witnessed in the past few years, the reduction in yield and interest rate started much earlier, indicating efficiency gains in the government securities market.

TABLE 9: Cross-Country Performance Analysis of Banks

(Per cent)

	Country	2001	2002	2003	Latest
	Gross Non-Performing Loans to Total Loans				
Latin America	Argentina[1]	13.2	17.5	22.7	November
	Brazil	5.7	5.3	5.7	June
	Mexico	5.1	4.6	3.7	September
Asia	China	29.8	25.5	22.0	June
	India	11.4	10.4	8.8	March
	Indonesia	11.9	5.8		
	Malaysia	17.8	15.9	14.8	June
	Philippines	16.9	15.4	15.2	September
	Singapore	3.6	3.4	3.5	September
	Thailand	10.5	15.8	15.5	August
Memo	US[3]	1.4	1.6	1.3	September
	UK	2.6	2.6	2.2	June
	Japan	6.6	8.9	7.2	September
	Profitability of Major Banks				
Latin America	Argentina	-0.2	-9.7	-2.5	August
	Brazil	0.2	1.9	1.9	June
	Mexico	0.8	-1.1	1.6	September
Asia	China	0.1	0.1	..	
	India	0.5	0.8	1.0	March
	Indonesia	0.8	1.3	..	
	Malaysia	1.0	1.3	..	
	Philippines	0.4	0.8	1.0	September
	Singapore	0.8	0.8	0.8	September
	Thailand	-0.1	0.4	1.1	August
Memo	US[1]	1.1	1.4	1.4	September
	UK[2,3]	0.5	0.9	0.5	June
	Japan[2]	0.1	0.0	..	September

.. Not available.

[1] With asset exceeding US $ I billion.

[2] Before tax.

[3] Includes mortgage banks.

Source : Global Financial Stability Report, April 2004.

TABLE 10: Outstanding Stock of Central and State Government Securities

(Amounts in Rs. Billion, Ratios in Per cent)

	1992	1995	2000	2003	2004
Centre	769	1,375	3,819	6,739	8,243
	(10.3)	(11.6)	(18.1)	(27.3)	(29.7)
States	190	312	739	1,331	1,795
	(2.5)	(2.6)	(3.5)	(5.4)	(6.5)

Note : Figures in bracket are outstanding debt as a ratio of GDP at current market prices.
Source : Reserve Bank of India.

TABLE 11: Share of Market Borrowing in Financing of Fiscal Deficit of Central Government

(Per cent)

	Market Borrowing	Other Sources
1991-92	20.7	79.3
1992-93	9.2	90.8
1993-94	48.0	52.0
1994-95	35.2	64.8
1995-96	54.9	45.1
1996-97	30.0	70.0
1997-98	36.5	63.5
1998-99	60.9	39.1
1999-2000	67.1	32.9
2000-01	61.4	38.6
2001-02	62.2	37.8
2002-03	79.3	20.7
2003-04	67.2	32.8

Source : Reserve Bank of India.

TABLE 12: Range of Yield by Maturity of Primary Issues

(Per cent)

	Under 5 years	5-10 years	Over 10 years
1995-96	13.25-13.73	13.25-14.00	–
1996-97	13.40-13.72	13.55-13.85	–
1997-98	10.85-12.14	11.15-13.05	–
1998-99	11.40-11.68	11.10-12.25	12.25-12.60
1999-00	–	10.73-11.99	10.77-12.45
2000-01	9.47-10.95	9.88-11.69	10.47-11.70
2001-02	–	6.98-9.81	7.18-11.00
2002-03	–	6.65-8.14	6.84-8.62
2003-04	4.69	4.62-5.73	5.18-6.35

Source : Reserve Bank of India.

TABLE 13: Weighted Average Yield and Maturity of Outstanding Stock

(Maturity in years and Yield in Per cent)

Years	Weighted Average Yield	Range of Maturity of New Loans	Weighted Average Maturity	Weighted maturity of outstanding stock
1995-96	13.75	2-10	5.7	N.A.
1996-97	13.69	2-10	5.5	N.A.
1997-98	12.01	3-10	6.6	6.5
1998-99	11.86	2-20	7.7	6.3
1999-00	11.77	5.26-19.61	12.6	7.1
2000-01	10.95	2.89-20	10.6	7.5
2001-02	9.44	5-25	14.26	8.2
2002-03	7.34	7-30	13.83	8.86
2003-04	5.74	4-30	14.94	9.78

Source: Reserve Bank of India.
N.A. : Not available.

Between the mid- and late-1990s, there has been a substantial widening of maturity profile of government securities, which has reduced the roll-over risk of government debt. Apart from reduction in yield, the dispersion of yield rate on different types of government securities has also declined considerably. These positive developments, to a large extent, reflect the improved market structure for the government securities since the initiation of reforms. Reflecting the buoyancy of the fixed-income securities market in India, despite almost secular decline in yield rate across the maturity spectrum, the turnover in the market has increased over ten-times between 1998-99 and 2003-04 (Table 14) (Mohan, 2004).

TABLE 14: Turnover in Government Securities Market

(Rs. billion)

Years	Outstanding	Repos	Total
1995-96	176	928	1,272
1996-97	599	254	1.229
1997-98	1,185	208	1,857
1998-99	1,431	381	2,272
1999-00	4,053	757	5.393
2000-01	5,091	1,091	6,981
2001-02	11,385	3,359	14,744
2002-03	13,781	5,635	19,416
2003-04	16,852	9,547	26,399

Source : Reserve Bank of India.

Foreign Exchange Market

The reforms measures in the foreign exchange market have resulted in significant deepening of the market in terms of both instruments and variety of players. Despite certain fluctuations, daily average turnover in the Indian foreign exchange market has shown a general increase. A survey by the Bank for International Settlements on the foreign exchange market turnover during 2001 in which 43 countries including India participated reveals that while foreign exchange market turnover declined the world over considerably as compared to 1998, it increased in India. The turnover has increased particularly in recent years (Table 15).

TABLE 15: Turnover in Indian Foreign Exchange Market

(US $ billion)

Year	Average Daily Turnover
1998	5.22
1999	5.31
2000	4.74
2001	5.74
2002	5.95
2003	6.34

Source : Reserve Bank of India.

In recent years, the turnover in the foreign exchange market has been nearly 6 times higher than the aggregate size of India's balance of payments. While inter-bank transactions accounted for about 80 per cent of the turnover in the foreign exchange market, merchant transactions registered high growth rates in recent years. The increased turnover can be taken as an indicator of the extent of liberalisation of the Indian foreign exchange market and the consequent deepening of the foreign exchange market. Full convertibility on the current account and extensive liberalisation of the capital account transactions have facilitated not only transactions in foreign currency, these have enabled the corporates to hedge various types of risks associated with foreign currency transactions.

Authorised Dealers (ADs) are the leading agencies in the transmission of the liberalisation measures in the context of foreign exchange market as well as widening and deepening of such markets. ADs also facilitate corporates in hedging foreign currency risk exposures. With the deepening of foreign exchange market and increased turnover, income of commercial banks through such transactions increased considerably. In recent years, profit from foreign exchange transactions accounted for 20-30 per cent of the total profit of the public sector banks.

Despite liberalisation of the capital account and introduction of a market determined exchange rate, the foreign exchange market in India remained stable barring a few episodes of mild volatility (Table 16). Therefore, India's current exchange rate policy of managing volatility without fixed target levels has yielded satisfactory results.

It is, however, important to point out that RBI intervention in the foreign exchange market has been relatively small in terms of volume. During 2002-03, a year considered to be characterised by considerable intervention by the Reserve Bank, gross intervention by the Reserve Bank of India accounted for less than 3 per cent of the turnover in the foreign exchange market. This shows the predominant role of market forces in determination of the external value of the rupee.

Reflecting the resilience of the Indian economy, in particular the financial sector, there has been a large inflow of funds towards the country in recent years. This has reflected in large accumulation of foreign exchange reserves (Table 17).

An analysis of the sources of reserve accretion indicates that buoyancy in services exports, large unilateral private transfers reflecting mainly remittance from Diaspora, and various types of non-debt creating capital inflows have been the major source for the accumulation of foreign exchange reserves. It is interesting to note that while financial sector reforms started at the backdrop of external sector crisis, India's foreign exchange reserves reached historical peaks when the country has substantially liberalised norms governing flows of foreign exchange. Accumulation of foreign exchange reserves also reflects monetary policy response in face of large capital

TABLE 16: Trends in External Value of the Rupee

(Per cent)

Year	Export-Based Weights				Trade-Based Weights			
	REER	% Variation	NEER	% Variation	REER	% Variation	NEER	% Variation
1990-91	73.3	-5.2	66.2	-7.6	75.6	-3.6	67.2	-6.9
1991-92	61.4	-16.3	51.1	-22.8	64.2	-15.1	52.5	-21.9
1992-93	54.4	-11.3	42.3	-17.3	57.1	-11.1	43 5	-17.2
1993-94	59.1	8.6	43.5	2.8	61.6	7.9	44.7	2.8
1994-95	63.3	7.1	42.2	-2.9	66.0	7.2	43.4	-2.9
1995-96	60.9	-3.7	38.7	-8.2	63.6	-3.7	39.7	-8.4
1996-97	61.1	0.3	38.1	-1.7	63.8	0.3	39.0	-1.9
1997-98	63.8	4.3	38.9	2.2	67.0	5.0	40.0	2.7
1998-99	60.1	-5.7	35.3	-9.3	63.4	-5.3	36.3	-9.2
1999-00	59.7	-0.7	34.3	-2.9	63.3	-0.2	35.5	-2.4
2000-01	62.5	4.6	34.2	-0.2	66.5	5.1	35.5	0.2
2001-02	64.4	3.0	34.5	0.9	68.4	2.8	35.8	0.7
2002-03	67.9	5.5	35.4	2.5	72.8	6.3	37.1	3.6
2003-04	69.7	2.6	349	-1.5	74.1	1.9	36.3	-2.2

REER : Real effective exchange rate. NEER : Nominal effective exchange rate.
Note : Both REER and NEER are based on 36 country bilateral weight-based index.
Source : Reserve Bank of India.

TABLE 17: India's Foreign Exchange Reserves

(US $ million)

Year	Cold	SDRs	Foreign Currency	Total	Reserve Position in the Fund	Outstanding Position Use of IMF Credit
Mar-93	3,380	18	6,434	9,832	296	4,799
Mar-94	4,078	108	15,068	19,254	299	5,040
Mar-95	4,370	7	20,809	25,186	331	4,300
Mar-96	4,561	82	17,044	21,687	310	2,374
Mar-97	4,054	2	22,367	26,423	291	1,313
Mar-98	3,391	1	25,975	29,367	283	664
Mar-99	2,960	8	29,522	32,490	663	287
Mar-00	2,974	4	35,058	38,036	658	26
Mar-01	2,725	2	39,554	42,281	616	0
Mar-02	3,047	10	51,049	54,106	610	0
Mar-03	3,534	4	71,890	75,428	672	0
Mar-04	4,198	2	107,448	112,959	1,311	0
Sept. 17, 2004	4,140	1	112,919	118,359	1,299	0

Source : Reserve Hank of India.

inflows. The process has been successful in maintaining price stability. Available indicators of reserve adequacy suggest that India's current level of foreign exchange reserves can be considered adequate as a cushion against potential disruptions to trade and current transactions as well as external debt servicing obligations. In the absence of an international lender of last resort, the reserves also provide the country a level of self-insurance against destabilising and costly financial crisis.

Other Fianancial Intermediatries

In line with banks, there has been an almost across-the-board improvement in the financial health of other financial intermediaries as well in terms of improvements in capital position and reduction in NPLs. Among the cooperative banks, there have been improvements in capital position, reduction in spread and operating expenses. Despite the decline in NPLs as a proportion of total assets for a majority of the cooperative banks, the ratio for some of the large cooperative banks increased significantly, mainly on account of inappropriate risk-management and corporate governance practices. Measures have been put in place to guard against repetition of such episodes, but this remains a burden.

Capital adequacy levels of most of the major DFIs have improved while NPL levels declined since the mid-1990s. Moreover, reflecting the adaptability of DFIs to changed business environment under the reform process, the share of para-banking activities such as underwriting, direct subscription and guarantees has increased from 10 per cent in the early-1990s to over 30 per cent in recent years. Some of the DFIs, however, have not been able to adjust as well as the others in the new environment mainly because of their past investment behaviours. Moreover, a few of the large DFIs felt that they could perform better as banks under the new environment. ICICI has already transformed itself into a bank and similar moves are underway for the Industrial Development Bank of India (IDBI). There has also been a large transformation in the NBFC sector, whereby a large number of NBFCs have discontinued their public deposit taking activities.

Under the strategy of sequenced reform, such measures in the insurance sector were introduced later than the banking sector. Despite this relatively late start, the insurance sector has witnessed considerable changes over the past few years. A large number of private insurance companies, generally with foreign capital participation, have entered the sector. The current profile of the Indian insurance industry reflects that, notwithstanding the entry of private sector players, in terms of both assets and liabilities, insurance companies from the public sector continue to dominate the industry. Despite this, given the fast pace of growth in the insurance industry, private players have been able to market their products (IRDA, 2002).

Perhaps more importantly, liberalisation of entry norms in insurance segment has brought about a sea change in product composition. While in the past, tax incentives were the major driving force of the insurance industry, particularly life insurance industry, in the emerging situation the normal driving force of an insurance industry is taking important roles (IRDA, 2002). Driven by competitive forces and also the emerging socio-economic changes including increased wealth, education and awareness about insurance products have resulted in introduction of various novel products in the Indian market. Along with the changing product profile, there have also been salutary improvements in consumer service in recent years, driven largely by the impact of new technology usage, better technical know-how consequent upon foreign collaboration and focused product targeting, dovetailed to specific segments of the populace as well as cross-selling of products through bancassurance. Insurance companies are also taking active steps to venture into innovative distribution channels for their products over and above creating strong agency network.

Equity Market

The 1990s have been good for the Indian equity market. The market has grown exponentially in terms of resource mobilisation, number of stock exchanges, number of listed stocks, market capitalisation, trading volumes, turnover and investors' base (Table 18). Along with this growth, the profile of the investors, issuers and intermediaries has changed significantly. The market has witnessed a fundamental institutional change resulting in drastic reduction in transaction costs and significant improvement in efficiency, transparency and safety (NSE, 2003). In the 1990s, reform measures initiated by SEBI such as, market determined allocation of resources, rolling settlement, sophisticated risk management and derivatives trading have greatly improved the framework and efficiency of trading and settlement. Almost all equity settlements take place at the depository. As a result, the Indian capital market has become qualitatively comparable to many developed and emerging markets.

TABLE 18: Select Stock Market Indicators in India

(Per cent)

Year (end-March)	1961*	1971*	1980*	1991	2000	2002	2003
Number of stock exchanges	7	8	9	22	23	23	23
Number of listed companies	1,203	1,599	2,265	6,229	9,871	9,644	9,413
Market capitalisation (Rs. Billion)	12	27	68	1,103	11,926	7,493	6,319

* End-December, the Stock Exchange, Mumbai only.

Source : The Stock Exchange (BSE), Mumbai and National Stock Exchange (NSE).

The liberalisation and consequent reform measures have drawn the attention of foreign investors leading to a rise in portfolio investment in the Indian capital market. During the first half of the 1990s, India accounted for a larger volume of international equity issues than any other emerging market (IMF, 1995). Over the recent years, India has emerged as a major recipient of portfolio investment among the emerging market economies. Apart from such large inflows, reflecting the confidence of cross-border investors on the prospects of Indian securities market, since 1993, when entry of FII was permitted for the first time, except for one year, India received positive portfolio inflows in each year. The stability of portfolio flows towards India is in contrast with large volatility of portfolio flows in most emerging market economies.

VI. Issues

As the foregoing analysis suggests, there has been a structural transformation in almost all segments of the Indian financial sector since the initiation of reforms. The reform process has strengthened the health of financial intermediaries, deepened financial markets and enhanced the instruments available in the financial system. At the level of individual institutions as well as at the systemic level, there has been considerable reinforcement of the framework for stability. There have also been discernible improvements in the competitiveness, efficiency and productivity of the Indian financial system. What then are important issues facing the Indian financial system now?

Even after one and a half decades of financial sector reforms, continued predominant public sector entities in the sector has often been a topic of debate. India's experience in this respect is different from many other emerging market economies, especially the transition countries, where financial sector reforms resulted in privatisation of erstwhile public sector financial intermediaries. In the late 1990s, India too proposed legislative change to enable reduction in government ownership up to 33 per cent in the public sector banks. It was proposed that notwithstanding such ownership pattern change, these banks "would retain their public sector character". The proposal, however, failed to meet parliamentary approval, indicating a lack of political acceptability on privatisation so far. Meanwhile public sector banks continue to raise capital from market and in nine public sector banks, including the State Bank of India, the largest Indian bank, private ownerships have become close to 40 per cent. It is also important to recall that this paper has shown that since the initiation of reforms, financial health as well as efficiency of the public sector banks closely matched and some times surpassed those of the private sector including foreign banks. Therefore, there is no definite observed link between efficiency and ownership in the contemporary Indian banking system. The competition induced by the new private sector banks has clearly re-energised the Indian banking sector as a whole: new technology is now the norm, new products are being introduced continuously, and new business practices have become common place.

India's approach towards treatment of insolvent banks is yet another interesting issue. Rather than closing them down, policymakers in India have shown a preference to merge such banks with healthy public sector banks. It has been felt in certain circles that such an approach may give rise to a moral hazard problem. However, two issues need consideration in this context. First, commercial banks are the most dominant and systemically important segment of the financial system. Second, over 70 per cent of the bank depositors in India are small depositors. Therefore, systemic concerns coupled with the necessity to safeguard the interest of small depositors have been paramount in the minds of policymakers while dealing with insolvent banks. This issue had not received much attention in the context of a predominantly government owned banking system. As the weight of private banks increases further thinking will need to be done on this subject, both in terms of prevention of insolvency through advance regulatory supervision and action, and post insolvency measures that discourage moral hazard and eventual fiscal cost.

Certain banking sector and related indicators on select emerging market economies (EMEs) have been presented in Annex I. Some broad points can be drawn from these data. First, while almost all EMEs have been successful in reducing domestic inflation rates since the 1990s, most of them experienced occasional inflationary spikes in this period. Reversing the situation, in the new millennium, countries such as China and Singapore experienced deflationary situations. Along with sustained reduction in inflation during the reform period, India has been able to avoid both the extreme situations. This can be taken as an indicator of the quality of financial sector reforms and monetary management in the country. Second, though lower than most of the East Asian EMEs, India maintained reasonably high and generally rising savings and investment rates since the 1990s. Stability in the financial market under the reform process has facilitated this process. Third, compared to most other EMEs, India maintained a stable real interest rate situation under the reform process. The generally increasing trend of the real rate, however, is an issue that needs greater attention of the authorities. Various steps have already been initiated in this context. Fourth, while banks in India needed to keep high proportions of their assets as liquid assets at the start of reform process, such requirements have been relaxed in a sequenced manner. Currently, these requirements in India are on the lower side among the EMEs. Lastly, despite substantial deepening of the Indian financial system as measured by the domestic bank credit to GDP ratio and domestic credit to private sector to GDP ratio, such processes are yet to catch-up the levels of the East Asian EMEs. This is yet another area where the Indian financial sector needs to make significant strides in the coming years.

Judged by the conventional measures such as share of foreign holdings in the Indian financial market, the extent of globalisation of Indian financial sector may look quite limited as compared to many other EMEs. Moreover, association of the authorities in the financial system either in the form of government ownership of financial intermediaries or intervention in the financial market may appear to be high. The conduct of the Indian financial sector in the face of various uncertainties and crises in various parts of the world, however, drives home the point that "On balance, there appears to be a great advantage in well-managed and appropriate integration into the global process...markets do not and cannot exist in a vacuum, *i.e.,* without some externally imposed rules and such order is a result of public policy" (Reddy, 2003). Similar views have been expressed in the influential work of Prasad and others (Prasad *et al.*, 2003), "The empirical evidence has not established a definitive proof that financial integration has enhanced growth for developing countries. Furthermore, it may be associated with higher consumption volatility. ...(I)mproving governance, in addition to sound macroeconomic frameworks and the development of domestic financial markets, should be an important element of such strategies." It is important to point out that despite the earlier apprehensions about the outcome of India's approach of sequenced implementation of international best practices in the financial sector and gradual opening up of the sector to international competition, such measures have enabled the country to avoid major financial sector crisis experienced by many emerging market economies since the 1990s. A list of such crises is given in the Annex II and the country experiences show that premature globalisation financial market and lack of prudential framework for financial regulation and supervision have been two major reasons for financial crises in emerging market economies. Indian policymakers have been conscious of the fact that international financial market acts in a strongly pro-cyclical manner in the case of EMEs. At the same time, these countries, especially disadvantaged strata within these economies, are seriously constrained in managing the impact of such volatility. Therefore, maintenance of stability becomes a part of public policy in the emerging market countries (Reddy, 2003). Accordingly, concern for stability has been a major plank of the financial sector reforms in India. Available indicators reinforce India's resolve for the continuance of this approach.

Despite the considerable progress in terms of both efficiency and stability of the financial sector under the reform process, it needs to be reiterated that India has miles to go in deepening the process. Despite considerable improvements, the current level of efficiency of the Indian financial sector is far from satisfactory. Reduction in transaction costs and improving the credit delivery mechanism are two areas, which require focused attention at the current stage of reforms. There are needs for the consolidation of the banking system in India and at present there are still various institutional and legal reforms that still need attention.

Effective implementation of corporate governance practices in financial intermediaries has been a longstanding concern of the regulators and supervisors across the world. In India too, instances of inadequacies in the implementation of corporate governance norms and disregard to prudential practices on internal control have come to light. Such instances have seriously compromised the financial health of a few private sector commercial banks and cooperative banks. Prompt corrective actions including criminal proceedings against the errant individuals have been initiated by the authorities in such cases. In order to guard against recurrence of such practices the Reserve Bank has taken various measures including implementation of important facets of international best practices in corporate governance and internal control, strengthening of the role of statutory auditors, recasting of the supervisory framework and increased disclosure to strengthen the role of market discipline. In the cooperative banking sector, continuation of multiple regulators has been identified as a major challenge before the authorities in effective regulation and supervision including implementation of corporate governance and internal control norms. The Reserve Bank has suggested jurisdiction of a single regulator to deal with this banking segment.

Despite decline, continuation of considerable stock of NPLs in the banking system continues to be a cause for concern. Improved institutional and legal arrangements and strengthening of risk management practices by banks is likely to keep incremental NPLs low. Initiatives such as setting up of Asset Reconstruction Companies and greater emphasis on compromise settlements are likely to deal with the stock problem for NPLs. Banks may need to adopt a more pro-active approach in dealing with these issues.

Enforcement of creditors rights will need continuous strengthening. The implementation of recent legislation will progressively be subject to judicial testing as it gets more accepted and as problems occur in its application. The legal provisions and practice in bankruptcy of the real sector are still inadequate and need further reform.

Another area of concern relates to the decline in direct bank credit towards disadvantaged but socially important sectors such as agriculture and small-scale industries. It is felt that in the past inadequate risk management practices constrained banks to more vigorously pursue financing of such sectors. With improved risk management, it is likely that banks would deploy larger portions of their funds in these sectors. As this assessment and risk management practices improve, banks should be able to distinguish the risk quality of individual borrowers, rather than treating borrowers of a particular class as equally risky. The introduction of credit information bureau is in its infancy: the large scale availability of credit histories of borrowers at low cost is essential for better credit delivery, particularly for smaller borrowers.

Debt Market

The Indian debt market ranks third in Asia, after Japan and South Korea, in terms of issued amount. Outstanding size of the debt floatation as a proportion of GDP, however, is not very high in India. Moreover, although in terms of the primary issues Indian debt market is quite large, the Government continues to be the large borrower, unlike in South Korea where the private sector is the main borrower. The corporate debt market in the country is still at a nascent stage. Factors such as lack of good quality issuers, institutional investors, supporting infrastructure and high cost of issuance, market fragmentation, etc. have been identified as the reason for lack of depth of the corporate debt market in India (Mohan, 2004). However, to place India on a high and sustained growth trajectory and particularly to meet the huge financing needs of the infrastructure projects, it is necessary to develop the corporate bond market.

As the debt market becomes larger, both for government securities and for corporate debt, its efficient functioning will depend a great deal on deepening of liquidity in the market so that trading becomes easier and more efficient. The government securities market needs to be widened much more to non-bank participants such as insurance companies, pension and provident funds, and many real sector participants who need fixed instruments for their treasury management. This will need greater trading of debt in the stock exchanges and better price discovery through anonymous, screen based, order matching systems. With increasing interest rate movement, in both directions, the efficient functioning of the debt market will also be aided by further development of the derivatives market. However, this has to be done in a careful manner, while ensuring that market participants have adequate risk management systems.

Financial sector reforms in India were initiated early in the reform cycle. Complementary measures in other areas including fiscal and external sector provided the crucial support to the financial sector reform process. In order to deepen the financial sector reforms further, it is essential that significant reform measures are initiated in other segments of the economy including real sectors. Since the early 1990s, India as well as the world economy have undergone a structural transformation. An enduring development has been the changed perception about India — both internally and from the rest-of-the-world. While India assumes a more pivotal role in the global arena, internally the country needs to reassess the future course of restructuring process. Managing heightened expectations is going to be the major challenge of future public policy in India since, this, on the one hand, provides the country to take a quantum jump in terms of development, but, on the other hand, even a small slippage in the policy framework may prove to be the undoing of the past painstaking reform efforts. As envisaged by the 10th Plan, India is posed to attain 8 per cent per annum growth rate on a consistent basis. This was even outside the realm of wishful thinking a few years back. Appropriate sequencing and repackaging of reform measures with changed emphasis and relative speed of reforms at various sectoral levels would ultimately determine whether India would be able to leapfrog into the new growth trajectory.

NOTES

1. See, for example, Hanson and Kathuria (1999) and Reddy (2002a).
2. In fact, in some cases, prudential norms in India have surpassed the international best practices and many of the proposals of Basel II are already under the process of phased implementation.
3. In the early 1990s through the use of SLR and cash reserve ratio (CRR)

as much as 63.5 per cent of the bank resources were pre-empted. Since the introduction of financial sector reforms these rates have been cut considerably in a sequenced manner. SLR has been reduced to the statutory minimum of 25 per cent, while CRR is currently at 5.0 per cent.

4. Distribution of banks according to CRAR for 1995-96 given in Table 3 follows a slightly different classification whereby banks have been grouped in terms of CRAR into groups of 4 to 8 per cent and 8 to 10 per cent.
5. Securitisation and Reconstruction of Financial Assets and Enforcement of Security Interest Act, 2002.

REFERENCES

Ahluwalia, M.S. (2002). "Economic Reforms in India since 1991: Has Gradualism Worked?" *Journal of Economic Perspectives*, 16 (3), 67-88.

Government of India (GoI) (1998). *Report of the Committee on Banking Sector Reforms* (Chairman: Shri M. Narasimham), Government of India, New Delhi.

Hanson, J.A. and S. Kathuria (1999). *India: A Financial Sector for the Twenty-First Century*, New Delhi.

Insurance Regulatory and Development Authority (IRDA) (2002). *Annual Report*, IRDA, Mumbai.

International Monetary Fund (IMF) (1995). IMF *Survey*, IMF, Washington, D.C.

Mohan, R. (2002). "Transforming Indian Banking: In Search of a Better Tomorrow", Valedictory address at the Twenty-Fourth Bank Economists' Conference, Bangalore, printed in *Reserve Bank of India Bulletin*, January 2003.

—— (2004). "A Decade of Reforms in the Government Securities Market and Agenda for the Future", Keynote Address at FIMMDA-PDAI Conference, Dubai.

National Stock Exchange (NSE) (2003). *Indian Securities Market Review*, NSE, Mumbai.

Prasad, Eswar, Kenneth Rogoff, Shang-Jin Wei, and M. Ayhan Kose (2003). "Effects of Financial Globalisation on Developing Countries: Some Empirical Evidence", mimeo., International Monetary Fund.

Rangarajan, C. (1998). "Banking Sector Reforms: Rationale and Relevance", *SICOM Silver Jubilee Memorial Lecture*, Mumbai.

Reddy, Y.V. (2002). "Public Sector Banks and the Governance Challenge: Indian Experience" Paper presented at World Bank, International Monetary Fund, and Brookings Institution Conference on Financial Sector Governance: The Roles of the Public and Private Sectors, New York, USA.

—— (2002a). "Monetary and Financial Sector Reforms in India: A Practitioner's Perspective", Presentation at the Indian Economy Conference, Cornell University, USA.

—— (2003). "Towards Globalisation in the Financial Sector in India", Inaugural address at the Twenty-Fifth Bank Economists' Conference, Mumbai.

Reserve Bank of India (1991). Report of the Committee on the Financial System (Chairman: Shri M. Narasimham), Reserve Bank of India, Mumbai.

ANNEX I
BANKING SECTOR INDICATORS OF SELECT EMERGING MARKET ECONOMIES

TABLE A.1: Bank Liquid Reserves to Bank Assets Ratio

	1991	1995	2000	2002
Singapore	4.1	4.0	2.5	2.5
Korea, Rep.	6.5	6.2	2.0	2.6
South Africa	..	2.9	2.7	2.7
Chile	6.0	5.2	3.1	3.0
Czech Republic	..	12.7	18.9	3.8
India	16.0	16.2	8.0	5.6
Poland	14.6	7.8	4.9	5.6
Philippines	23.4	11.2	7.4	8.5
Argentina	8.2	3.6	2.5	9.5
Mexico	3.0	22.3	5.5	11.1
Indonesia	9.0	1.9	7.0	11.1
China	17.8	18.0	12.7	12.1
Malaysia	6.4	14.4	13.6	12.5
Russian Federation	..	12.0	15.4	13.9
Brazil	7.3	7.7	7.7	23.6
High Income: OECD	1.7	1.5	0.9	..

Source: World Development Indicators online, World Bank.

TABLE A.2: Domestic Credit Provided by Banking Sector (Per cent of GDP)

	1991	1995	2000	2002
Mexico	36.8	42.3	26.7	26.6
Russian Federation	..	25.5	24.7	26.6
Poland	34.8	32.0	34.1	36.2
Czech Republic	..	75.9	54.5	45.8
India	51.3	44.3	53.3	58.5
Indonesia	45.6	52.7	67.4	59.5
Philippines	23.9	64.3	66.9	60.5
Argentina	22.8	27.9	34.5	62.4
Brazil	93.8	44.8	49.5	64.8
Chile	63.9	60.3	72.6	77.6
Singapore	75.9	76.0	90.4	84.8
Korea, Rep.	66.4	64.7	103.1	116.9
South Africa	..	140.2	158.4	150.9
Malaysia	79.0	126.7	148.2	154.2
China	92.6	91.2	132.7	166.4
High Income: OECD	135.3	154.2	175.2	170.0

Source: World Development Indicators online, World Bank.

TABLE A.3: Domestic Credit to Private Sector (Per cent of GDP)

	1991	1995	2000	2002
Mexico	21.0	29.3	13.0	12.6
Argentina	12.6	20.0	23.9	15.3
Russian Federation	..	9.4	13.3	17.6
Indonesia	46.2	53.5	21.9	22.3
Poland	24.0	18.5	27.7	28.8
India	24.2	22.8	29.0	32.6
Czech Republic	..	75.2	54.0	33.4
Brazil	42.7	37.3	34.7	35.5
Philippines	21.5	45.1	43.8	36.4
Chile	44.8	54.4	63.7	68.1
Singapore	96.9	106.4	111.0	115.5
Korea, Rep.	65.2	64.7	101.0	115.6
South Africa	..	119.3	138.9	131.7
High Income: OECD	109.5	119.3	138.0	133.7
China	89.9	88.3	124.6	136.5
Malaysia	..	124.4	140.4	146.1

Source: World Development Indicators online, World Bank.

TABLE A.4: Gross Domestic Savings (Per cent of GDP)

	1991	1995	2000	2002
Poland	18.0	22.1	18.4	15.7
Mexico	20.4	22.5	21.8	18.3
High Income: OECD	23.0	22.4	22.0	18.4
Philippines	17.2	14.6	23.1	18.8
South Africa	21.7	18.9	18.3	19.2
Indonesia	33.2	30.6	25.6	21.1
Brazil	20.5	20.5	20.0	22.4
India	21.9	25.3	21.9	22.5
Czech Republic	30.1	29.3	26.3	25.8
Chile	27.0	27.6	23.5	26.8
Argentina	16.2	17.5	15.6	26.9
Korea, Rep.	36.8	35.7	31.3	27.5
Russian Federation	36.6	28.8	38.7	31.8
Malaysia	34.1	39.7	47.2	41.9
China	38.1	43.1	39.0	43.4
Singapore	45.1	50.2	48.1	44.7

Source: World Development Indicators online, World Bank.

TABLE A.5: Gross Fixed Capital Formation (Per cent of GDP)

	1991	1995	2000	2002
Argentina	..	17.9	16.2	12.0
South Africa	17.2	15.9	14.8	15.1
Russian Federation	23.3	21.1	16.9	17.9
Poland	19.5	18.6	23.9	18.6
Mexico	18.7	16.2	21.4	18.9
High Income: OECD	22.6	21.2	21.9	19.0
Philippines	20.0	22.2	21.2	19.2
Brazil	18.1	20.5	21.8	19.3
Indonesia	27.0	28.4	21.8	20.2
Chile	19.9	23.9	21.0	21.6
India	22.0	24.4	22.0	22.5
Malaysia	36.4	43.6	25.6	23.2
Singapore	33.6	33.4	30.0	25.7
Czech Republic	24.1	32.0	28.3	26.3
Korea, Rep.	39.0	36.7	28.4	26.7
China	27.5	34.7	36.5	40.2

Source: World Development Indicators online, World Bank.

TABLE A.6: Inflation, Consumer Prices (Annual %)

	1991	1995	2000	2002
China	3.5	16.9	0.3	-0.8
Singapore	3.4	1.7	1.4	-0.4
Czech Republic	..	9.2	3.9	1.8
Malaysia	4.4	3.5	1.5	1.8
Poland	76.7	28.1	10.1	1.9
Chile	21.8	8.2	3.8	2.5
Korea, Rep.	9.3	4.4	2.2	2.8
Philippines	18.5	8.0	4.4	3.1
India	13.9	10.2	4.0	4.4
Mexico	22.7	35.0	9.5	5.0
Brazil	432.8	66.0	7.0	8.4
South Africa	15.3	8.7	5.3	9.2
Indonesia	9.4	9.4	4.5	11.5
Russian Federation	..	197.5	20.8	15.8
Argentina	171.7	3.4	-0.9	25.9

Source: World Development Indicators online, World Bank.

TABLE A.7: Real Interest Rate (Per cent)

	1991	1995	2000	2002
Russian Federation	..	72.3	-9.6	0.4
Malaysia	4.4	3.9	1.7	2.7
Mexico	..	15.7	4.2	3.4
Czech Republic	..	2.3	6.0	3.5
Philippines	5.6	6.6	4.3	4.1
Korea, Rep.	-0.8	1.8	9.8	5.0
Chile	6.1	8.1	10.2	5.0
Singapore	3.0	4.2	1.3	5.2
China	1.8	-1.0	4.9	5.6
South Africa	4.0	6.9	6.8	6.6
India	3.6	6.0	8.2	8.7
Poland	-0.4	3.8	7.6	10.3
Indonesia	15.4	8.3	8.1	11.0
Argentina	..	14.2	9.9	16.2
Brazil	..	..	42.9	50.1

Source: World Development Indicators online, World Bank.

ANNEX II

MAJOR FINANCIAL CRISES SINCE THE 1990s

Nature of Crises	Reasons
ERM crisis of 1992-93, affected the countries under the Exchange Rate Mechanism	The ERM crisis brought into focus the ability of speculators to precipitate a crisis and the limited ability of available foreign exchange reserves to stem the run on a currency in a world of volatile capital flows. The ERM crisis also highlighted the trade-off between monetary and exchange rate management policies under a convertible currency.
Currency crisis in Mexico in 1994-95 which graduated into a debt crisis	Volatile capital flows resulted in a currency crisis, which graduated into with the inability a debt crisis of the government to redeem the 'tesebonos', which were short-term debt instruments repayable in Pesos but were indexed to the US dollar issued by the Mexican Government.
East Asian currency crisis which started with the collapse of the Thai Baht in July 1997 engulfed other Asian countries like South Korea, Indonesia, Philippines and Malaysia	The crisis reflected a typical case of structural imbalance and some major deficiencies in the affected economies. Uncontrolled capital account on the liberalisation back of weak financial systems that were characterised by poor monitoring and surveillance, inappropriate policy stances such as pegged exchange rates and unlimited access to foreign currency loans for the private sector led to the crisis. Lack of timely and adequate financial assistance from the multilateral institutions, at least initially, seems to have exacerbated the crisis.
Russian currency crisis in August 1998	Faced with significantly large capital outflows in the face of inadequate reserves, Russia defaulted on its domestic and external debt in August 1998. It subsequently devalued its currency, thereby disrupting the international economy to a certain extent.

ANNEX II (Contd.)

Nature of Crises	Reasons
Brazilian currency crisis in February 1999	In February 1999, following months of speculative pressure and in spite of a large IMF rescue package, the Brazilian Real was devalued. Reasons included volatile capital flows and fundamental problems associated with the adoption of the Real Plan (1994) to control hyperinflation. Inadequate fiscal consolidation also led to fears of default, high interest rates, and a consequent debt spiral.
Argentinean crisis in September 2001	In September 2001, Argentina defaulted on almost US $ 3 billion debt owed by it to the IMF. Interactions between an unsustainable fiscal regime and the existing currency board arrangement in the face of unfavourable external developments were the most crucial elements in the Argentine crisis.
Crisis in Turkey in 2001	The immediate cause of crisis in Turkey in 2001 was a combination of portfolio losses and liquidity problems in a few banks, which triggered a loss of confidence in the entire banking system leading to a reversal of capital flows. The Turkish Lira was devalued by 30 per cent in February 2001 and the Government adopted a floating exchange rate regime to keep most of its reserves intact.

2

TOWARDS UNDERSTANDING GLOBALISATION PROCESS

AMEER BATCHA

Introduction

The term 'globalisation' means different things to different people. To elaborate, globalisation as a concept is being looked upon very closely by people in all walks of life, be it economists, technocrats or common man. Some use the term 'globalisation' to refer the disintegration of the traditional social fabrics, multi-cultural and pluralistic nature of the society. In a way, it has integrated and internalized the culture, habits and values of the developed countries by the people living in other parts of the world. Globalisation also refers to the emergence of consumerism, cyber culture, changing work ethics and work rhymes, rise of extremism, fundamentalism or terrorism with global network. From another viewpoint, globalisation represents the speed and swiftness of communication across the globe, the frequency and the speed of travel and transportation from one place to the other at less and less transaction cost. In this paper, we look at globalisation as a process sweeping across nations over time with a sort of inevitability. In short, it is a revolution not seen by the world so far. Hence, it was given the nomenclature 'globalisation'. The effects are far-reaching, never dreamt of in the past and represent a paradigm shift. However, our effort will be to analyse it within the framework of economics with the understanding that all the emerging economic developments will have their own socio-politico and cultural counterparts.

2. Within the framework of economics, the term globalisation refers to a world characterised by the absence of restrictions for the movement of the factors of production amongst nations. Taken to the extreme, the concept of nation states will wither away. Such a state of affairs is yet to pass the globe, though it is difficult to rule out that at least in the distant future. Then, all about globalisation refers to the impact that is being felt due to the onset of processes which unite the nation states irreversibly. Such processes ultimately lead to accelerated movement of physical and financial capital, labour (to a limited extent), diffusion of technology, etc. Globalisation has not dawned overnight and each aspect of globalisation gradually unfolds itself. The driver of such process is ultimately the events, which, in turn, manifest themselves due to the underlying process. Therefore, there is a bi-way causality between the events and process. Due to the above, it is not possible to separate them as they are closely related. However, such a separation would enhance the understanding of the globalisation. This article is an attempt to understand (a) the underlying processes which drive the overall globalisation and (b) the role of events as catalysts to the underlying processes.

3. To understand the process of globalisation, one has to know the framework of capitalism within which the process of globalisation has emerged. This would be dealt in Part I. The process of globalisation receives its impetus from a number of events like, collapse of the fixed exchange rate system, emergence of 'euro', proliferation of the MNCs in the financial sector, growth of East Asian countries, etc. The above are dealt in Part II. The role and importance of the financial intermediation in the globalisation process is the focus of Part III. The paper is concluded in Part IV.

PART I

Characteristics of Capitalism

4. The capitalistic frameworks in its basic form encompasse two sets of people, *viz.*, the employer and the employee. It is based on the contractual relationship entered into with the free will of the contracting parties. No doubt, it is superior to the 'mode of production' based on slavery and the subsequent

serfdom under the feudal system. Further, market mechanism is used for pricing the services of labourers. The employer in the capitalistic system is generally the owner of the means of production instead of only land under the feudal system. Accordingly, instead of ownership of land as the instrument for expropriation, now, under the capitalistic system, capital needs to be used as an instrument to garner the surplus. Capital can be viewed as a sum of financial resources invested by the owner. It is available to the firm as means of production like machines and other inputs necessary for production. The owner of capital under the capitalistic system needs to assume the risk arising from the operation of the particular unit in a market environment subject to a number of uncertainties in regard to generation of surplus or profit. This is one of the defining characteristics of capitalism as the expropriation of surplus is the reward for assuming the risk of loss. Whereas in the case of feudal system, expropriation is done by virtue of the ownership of land resources gifted by the nature free of cost. In the case of capitalism, a firm may incur losses due to inefficiency in the use of financial and physical resources, or due to the uncertainties prevalent in the market environment, hence it is subject to uncertainty. Whereas the expropriation under the feudal system is more or less certain with all the risk borne by the tenants or serfs themselves. Thus, ownership of capital and organisation of production to earn profit is an important characteristic of the capitalistic system.

5. Another important feature of the capitalistic system is that decision for production of goods and services and distribution of income arising therefrom is atomised through the market mechanism which co-ordinates the decisions of all the players in the market through generating the price impulses for all goods and services and factor payments.

The Role of Money and Finance in the Rise of Capitalism

6. The rise of capitalism is not an accident and on the other hand, it was the result of a number of concomitant factors. The most important among them being the evolution in money creation and the role of banking. Even though, they are separate in themselves, they are closely related. If mode of production changed according to the stage of civilization,

the form of money that was in use by different groups of people at different time also underwent evolution depending upon the stage of the civilization. The money changed its form from commodity money to metallic money and subsequently to paper money.

7. However, the evolution from paper money to the bank money could be considered as the most revolutionary. Bank money is nothing but a dematerialised form of paper money. Looked at another angle, it is a dematerialised form of wealth in the most liquid form. After the advent of the banking system, money can be created out of thin air, to quote Schumpeter. Prior to the advent of banking, accumulation of wealth was mostly in the form of land and cattle, gold and jewellery and other physical assets. It is very difficult to store wealth beyond a point if the wealth is perishable or deteriorates in quality or if it loses the market value. The maintenance of wealth is possible at a heavy transaction cost. Wealth in dematerialised form at marginal or zero cost of maintenance became possible with advent of the banking system. Further, it was possible to earn income on the wealth maintained with the bank. Hence the accumulation of wealth in the capitalistic era is unheard of. Plastic money and digital money has again revolutionised the concept of money as it eased the use of deposit and credit at will at different convenient time and locations. It also enabled quick transfer of purchasing power at almost negligible transaction cost. One of the important characteristics of globalisation is that wealth or purchasing power moves across the globe almost on a real time basis.

Capitalism *vs* Socialism

8. The new forces, unleashed due to the French Revolution followed by the industrial revolution, transformed the feudal system into capitalistic system. The marxian framework postulated that capitalism would grow into socialism and ultimately to communism. The great 'October Revolution' of 1918 gave a practical shape to the ideology of socialism and communism propounded by the Karl Marx. The world development and its evolution so far, has neither traversed

the path envisaged by Karl Marx, nor the capitalism collapsed as per Schumpeterian propositions.

9. Though capitalism did not collapse as predicted, however, it evidenced vulnerabilities on a number of occasions. The chief among them being the great depression of 1929-33. The lessons learnt during the great depression became a subject in itself and the whole Keynesian framework evolved out of it. The stagflation appeared during the seventies made the Keynesian framework obsolete relegating it to the position of depression economics and not applicable at all times. The Classical framework re-asserted itself in the form of new Classicals, rational expectationists, etc. One of the main proposition of the above school is that markets work better with least intervention from the nation governments. In a way, the above development sowed the seeds of globalisation. Capitalism in the process of its development had its own events depicting its serious pitfalls in its framework. However, it is to the credit of the resilience of the capitalism that it restarts its journey with renewed vigour relegating the events affecting it to the world of history.

10. On the other hand, the other system, *i.e.*, the socialism which grew significantly during the initial periods started showing signs of stresses and strains in the form of shortages of essential commodities, long queue in the ration shops, etc. especially after seventies. The gradual weakening of the socialist states like, the USSR, and the rise of globalisation was a simultaneous process. The ultimate dissolution of the USSR in the beginning of the nineties gave a new impetus to the process of globalisation.

Four Stages of Capitalism — Organisation of Production

11. Capitalism when it appeared in the scene with the industrial revolution, production was mostly organised in the sole proprietor and partnership units. The important characteristic of the above was that ownership and management were in the same hands. The stage two of the capitalism is marked by the separation of ownership and management giving rise to corporate form of organisation. Another important characteristic of the separation is that ownership was divided into tiny parts called shares and

distributed to multitude of owners called shareholders. It has served two important objectives. Firstly, it became possible to conceive mammoth production facilities on the basis of very small contribution mobilised from a large number of people scattered across the country/regions. Secondly, the risk arising out of a particular activity was distributed and transferred depending upon the risk bearing capacity and willingness of the shareholders. The risk transfer from one entity to the other is the major hallmark of globalisation, the genesis of which was sown in the second stage itself with corporate form of organisation. In the third stage, the corporate form of organisation ultimately evolved into Multi-National Corporations (MNCs). The group of such MNCs organised within the same group called conglomerates dominated the scene of capitalism. In the fourth stage, *i.e.,* in the days of globalisation, conglomerates are breaking up on the basis of core competency and the forms of organization is undergoing change and the conglomerates are considered to be inefficient and unwieldy to face the challenge from new and small entities leveraging the information technology. It is to be noted that the process of globalisation does not bring about any change in the 'mode of production' of the capitalistic system, *i.e.,* the contract labour system. On the other hand, the system of contracting labour itself has evolved significantly. The concept of 'life-time employment' has given way to contracted period say, for two to five years.

The Challenge for Capitalism

12. But the continued path of expansion with capitalistic process depends upon the aggregate demand emanating from all the groups of the economy and especially the workers. According to Kalecky, 'workers spend what they get, and capitalists get what they spend'. When the income generated by the labour force fluctuate in the aggregate, it would create fluctuations in the overall economic activity. When it occurs with a pattern, the economy will be subjected to cyclical movements, *i.e.,* the economic activity resulting in alternate increase and decrease in employment rate in succession. The cyclical trend in the economic activities are caused by a number of other factors. However, they ultimately get manifested

in the rate of unemployment. Increase in the rate of unemployment is associated with pains and adjustments in the overall structure of the economy to purge the uneconomical units from the system, ultimately leading to efficient allocation of resources. The challenge is, therefore, to maintain the economy from the extreme downtrends while at the same time carrying out adjustments in the economic system to increase the overall efficiency.

International Trade and Capitalism

13. Globalisation represents the interactions amongst the nation states. The international trade constituted the most important form of interaction amongst the nation states from time immemorial due to mutual benefits accruing to the participating nations in the international trade. International trade transactions are, in general, voluntary in nature. Hence, it happens only when it benefits both the parties to the transactions. However, the benefits shared by the nations are not equal. The terms of contract entered into depend on the intensity or the necessity of the parties to the contract, the higher the necessity the more unfavourable the terms of the contract will be, similar to the situations faced by a wage labourer.

14. The theory of comparative advantage propounded by the classical economist, David Ricardo, merely emphasises the mutual benefits accruing to nations participating in the international trade. The distribution of gains arising from international trade among the trading nations is governed by the price mechanism operating at the international level. The price represents the forces of demand and supply and as such the price mechanism, *per se*, would not ensure equitable distribution of gains from trade. Depending upon their necessity to trade, benefits might accrue to one country more than the other. Taking into account the narrow export base of the developing countries and also their import requirements for economic development, they may very often find themselves in the perennial trade deficit due to unfavourable terms of trade and narrowness of export sector.

15. Due to the above reasons, the benefits gained by the less developed countries (LDCs) declined from 1.7 per cent

in 1970 to 0.6 per cent in 2002.[1] The situation faced by the less developed countries is very aptly described by Kofi Annan, United Nations Secretary General in the following words, "Notwithstanding the remarkable growth in international trade over the past century, too few countries in the developing world have shared in the benefits. These countries do not lack potential to participate competitively and constructively in the international market place. Rather, the challenge facing the global community is to ensure that these countries have an unfettered opportunity to realize their potential, thereby enabling them to make real progress towards achieving the Millennium Development Goals."[2]

16. The term 'Globalisation' indicates a more comprehensive relationship existing amongst nations. Trade relation constitutes a subset of globalisation. Taking the case of trade relations existing among countries as an example, the purpose of the above analysis is to indicate that globalisation as a process need not always benefit all the countries across the globe. The possibilities of leaving behind the scores of underdeveloped countries while surging ahead in the path of globalisation process is a distinct reality that the nations must be aware of. Then the question arises as to whether is there any scope for underdeveloped countries and developing countries to participate in the globalisation process and achieve progress. The answer is both yes and no depending upon the country specific situations.

17. The above analysis is an attempt to derive home the point that Globalisation process is basically an evolutionary process in the womb of capitalism and it will also attract criticisms similar to capitalism in its earlier stages. However, globalisation, *per se*, is subjected to a number of criticisms.

PART II

18. Trade relation amongst countries is viewed by many as constituting the core of globalisation process. The rate of growth achieved in world trade in the eighties and nineties is not substantially different from the earlier decades. Then the question as to why so much hype is created about globalisation. The answer, perhaps, lies with the fact that globalisation has to do more with the rapid movement of

finance or capital, an another factor of production. Liberalisation and the rapid advancement in the information and communication technology, *inter alia*, facilitated such movement of funds. Since the mid-eighties, world flows of foreign direct investment have been growing nearly at 14 per cent annually, almost twice the growth rate of world exports.[3]

19. A number of other factors contributed to the process of globalisation. They include, falling trade barriers, fast paced technological advances, declining communication and transportation costs, international migration, and highly mobile investment. The following is an attempt to dissect those factors. The factors enumerated are not to be viewed as independent of each other. Rather, they are closely inter-related that it is not possible to discuss one factor in isolation of other factors. Of the above factors, Information Technology and capital flow played became the most crucial.

Era of Information Technology

20. The human kind progressed in its civilization through inventions and discoveries. The invention of machines with computing power and memories called, computers, marked an important step in the march towards the new millennium. Further, the price of computer processing power has fallen by an average of 30 per cent in real terms over the last 20 years.[4] The advancement made in transmitting information made possible through optical fibre cables replacing the copper wires, communication through broadcasting the electronic signals using transmitters and transponders, etc., brought about instant revolution in the communication. It transformed the world into global villages. Information is being disseminated across the globe with lightening speed while reducing the transaction cost to the minimum. Convergence between the computer and telecommunication in the form of e-mails and internet, etc. marked a paradigm shift in the whole development process.

Capital Flow

21. Due to the surge in the capital flow across the globe, the dynamism in the Balance of Payment (BOP) has shifted from current account to the capital account as nearly 90 per

cent of the forex market transactions takes place on account of the capital account also known as inter-bank transactions rather than the current account. In this regard, it would be worth-while to look closely into the events and processes that have transformed the financial systems of the world.

Global Scenario

22. The golden age of capitalism (1945-70) was characterised by more or less fixed exchange rate, high growth in trade and high growth of income in the developed countries. However, due to the ever increasing demand for dollar as an international reserve currency, the US pumped enormous US Dollars in the international markets. Subsequently, with engagement of the US in the Vietnam and Korean war, the supply of US Dollar increased excessively.

23. The above resulted in loss of international confidence in the US dollar and a number of countries started redeeming their Dollar holdings at the rate of 1 ounce of gold per 35$ depleting gold reserves maintained by the Federal Reserve in the process. The convertibility clause of the USA was abrogated by the Nixon Administration in 1971 to preserve the gold holdings of the Federal Reserve; a death knell to fixed exchange rate system advocated and maintained by the IMF.

First Oil Shock — 1973

24. With the onset of inflation in the US economy, the purchasing power of the US dollar got eroded. When the US dollar is serving as the major invoicing currency, countries exporting goods including petroleum goods denominated in US dollar found that they are selling their good cheap even though the dollar price has remained the same over the years. With a view to realising more purchasing power from the sale proceeds, oil rich countries formed a cartel known as 'Organisation of Petroleum Exporting Countries' (OPEC) and raised the price of oil sold in the international market. Due to such price hikes and also due to the emergence of stagnation in the growth of real income, a situation of stagflation came into existence. Till the seventies, Philips curve trade off between the unemployed and inflation guided the policy formulation especially the monetary policy. However, increasing the growth

prospects through subjecting the economy to higher inflation broke down completely as the world experienced both high rate of unemployment and inflation. The increase in the rate of inflation made the financial system unhealthy as significant rise in the rate of inflation invariably led to increase in the level of interest rate. The increase in the interest rate affected differently the assets and liabilities side of banks' balance-sheet giving rise to unsustainable reduction in the net interest income generated by banks. For the first time, the financial system was made to realise the risk involved in borrowing in short-term and lending for long-term. Since then, the concept of the asset-liability manangement and risk management demanded the attention of the bankers.

Rise of Monetarism

25. The Keynesian macroeconomic framework received its jolt from the monetarist school in the wake of the breakdown in the Philips Curve relationship. Monetarist school advocated rule based policy for money supply expansion to insulate the economy from the shocks created by the discretionary policy followed by the monetary authorities.

Regulation Q and the Rise of Euro Dollar Market

26. To circumvent the Regulation Q, the depositors as a part of innovation in banking started keeping their savings denominated in the US Dollars in the European market, thus giving impetus to the Euro-Dollar Market. Further, following the prescription of monetarism, with a view to controlling the money supply within the target level, the Federal Reserve targeted growth in the money supply indicators, hence controlling the growth in the deposits in the USA. Hence, some market players chose to keep the dollar deposits in the Euro-Dollar market which is outside the purview of the Federal Board.

The Rise of Euro Dollar Market

27. The emergence of Euro-dollar market is traced back to the sixties since the erstwhile socialist countries wanted to keep their US dollar balances out of the reach of the American hands. However, it emerged as an important market with the inflow of Petro-Dollars of OPEC countries. The resources were

channelised into countries facing BOP deficit due to sudden oil price hike. It was considered as a footloose market as it was not within the control of the USA. Subsequently, the 'euro market' developed for all other major currencies. Hence, the term 'euro currency market' was evolved to indicate the market for deposits and funds denominated in foreign currencies traded outside their respective home country. The USA also subsequently encouraged the growth of such markets in America.

Reform and Liberalisation

28. Consequent to the banking crisis in the Great Depression of 1929-33, the USA sought to demarcate banks from other financial market entities. The Glass-Steagall Act, 1933, enacted in the USA is an effort to create fire wall between banks and other financial institutions. Unlike banks in the German and Japan, the role of banking system in the United States was mainly to provide short-term capital and the activities of the banking system were confined within defined limits of the Glass-Steagall Act, 1933.

29. Fixed Exchange Rate regime prevailing before seventies co-existed with regulations of the banking and financial system in the matters of their deposit taking activities and pricing in a number of countries including the USA. When the euro-market emerged as an important market for accessing funds from the international market, the control exercised by the central banks of OECD countries on the banking system became difficult as the euro-market emerged as the footloose market and not within the control of any central banks. When the funds recycled in the euro-currency market became significant, the central banks that matter had no option except to align the policies taking the clue from the Euro Market developments. London market was the first to derive the benefits out of the Euro-market due to its strategic location, technical know-how, well laid out infrastructure in the form of network of banks and other financial institutions. To vest the London market with a permanent hold as an important financial centre, and also to benefit the British economy, Margaret Thatcher, the then British Prime Minister adopted what is called 'big bang' approach to reform the economy

including the financial sector. Various countries adopted policy measures, which would transform their economy into liberalised economy. Many of them instead of adopting big bang approach adopted what is called gradual approach. There is no firm conclusion in the literature about the merit of the alternative approaches. Either way, a number of countries including the USA went ahead in the path of liberalisation and deregulation.

The Debt Crisis

30. The countries which received funds from Euro-Dollar Market used them for the import of capital goods, defence supplies or even to import luxurious items. The European and the American commercial banks which were actively involved in recycling the Euro-Dollar fund did not take adequate care about the end-use of such loans as they were backed by the sovereigns. Any loan which is sanctioned solely on the strength of collateral without reference to the end-use is bound to fail. Even the sovereign guaranteed loan is no exception to this rule.

31. A number of highly indebted countries especially in the Latin American region found themselves in an inexorable position of servicing huge foreign debt at commercial rate of interest determined in the Euro market. The vulnerabilities of such countries was heightened with increase in the rate of interest resulting from surge in the inflation and other factors. Further, the external debt has to be serviced using foreign currency reserves, which has to be generated ultimately from current receipts including exports. The debt servicing becomes burdensome especially when there is a global slowdown worsening the possibilities to generate the foreign exchange inflow either through current or capital account. Beyond a point, such countries were left with no option except to declare moratorium. Naturally, the asset quality of a number of banks with exposures to such loans suffered a severe setback. Again, international financial system being market determined, the market had to provide answer for such developments.

32. By the middle of the eighties, a number of banks in the USA and elsewhere faced closure, merger and amalgamation, etc. due to the emergence of weakness in the banking system. The closure of a number of banks posed

systemic instability putting the payment and settlement system in jeopardy damaging the prospects for the growth of the real economy.

33. Due to its systemic impact and to protect the interest of the depositors, weak banks were ultimately bailed out at a considerable cost to the central banks and exchequer giving rise to the phenomenon called 'moral hazard' on the part of banks.

Reform and Debt Crisis

34. The debt crisis faced by the Latin American Countries considerably changed the policy environment in favour of liberalisation. To quote John Williamson, "as the region emerged from the debt crisis and the Berlin wall came down, there was a historically unusual degree of consensus about the main elements of policy agenda that Latin American countries need to pursue. Just like the OECD countries, Latin American countries need to stabilise, to open up their economies to trade and FDI and to liberalise".[5]

Basel Accord — 1988

35. Chastened by the experience of bailing out the highly leveraged commercial banks at a considerable cost to the economy and also with a view to bailing in the private sector for their excesses, it was agreed by G10 countries under the auspices of Bank for International Settlement, Basel, that commercial banks should recapitalise themselves in relation to their riskiness in their asset portfolios. The agreement is known as the Capital Accord of 1988. This accord changed the entire framework within which the erstwhile international banking system was functioning. India is no exception to this especially after the acceptance of recommendations made by the Narasimham Committee in 1992.

Collapse of the Soviet Union and Communist Bloc

36. The reason for the demise of the Soviet bloc was dealt in brief earlier.[6] The point to be noted here at this point is that the collapse of the USSR strengthened significantly the forces of globalisation as the East European and Asian countries of the erstwhile USSR camp adopted the path of transition towards market based economy.

TABLE I: Net Private Capital Flows to Emerging Market Economies[1]

(In billions of US dollars)

	Annual Average 1990-2000	2001	2002	2003
Emerging Market Economies[2]				
Total flows	111	57	66	171
Direct investment	76	129	96	76
Portfolio investment[3]	50	-21	-28	29
Other private flows[4]	-15	-51	-3	66
Memo: Current account balance	-24	45	107	142
Changes in reserves[5]	-56	-89	-177	-282
Asia[6]				
Total flows	35	31	41	111
Direct investment	35	42	47	45
Portfolio investment[3]	12	-12	-18	36
Other private flows[4]	-12	1	12	30
Memo: Current account balance	14	66	99	123
Changes in reserves[5]	-37	-82	-151	-215
Latin America[7]				
Total flows	62	36	-3	16
Direct investment	34	59	34	24
Portfolio investment[3]	30	1	-13	-5
Other private flows[4]	-2	-24	-24	-3
Memo: Current account balance	-39	-47	-8	9
Changes in reserves[5]	-11	3	0	-27
CEE[8]				
Total flows	20	-10	28	43
Direct investment	12	16	14	6
Portfolio investment[3]	9	-2	4	-2
Other private flows[4]	-1	-24	10	39
Memo: Current account balance	-2	27	16	12
Changes in reserves[5]	-12	-7	-23	-33

[1]Estimates of capital flows based on national balance of payments data and IIF. [2]Comprises the economies in Asia, Latin America and CEE listed in the footnotes and South Africa. [3]Debt and equity assets and liabilities. [4]Includes net flows intermediated by commercial banks and other private sector agents (not including financial derivatives). [5]A negative value indicates an increase. [6]China, India, Indonesia, Korea, Malaysia, the Philippines, Taiwan (China) and Thailand. [7]Argentina, Brazil, Chile, Colombia, Mexico, Peru and Venezuela. [8]The Czech Republic, Hungary, Poland, Russia and Turkey.

Sources: Central banks: IMF; Institute of International Finance (IIF).
— As published in BIS Annual Report — 2003-04.

Emergence of China

37. The demise of the USSR in the nineties is not the end of the socialist regimes as China still survives. However, the survival of China facilitated the globalisation process further. The Peoples' Republic of China under the leadership of Den Xio Ping participated in the globalisation process through its policy of 'export led growth' and active encouragement to the forex inflows. China is far ahead of India in terms of the quantum of FDI received by them every year as is evident in Table II.

Emergence of MNCs

38. Concomitant with other developments enumerated above, the decade of 70s and 80s were characterised by the emergence of MNCs as an important factor to be reckoned with. With the predominance of MNCs as an important player in the product market and increasing their share over a period of time in a significant manner, the movement of merchandise in the international market was no longer governed by the principles of comparative advantage of a particular country. On the other hand, the movement would rather reflected the convenience and the decisions of the MNCs about their production process.

MNCs in the Financial Sector

39. As we have already noted, globilisation process is mainly spearheaded by the movement of capital across countries. Such movement was partly facilitated by the emergence of MNCs in the financial sector. MNCs in the financial sector include, banking, insurance, pension and mutual funds, also known as Foreign Institutional Investors (FIIs). After the proliferation of derivatives as a financial product, a new genre of MNCs called hedge funds have also come into existence. The reform and liberalisation process ensured that the level and the movement in exchange rate and interest rate reflect the market forces. Volatility in them created profitable opportunities in the form of arbitrage avenues between different currencies and fund markets. The inflation rate differentials across the countries and its linkages with interest rate differentials and expected exchange rate

TABLE II: Global Private Financial Flows — Selected Countries

Country	Net private capital flows $ millions		Foreign direct investment $ millions		Portfolio Investment flows $ millions: Bonds		Portfolio Investment flows $ millions: Equity		Bank and trade-related lending $ millions	
	1990	2002	1990	2002	1990	2002	1990	2002	1990	2002
Brazil	666	9,861	989	16,566	129	1,519	103	1,981	-555	-10,205
Canada			7,581	20,501						
China	8,107	47,107	3,487	49,308	-48	-1,289	0	2,249	4,668	-3,161
Hong Kong, China				12,794						
Egypt, Arab Rep.	668	437	734	647	-1	0	0	-212	-65	3
France			13,183	52,020						
Germany			3,005	37,296						
India	1,842	4,944	237	3,030	147	-272	0	967	1,458	1,219
Indonesia	2,923	-6,966	1,093	-1,513	26	-406	0	877	1,804	-5,924
Italy			6,411	14,699						
Japan			1,777	9,087						
Korea, Rep.			788	1,972						
Malaysia	476	4,807	2,332	3,203	-1,239	1,962	0	-250	-617	-110
Mexico	9,600	10,261	2,549	14,622	661	-3,899	1,995	-104	4,396	-359
Netherlands			10,676	28,534						

Source: 2004 World Development Indicators.

movements engaged the attention of the fund managers. They moved their funds from one location to the other. Another important factor, which facilitated the movement of funds across the globe, was the rapid strides made in the information technology front. Technology enabled movement of funds ensured reduction in both the transaction time and costs. However, putting in place an appropriate technological and risk management framework involved heavy capital outlay. Hence, the benefits could accrue only to big players in the financial markets. The route of mergers and amalgamations were resorted to by the various players in the financial market to transform themselves into global players.

40. When the financial system is subjected to the impact of frequent and quick movement of enormous liquidity, it becomes vulnerable to panic and instability. Further, the rate prevailing in the market may not be in alignment with the requirements of the real sector giving a rise to misallocations of resources and ultimate bursting of the bubble termed as 'casino effect'.

East Asian Economy

41. After the weakening of the Dollar, the Deutch Mark (Germany) and the Japanese Yen emerged as important international reserve currencies. Yen appreciated continuously over the Dollar along with steady increase in the wage rate in the Japanese economy resulting into Japan graduating into high cost economy. The growth process emanated from Japan spilled over into the neighbouring countries to take advantage of cheap labour and other advantages of late starter. South Korea, Hong Kong, Taiwan, and Singapore gained in the first place and subsequently, developing countries like, Malaysia, Indonesia, Thailand and Philippines benefited from the process. The above countries in general followed the strategy called 'export led growth'. The growth rates achieved by some of the above countries were in the range of 6-8 per cent during 1961-96.[7]

42. Consequent to switching over to the policy of export led growth and liberalising forex inflows, the above countries experienced a very high rate of growth in the region of six to eight per cent in the eighties and the first half of the nineties.

The high level of performance achieved by such countries became a sort of eye-opener for other developing countries especially India to review the inward looking policies pursued by them. In fact, the argument for implementation of reform in India derived its strength partly due to the success achieved by the above countries. There were a number of reasons as to why this region became successful compared to other countries. Firstly, the continued prosperity in Japan ensured shifting labour intensive industries to other neighbouring South-East Asian countries. Secondly, the above countries incidentally increased the outlay on human resources development through ensuring better access to education and health. Thirdly, over a period of time, the labour force became skill-intensive and at the same time cheap as compared to the Japanese economy.

European Economic Community

43. The region comprising 15 EEC countries included a number of developed countries *viz.*, German, France, Italy, United Kingdom. Due to historical reasons of mutual co-operation among the EEC countries, it was agreed that 11 countries who were willing and complied with the convergence criteria came under Economic and Monetary Union (EMU) to merge their currencies into a single currency called 'Euro' in three phases which started from January 1, 1999 and ending with June 30, 2002.

Euro

44. Such an economic and monetary union ensures free movement of men, material and capital funds among the 12 Euro-Member countries[8] (Greece joined subsequently) and a single border for customs *i.e.*, goods entering into any member country can be freely shipped into other member countries. The ultimate integration is possible with the monetary union with a single currency called 'euro' as each of the constituent surrenders the freedom to frame their own monetary policy.

Reasons for the Emergence of Euro

45. EEC is, in a way, can be looked upon as a political movement to create a counterweight to the dominance of the USA. The impetus to the above arrangement was provided by the emergence of the MNCs as they will be able to operate in

a bigger territory than hitherto. The European MNCs, thus, would be able to derive the competitive advantage *vis-à-vis* the MNCs of the USA and also from Japan. The single market is not without its costs especially for MNCs in the financial sector in terms of reduction in spread and also in the fee based income and other charges and prices to be paid in the process of converting one currency to the other. Hence, in the single economic community, the scope for merger and amalgamation becomes higher to take advantage of the scale economics and also to face the competition more effectively. However, for the EEC as a whole, there would be static and dynamic benefits. The static benefits are in the form of free movement of factors of production and more so of capital, from one place to the other, economy in the form of conversion costs and also the cost incurred to hedge against the movement of currencies of one Euro member country and the other. The dynamic benefits would accrue in the form of less transaction costs, improved efficiency, increased savings and investment and ultimately leading to more growth for the community.

General Agreement on Tariff and Trade (GATT)

46. With a view to protecting the international trade from the protectionism, trade talks were used to be held so that the barriers to the trade are brought down over a period of time in the form of quotas and tariffs. The scope of GATT which initially covered only merchandise trade was widened to cover trading in the services and other investment measures. Hence, GATT associated itself with matters like intellectual property rights, investment measures and trade in services reflecting the emergence of service sector in the share of overall GDP. According to a UNCTAD study, service sector constitute about 68 per cent of GDP in developed countries and around 50 per cent in developing countries. Trade in services represents 16 per cent of all trades. Services now generate about half of all jobs in the formal sector.[9]

World Trade Organisation

47. Consequent to the Uruguay Round, with a view to formalise the arrangement for trade talks, a separate institution called World Trade Organisation (WTO) was established in

April 1995 initially with 77 members as a permanent body. Similar to GATT, the main objective of WTO is to provide for the member countries a forum for negotiation and dialogue in respect of trade matters. The WTO is also entrusted with the task of enforcing the agreements already entered into. Being the signatory to the WTO agreements, the countries are liable for adjudication under WTO arrangement. As WTO is a permanent body and the ministerial conference is being held every two years to review the progress made in the earlier ministerial conference and to start negotiations on new areas to further the objectives of WTO.

PART III

CONDITIONALITIES FOR REAPING THE BENEFITS OF GLOBALISATION

Globalisation and Financial Markets

48. While the globalisation is an inevitable and irreversible process, it is not an unmixed blessing. Integrating the domestic economy with the rest of the world is fraught with risk of exposing the domestic economy to the vicissitudes of global arena. To reap the benefits of globalisation, it is important to ensure that the market mechanism becomes wider and deeper and further endowed with flexibility to achieve the appropriate price discovery in the market place. The price signal, be it the price of goods and services or the factor prices, should reflect the market condition. This is because the whole process of globalisation works on the strength of the underlying market mechanism. Naturally, reaping the benefits of globalisation depends on the robustness and resilience of the market mechanism.

49. Channelising the forces of globalisation for the purpose of development is an arduous task as it demands utmost discipline especially in the matters of fiscal policy and also in the matter of monetary policy. Otherwise, it would lead to monetary instability in the form of high rate of inflation, unsustainable high interest rate and depreciation of the domestic currency. Monetary instability would deprive the country the benefits of liberalisation and it would further damage the growth prospects of the economy for a long time rendering the recovery process more difficult and complex.

50. The financial system has to play a very important role as it acts as a funnel to channelise the resources into the domestic economy among the competing sectors/industries/units in a such a manner that the growth is maximised. To achieve such allocational efficiency, the financial system needs to function in a viable and sustainable manner which, in turn, depends upon the operational efficiency. The operationally efficient financial system would benefit the economy in the form of lower spread between the cost of deposits and the lending rate. The achievement of operational and allocational efficiency requires that the financial system functions with necessary autonomy and manoeuvrability.

51. The freedom to operate the financial system has to be seen with reference to the freedom to allocate the resources among the competing sectors, products, manpower recruitment, deployment and remuneration. The interest rate emanating from market discovery process should remain stable and discourage the unproductive use of resources. Instability in the working of the financial system would lead to high interest rate, which, in turn, could lead to high level of non-performing assets going by the theory of adverse selection. Thus, an economy with efficient and robust financial infrastructure deriving the benefits of globalisation are higher than that of an economy with weak and inefficient financial infrastructure. In short, the economy needs to become resilient enough to weather any unforeseen shocks and contagion effects. Reform in the financial sector is, therefore, a necessary condition. According to John Williamson, "What is needed here, in addition to the strengthening of prudential supervision, is a whole series of apparently minor changes like improving transparency, upgrading accountancy, strengthening the rights of minority creditors, facilitating the recovery of assets pledged as collateral, and developing credit registries. While such reforms may appear minor, in fact they are of fundamental importance, but quite difficult to implement."[10]

52. As we have already noted, South East Asian countries like, Thailand, Indonesia, Malaysia, Taiwan, South Korea, Philippines, etc. experienced high growth in their national income in an uninterrupted manner over a long period of time following the strategy of 'export led growth'. The prospects

of high growth rate and the consequent high rate of return on investment attracted huge foreign capital. The inflow of such foreign capital was encouraged to bridge the domestic saving-investment gap to achieve higher rate of capital formation.

53. To make the foreign investment more attractive, the uncertainty arising from the exchange rate movements was mitigated through management of exchange rate at a fixed level or range. The above lulled the market participants into complacency about the risks arising from exchange rate movements. Further, there was no effective control over the activities of the financial institutions. While the foreign capital was flowing into such economies in an uninterrupted manner expecting a higher rate of return, the growth prospects and consequently the profitable opportunities available at different points of time underwent decline. With a view to ensuring higher rate of return for such capital investment, in the absence of appropriate investment opportunities, the financial system channelised them into more risky investments (real estate and stock and derivative markets). The high euphoria and consequent 'bandwagon effect' ensured that the investment decisions made by the financial system in the host country did not come under the scrutiny of either the lenders or the rating agencies. Later on, when the bubble ultimately bursts, to be exact on July 2, 1977, with the collapse of Thai baht by about 25 per cent, nobody ever thought that it will threaten the whole of newly industrialised countries and would subsequently spread to far away places like Russia and Latin American countries.[11] The internationally reputed rating agencies came under severe criticism for their failure to detect the weakness in such countries and forewarn the international investors. However, the rating agencies blamed it on the lack of transparency in the operations of the economy as well as the financial system.

54. Very often, vulnerability caused by the high level of non-performing assets (NPA) and the consequent liquidity crisis trigger panic reaction amongst the public. All the units of the financial system can survive as long as the investor reposes confidence in them. If the system loses its confidence of the investors, then even the most efficiently managed system becomes insolvent overnight. This is because all the lending

activity is being undertaken by the financial entity with the hope that all the depositors would not come back at the same time to demand their funds back. If that happens for any reason, the failure of the concerned entity becomes inevitable. The financial system is always vulnerable to instability and to the self-fulfilling prophecies. The vulnerability can be reducing by ensuing safety and stability of the financial system.

55. It is possible to prevent unit-level crisis through certain time-tested lender of the last resort facility offered by the central banks, deposit insurance, etc. and the recently evolved mergers and acquisitions of weak entities. However, when it happens to the financial system for a country as a whole in the form of sudden withdrawal of foreign capital, the crisis assumes systemic proportion. The vulnerability to such systemic risk increases especially when such capital flow is for a short-term or to realise gains out of movements in the equity scrip or exchange rate. Hence, the policy framework should take into consideration the above factors especially the state of the economy and the financial system infrastructure and the nature of capital flow. Further, the international investors should be in a position to track the profitability and viability of the financial system. Transparency in the financial system is therefore considered as very important to inspire the confidence of the international investors.

PART IV

Concluding Remarks

56. The analysis made in the preceding three sections brings out very clearly the fact that globalisation is an evolutionary process and is the logical extension of the earlier stage of capitalism. It will further evolve and get shaped with the passage of time and events. A number of drivers to the whole process of globalisation can be identified. The most important among them include, change in the mode of production, evolution in money, banking, form of organization, advancement in the science and technology, computer and telecommunication and the convergence between the above two, international trade and capital movement, etc. The above process brings about changes in the existing order or

configuration or structure of the economy. The adjustment by the economy to the continuing changes is not uniform or smooth due to the inherent resistance to changes caused by the redundancy created in the existing order of things. For example, introduction of IT based production process will make a part of the labour force used to manual operation redundant. Any difficulty in reducing the existing size of the labour force earlier needed for manual operation would result in decrease in productivity in general *vis-à-vis* a new entrant with the state of the art technology. Rigidity is not restricted to labour force alone. On the other hand, rigidity could be present in the pricing of goods and services, monetary and fiscal policies. For example, unwillingness on the part of the Government to allow the exchange rate to reflect the market forces could distort the entire price discovery process and introduce inefficiency in the functioning of the economy. When such maladjustments, inefficiencies are allowed to continue without timely correction, it would lead to crisis in one segment or the other. The positive side about the economic crisis is that it makes the necessary adjustments acceptable to the players in the market/economy/government. In this context, events could act as a guide to facilitate appropriate policy formulation. Globalisation is no exception to this and the events detailed in Part II accelerated globalisation process. The downside about the crisis associated with globalisation process is that it distorts the benefits accruing to the different nations and damages the growth prospects of domestic economy and other nations. To quote, Eswar Prasad *et al.*, "Crisis can be regarded as particularly dramatic episodes of volatility. In fact, the proliferation of financial crises is often viewed as one of the defining aspects of the intensification of financial globalisation over the last two decades."[12]

57. Another important point of discussion is that capitalism and its advancement owes a lot to the appearance and growth of the banking system, but for that, the unprecedented accumulation of wealth would not have been possible. In fact, it could be viewed as a concomitant process. Globalisation came about revolutionizing the money and wealth creating process further thanks to the IT revolution. The dark side to the above is that weakness in the financial system can destroy

the fabric of globalisation beyond recognition with severe consequences that it will take even decades to come out. Hence, globalisation process should be accompanied with measures to protect the stability of the financial system. Part III is an attempt to drive home the above point.

NOTES

1. P. 14 of Erica Meltzer.
2. P. 15 of Kofi Annan
3. P. 6 of Badrinath *et al.*
4. P. 6 of Badrinath.
5. P. 1475 of John Williamson.
6. Please see para on 'Capitalism *vs* Socialism.'
7. P. 13 of *Economic Survey.*
8. There is a proposal to admit another ten countries mainly the countries of the erstwhile USSR and satellite countries and also Turkey into the Euro area.
9. P. 14 of Erica Meltzer.
10. P. 1479 of John Williamson.
11. P. 89 Stiglitz J.
12. P. 4325 of Eswar Prasad *et al.*

REFERENCES

ABN AMRO Bank. *EMU & euro: the consequences.* Special edition — Ewoud Schuitemaker — February 24, 1997.

Badrinath and Ganeshan Wignaraja. *Building Business Competitiveness.* International Trade Forum — Feb. 2004 issue.

Bhagwati J., 2002. *Free Trade To-day.* Princeton N.J.: Princeton University Press.

Economic Survey — 2003-04. Government of India, Ministry of Finance, Economic Division, New Delhi.

Eicher Green B.J., 1996. *Globalising Capital, A History of the International Monetary System.* Princeton, N.J. Princeton University Press.

Erica Meltzer. *UNCTAD — Assuring Development gains from Trade.* International Trade Forum — Feb. 2004 issue.

Eswar Prasad, Kenneth Rogoff, Shang Jin Wei, M. Ayhan Kose. "Effects of Financial Globalisation on Developing Countries" Some Empirical Evidence. Special Articles. *Economic and Political Weekly* — October 11-17, 2003.

Ganti Subramaniam, S.V.S. Dixit, Arindam Roy, 1988. *EMU, EURO and India Development Research Group of RBI* — 1988.

John Williamson, 2003. "The Washington Consensus and Beyond." *Economic and Political Weekly*, p. 1475 — April 12-18, 2003.

Kofi Annan. *Message to International Trade Centre — Launching ITC's 40th Anniversary.* International Trade Forum — Feb. 2004 issue.

Kurien, C.T. *Global Capitalism and the Indian Economy — Tracts for the Times.* Series No. 6, 1994, Orient Longman Limited, Hyderabad.

Radhakrishnan, P. "Religion under Globalisation." Special Articles — *Economic and Political Weekly,* March 27-April 2, 2004.

Raghu G. Rajan and Lingui Zingales, 2003. *Saving Capitalism from Capitalists,* Crown Business, New York.

Reddy, Y.V. "IMF: Concerns, Dilemmas and Issues." *Economic and Political Weekly,* August 2-8, 2003.

Schumpeter, J.A. 1993. *The Theory of Economic Development: An enquiry into profits, capital, credit, interest and the business cycle.* New Brunswick; London; Transaction Publishers.

Stiglitz, J.E. 2002. *Globalisation and its Discontents.* New York, W.W. Norton.

3

Integration of Financial Markets in India

ARUN KUMAR MISRA & A.K. RAMANATHAN

1. INTRODUCTION

Economic activity, particularly finance, has become extremely global in recent decades. The world of finance has changed markedly over the past three decades or so. The change has been brought about by a number of events and circumstances. The growing dissatisfaction with the working of the fixed exchange rate system during the 1960s led many countries, especially of the industrialised world, to adopt floating exchange rate system by the early 1970s. In 1973, a new paradigm in the design of financial policies emerged. The theoretical underpinning of this thought was provided by Mckinnon and Shaw (1973) who forcefully challenged the Keynesian ideas and revived the predominant role of financial sector of the economic development. According to this theory, government and central bank regulations distorted financial markets and the distortion, in turn, adversely affected saving and investment decisions. Subsidized interest rate depressed savings and promoted inefficient investment. The phenomenon came to be known as financial repression.

There was also a growing realisation that achieving sustained growth with stability, necessitated open trade, liberalised external capital movements and a relatively flexible domestic monetary policy. With trade being subjected to multilateral negotiations, industrialised countries and emerging market economies took steps to liberalise capital account/movements across countries since 1970s. Simultaneously, efforts were made to remove distortions in the domestic financial sector through elimination or containment of reserve requirements and interest rate regulations. These initiatives coincided with the rapid technological improvements in electronic payments. The communication and technological advances of the recent years have radically changed access to information and markets and consequently, business and personal strategies. The world economy has become increasingly integrated in terms of trade, investment and financial flows among countries over the past decades. There has been enormous increase in the volume of financial flows across countries — both short-term speculative capital flows, searching for the highest rates of short-term financial returns across currency and interest rates, and of longer-term investment. The emergence of offshore banking centres in the developing world is nothing but the growing cross-border financial transactions. Those countries, on their part, have been practicing, since the early 1980s, market-oriented strategies of financial development, partly supported by the international financial institutions and partly to avail the large pool of resources available in international financial markets. Many developing countries have sharply contained 'financial repression' and undertook financial reforms with a view to enhance allocative efficiency and competitiveness.

Many countries reformed their financial markets and integrated their economies with the rest of the world. The driving force behind the international capital mobility is the prevalence of differential interest rates among the countries and hence the possibility of arbitrage opportunities. The integration of capital markets followed the policy initiatives, which were aimed at liberalisation and deregulation of the domestic markets in all the major industrialised economies. While the spontaneous flows of capital to highly indebted countries have remained limited, the Newly Industrialised Economies (NIE) of Asia expanded their links with the international financial markets both as users and suppliers of capital. Integrated financial markets of those economies are fast developing into a noteworthy segment of the international capital markets. Several Latin American and Asian Countries implemented financial reform policies in terms of elimination of government control over (i) domestic interest rates, (ii) credit allocation and (iii) exchange rate etc. in order to enhance financial integration. Countries like Korea, Malaysia, Chile, Argentina, Uruguay, Japan, Hong Kong, India and China are immediate examples in this regard. However, Bascom (1994) found that the financial reform programmes of Korea, Malaysia, Chile, Argentina and Uruguay were, more or less, aimed at macroeconomic stability of their economies. In other words, limited capital market reforms and prevalence of government controls on cross-border movements of capital tended to dampen the process of financial integration at the global level. At the same time, however, evidence has shown/ given the extent of financial reforms, in those economies led to more integration of various segments of domestic financial markets. Financial development, as a major objective of financial reforms, required the deepening and widening of the existing financial markets as well as the introduction of new products and instruments to cater to the needs of savers and investors. With financial development, secondary markets would become prominent and ensure that financial sector integration is rendered possible.

Since 1991, the process of financial sector reform programme has been continuing in India. Prior to that Chakravarty Committee (1985) recognised the major weakness of the Indian Money Market and recommended *inter alia* the setting up of a working group to study the weaknesses of Indian money market in detail. Accordingly, the Vaghul Working Group was appointed by the RBI, which recommended for the introduction of new instruments, such as, Commercial Papers (CPs), Certificates of Deposits (CDs), 182-day Treasury Bills besides the revival of inter-bank participation Certificates. In accordance with the recommendations of Narasimham Committee (1991), banking sector reforms and reforms in money market and capital market have been undertaken. Deregulation of interest rates and market based allocation of resources has infused competition in the financial markets. Deregulation of interest rates has led to the convergence of interest rates among the short-term markets — Money, Credit, and Gilt markets. Co-movements of various interest rates in uniform direction is an encouraging sign of the growing integration of financial markets in India. The call rates, forward premia and the certificate deposit rates are found to be highly correlated. The capital market, particularly the stock market, has undergone rapid transformation in recent years. The massive investment made by foreign institutional investors in the Indian stock market have increased its volume of trade. It has been found that the BSE-(100 scripts) Index and the NASDAQ Index are highly correlated (RBI, 2000).

The review provides a basis for the paper to initiate a process of measuring the integration of financial markets in case of India.

2. FINANCIAL INTEGRATION: CONCEPTS AND ITS PROPERTIES

Integration is a process by which segmented markets become open and unified so that participant enjoys the same unimpeded access to international trade and finance. It occurs through the removal of domestic and international controls on trade in financial assets, goods or services. Integration of markets is a tendency for prices of goods, services and financial assets of different markets to converge. Financial integration leads to rapid flows of funds from 'less returns markets' to 'high returns markets' and, in this process, it brings about equality in returns. Return differentials across markets could cause arbitraged shifts in portfolios of investors, ultimately, bringing about an overall equality of returns across markets. It is the deregulation and innovations in financial markets, in recent years that have contributed in bringing about integration of financial markets.

Financial integration can vary in strength from perfect integration to perfect disintegration or segmentation and also it can be direct or indirect. Perfect integration is said to prevail if goods and foreign exchange markets are integrated and there is no risk premium, even for political risk. If perfect integration takes place between two markets then, both the markets will behave as one. In case of direct financial integration, which is also known as capital market integration, it is expressed in deviations from the 'law of one price' for financial securities. Under direct financial integration investors can expect the same return on investments and borrowers can expect the same loan costs on different markets, after the requisite adjustment has been made for risk. Indirect financial integration refers to a situation in which the return on an investment in one country is indirectly linked to the return on investments in other countries.

An important objective of financial reforms has been to develop the various segments of the financial market into an integrated one. Economies that exhibit strong financial integration have very different macroeconomic properties from those, which exist in financial autarky. Financial integration is the opposite of the segmentation or partitioning or compartmentalisation of the financial markets in terms of maturitywise, geographical, institutional, seasonal and instrumental aspect. The macroeconomic consequences of strong financial integration are typically derived on the usual assumption that all domestic interest bearing assets are perfect substitutes. Five macroeconomic implications of strong financial integration are especially important. These implications are as under:

(a) Domestic Investment is Independent of Domestic Saving

Changes in excess supplies and demands of assets in a small economy have no influence on the world prices of the assets. Thus, shocks to domestic saving and investment schedules, which affect the domestic flow of excess supply and demand for the financial assets, leave the rates of return on assets unchanged confronting domestic agents. In particular, changes in domestic investment do not affect the rates of return on assets available to domestic savers, and changes in domestic saving do not affect the cost of capital for domestic firms. The implication is that economic growth is not limited by scarcity of domestic saving. It follows that policy measures to promote saving do not increase domestic investment but merely reduce the current deficit.

(b) Domestic Borrowing and Lending are Independent of Domestic Monetary and Fiscal Policies

The effects of domestic fiscal and monetary policies on aggregate demand also depends on the extent to which the economy is financially integrated with the rest of the world.

Under the fixed or predetermined exchange rates regime that characterises most developing countries, strong financial integration implies that in a small economy neither fiscal nor monetary policy can influence the terms for domestic borrowing and lending.

(c) Domestic Inflation is Influenced by International Inflation

The economy's steady-state inflation rate may be affected by the extent of its integration with world capital markets. The revenue that a government can collect from the inflation tax depends on the stock of base money and on the elasticity of base money demand with respect to the rate of inflation. Given the revenue to be raised through the inflation tax, the smaller the stock of base money and higher its elasticity with respect to the rate of inflation, the higher the steady-state inflation rate. Even under weak financial integration, domestic agents have more means at their disposal to escape an inflation tax than when the economy where financial sector is closed. This is likely to increase the elasticity of base money demand, implying that the inflationary consequences of a given fiscal deficit are magnified.

(d) Taxation and High Capital Mobility

Taxes on capital generally become more problematic under a situation of high capital mobility because taxes can be evaded by taking funds out of the country. With high capital mobility, the taxation of capital would leave the domestic economy with a sub-optimal capital stock because owners of capital would require an after-tax rate in the domestic economy equal to the pre-tax return available externally.

(e) Interest Rate and Capital Mobility

Interest rate policy in repressed economies, in which domestic interest rates are subjected to binding legal restrictions, is affected by the implications of financial openness. The pursuit of positive real interest rates in a closed economy, which the domestic marginal product of capital is the relevant opportunity cost of funds may easily be frustrated by capital inflows, if the economy is sufficiently open.

The above macroeconomic implications of strong financial integration are well-known, but not much work has been done to assess the position of developing countries. Although the vast majority of developing countries maintain controls on capital movements, the effectiveness of the controls is often questioned, and there is a widespread view that the mere existence of those controls does not justify treating the countries as closed economies.

3. EXPERIENCES OF DEVELOPED COUNTRIES

At the international level, the cross border movements of capital has to some extent helped in the integration of domestic financial markets of various countries. Many countries undertook open economy macroeconomic policies, which led to the movements of global capital. The interest rate differential and hence the arbitrage opportunities among countries is the driving force for the integration of financial markets. Conversely, the integration of international financial markets led to a global interest rate, like LIBOR, Euro-market etc., which exerts influence on markets of all over the world.

During the 1960s and 1970s, majority of the models of the interest-sensitivity of capital flows assumed that the US interest rates were unaffected by foreign influences. But reduced trade barriers and the internationalisation of the credit market in recent years, has indicated that even the US financial markets are exposed to foreign influence. Studies of the interest-sensitivity of the capital flows were reported in Branson (1968), Branson and Hill (1971), Kwack and Schink (1975) and Kenen (1978), among others. Cross-country results show that the capital flows are interest sensitive. However, the sensitivity is far from degree of infinite elasticity. Infinite elasticity is a feature of perfect market integration. The studies on Purchasing Power Parity and the international Fisher effect by various authors like, Mishkin (1984), Cumby and Obstfeld (1984) revealed a fairly low degree of financial integration. These authors reported a gap between real interest rates of countries and also absence of correlation among the values of the real interest rate pertaining to the countries. According to the authors, imperfect integration of goods markets rather than that of financial markets might be reason for deviations in the values of real interest rate.

By the second half of the 1970s, international economists

had to speak about the world financial system as characterised by perfect capital mobility. According to them, world financial integration started in 1973, with the removal of capital controls on the part of the USA, Canada, Germany, Switzerland and the Netherland. The steady progress of technical, institutional and financial innovations and the recycling of OPEC surpluses to developing countries helped the process of financial integration. It was expected that international capital mobility would lead to the integration of world financial markets.

4. EXPERIENCES OF DEVELOPING COUNTRIES

Since the mid-1970s several Latin American and Asian countries implemented financial reform policies or eliminated Government control of domestic interest rates, credit allocation and exchange rate etc. Countries like Korea, Malaysia, Chile, Argentina, Uruguay, Japan, Hong Kong, India and China have liberalised their economies. These countries undertook many policy decisions to reform their financial markets. One of the main aims of financial reforms programme of these countries has been to integrate the various segments of financial markets. Bascom's (1994), indepth study on financial reforms in developing countries revealed that developing countries particularly Korea, Malaysia, Chile, Argentina and Uruguay were forced to implement financial sector reform for macroeconomic stability of their economies. Financial reform in Korea, particularly the reform in the banking sector, deregulation of administered interest rate and policy initiatives for widening of primary and secondary markets in fact contributed to the movements of various market-determined interest rates in tandem. However, limited capital market reforms and Government controls on cross-border movements of capital and lack of capital account convertibility have led to the absence of integration of Korean financial markets with that of international financial markets. However, the reform in financial sector, led to more integration of various segments of domestic financial markets. In 1980s, many countries of Sub-Saharan Africa initiated major restructuring programme in their financial systems as a part of Structural Adjustment Programmes (SAP). However, SAP could not succeed in integrating the financial markets due to lack of proper financial institutions and regulatory authorities.

5. FINANCIAL INTEGRATION: THE INDIAN EXPERIENCE

The financial sector reform measures initiated during 1990s paved the way for the integration of financial markets in India. In their study on financial market integration Bhoi and Dhal (1998) found that deregulation of interest rates led to the convergence of interest rates among the short-term markets — Money, Credit, and Gilt markets —, but the capital market deviated from the integration path. However, the co-movements of various interest rates in uniform direction, is an encouraging sign of the growing maturity of financial markets in India. The study did not however, found integration between domestic and international financial markets, because of limited liberalisation of foreign exchange market and the policy on foreign investment in the country.

The Reserve Bank of India in its Report on Currency and Finance (2000) extensively studied the process of liberalisation of Indian financial markets and integration of various segments of domestic financial markets and the overall integration of domestic financial with the international financial market. The study found evidence for the gradual integration of call money and the foreign exchange markets. The volatility spillovers in the above two markets were found to follow the same path, indicating the intrinsic link between the two. The foreign exchange spot and forward markets were not found to be integrated, even though the high volatility in spot market increases the forward rates. This aspect indicates that the Indian foreign exchange market is not efficient. The other segments of Indian money market, particularly the Gilt market is found to be integrated with the call money market. The 90-day treasury bill instrument is evolving as the best indicative rate for the short-term interest rates. The call rates, forward premia and the certificate deposit rates are found to be highly correlated. However, the study could not find evidence for the integration of institutional deposit and lending rates with money market. The capital market, particularly the stock market has undergone rapid transformation in recent years. The massive investment made by foreign institutional investors in the Indian stock market have increased its volume of trade. The study has found that the BSE-(100 scripts) Index and the NASDAQ Index are highly correlated.

As far as the international integration is concerned, Bhoi and Dhal (1998) found that the interest rate parity condition does not hold in case of India. However, Pattanaik (1999) has found that the Purchasing Power Parity holds only in the long-run in case of India. The study on term structure interest rates also indicate the integration process of financial markets. Term structure interest rates refer to the alignments of short- and long-term interest rates of identical assets. In case of India term structure interest rates does not prevail, as yields of various maturities are still not perfectly correlated (Ghose and Nag, 2000). Joshi (1998) has found that the term structure theory holds good in case of call rates and cut-off yields on government of India 91-day treasury bill rates, medium term 364-day treasury bill rates and redemption yields on long-term government of India securities, indicating that the above instruments are integrated.

6. IMPLICATIONS OF FINANCIAL INTEGRATION

The process of deregulation and globalisation of financial markets gained momentum in the 1990s and it expanded the choices for investors. It also helped to improve the prospects of reducing the costs of financial transactions and improving operational and allocative efficiency of the financial system. A number of developing countries, especially in Asia, that moved early on to the path of economic liberalisation had experienced large capital inflows during the 1980s and the first half of 1990s. Large capital inflows, however, carried with it risk of financial sector vulnerability, where the flows is not buttressed by the applications of proper mix of macroeconomic and structural policy measures. The recent currency crisis and financial crisis in Mexico and Thailand, followed by Korea and Indonesia, provide many insights about the problems that would arise when exchange rates are inflexible and banking and financial systems are weak. The experience of the crisis-affected countries highlights the need for setting regulatory and supervisory framework, in proper place, to ensure the safety and stability of financial systems. Their experience also underscored the premise that financial development is only a necessary condition for sustainable growth, and by no means sufficient. In fact, with the incidence of the costs of financial crisis falling on the sovereign governments, the notion of financial stability has come to occupy a centre-stage in public policy along with the requirement of ensuring that the efficiency of financial sector is high.

There are several reasons why policymakers and economists focus on financial integration. The macroeconomic policy-mix depends crucially on the openness of the financial system (Fleming, 1962, Mundell, 1963). The more mobile is capital, the more substitutable are financial assets and the less flexible is the exchange rate, the more difficult for the country to set the interest rate policy independently. Thus, when domestic financial markets are integrated with the world financial markets this has crucial implications on the formulation of monetary and exchange rate policies. In the event of domestic financial integration, there will be alignment of various interest rates and the market itself will create a reference rate. All other interest rates will move in accordance with the reference rate. There will be close connection and effective linkages between various parts and sub-parts of financial markets, which will reduce the arbitrage opportunities and, thus, increase the efficiency of financial markets.

Integration of domestic financial market with the international financial markets has significant implications for the formulation of monetary and exchange rate policies. In the event of international integration of domestic financial markets, the monetary authorities lose their independence in the formulation of interest rate policy. The emergence of financial innovations consequent upon financial development and global integration has cast doubts about the effectiveness of having simple rules of monetary policy, such as, monetary targeting. As a result, domestic monetary policy formulation has to be adequately flexible to attain the specified objectives. This implies that there is a need for continuous interface between the financial market and monetary and exchange rate management. They need to be mutually reinforcing also. It is now recognised that the behavioural relations that evolve out of the interface would provide critical insights about the state of the development, diversification, efficiency and integration of financial markets and also the elements that constitute the transmission channels of monetary policy. In case of international integration of financial markets, the domestic interest rate is determined by international factors rather than domestic factors. The domestic saving-investment will be less correlated. The exogeneity character of money supply will not be there and the money demand function becomes unstable. In addition, when the necessary macro-economic fundamentals are lacking, banking systems are weak, and domestic distortions are pervasive, countries may experience capital flight rather than capital inflows, or they may be unable to use inflows efficiently. Inefficiency could be in terms of unstable growth. Now the question is how developing countries can respond to these challenges, drawing upon the evolving experience of the more rapidly integrating countries.

7. MEASUREMENT OF FINANCIAL INTEGRATION: METHODOLOGICAL ISSUES

The most crucial issue related to financial integration is its measurement. An economy is financially open when its residents are freely trade financial assets with other country. Several empirical methods have been developed to measure the financial integration. These include measures of magnitude of gross capital flows, the degree of arbitrage, the scope for sterilization, saving-investment correlation and tests based on the Euler Equation for the path of optimal consumption.

There are several ways of testing for market integration. In the past static high price correlations, across markets were considered to reflect market integration [Jones (1968), Harris (1979), Uri and Riffin (1985), Blyn (1983)]. The simple bivariate correlations, of various markets rates would indicate the degree of association of various rates and show the co-movements of various rates. However, the statistical correlation coefficient as a measure of market efficiency has been rejected on the ground of non-stationary nature of variables under consideration. To circumvent this problem, the regression analysis has been suggested. A notable contribution in this direction was made by Ravallion (1986), who proposed a dynamic model for testing market integration, through spatial price differentials. Subsequently, the Ravallion (1986) model was employed and extended by others [Monke and

Petzel (1984), Neal (1987) and Faminow and Benson (1990)]. A relatively less restrictive approach to market integration is the cointegration and error correction technique [Alexander and Wyelh (1994)]. If prices in two different markets bear a long run relationship, the prices are said to be cointegrated and the market are integrated. The cointegration approach to market integration has been considered as an alternative to the Ravallion model.

International parity conditions provide criteria for measuring the degree of integration between different world markets. Purchasing Power Parity (PPP) is the core upon which the international parity criteria are based. There are three interrelated criteria to measure the market integration—(1) Covered Interest Parity (CIP), (2) Uncovered Interest Parity (UIP) and (3) Real Interest Parity (RIP). Last four decades have witnessed a tremendous revival of interest rate parity theory.

7.1 Partial Adjustment Analysis

The Partial Adjustment Model (PAM) shows the degree and speed of integration of different segments of financial market. It also gives an estimate of the long run elasticity and mean-lag response of the variables with respect to the reference rate.

7.2 Cointegration and Market Integration

Cointegration technique identifies the long run structural relationship among the variables under consideration. It indicates that in the long run, the variables under study would move in the same direction without drifting apart from each other. Thus, when two variables are cointegrated then they have long run relationship, which, in turn, means they are integrated. Cointegration provides ideal framework for the study of financial market integration. It is through rates/ratios/ returns market integration is measured. If returns from two markets move in the same direction, then it can be inferred that the markets are integrated.

Prior to the estimation of the model, one needs to examine the stationarity of the processes, which can be checked using Augmented Dicky Fuller (ADF) and Philip-Perron (PP) tests.

Both bivariate and multivariate cointegration techniques have been used to measure the process of market integration. A final consideration in using the VAR model is the choice of the order of the process. In the present study, minimum Akaike Information Criteria (AIC) has been used to determine the optimum lag length.

For analysis of market integration the paper has considered money market, foreign exchange market and capital market. In the money market, call money (CMR), certificate deposits (CDR), short-term government treasury bill (G91 & G365) and commercial paper (CPR) have been considered as instruments for integration process. For banking sector, commercial bank lending rate (LRT) and deposits rate (DRT) have been considered. Similarly, in the foreign exchange market, forward premia of three-month and six-month (FRW3 & FRW6) have been chosen as the instruments.

Except stock indices, which are taken daily basis, frequencies of all other variables are monthly basis. The period of study is March 1993 to December 2003.

7.3 Identification of Reference Rate

To identify the process of integration, a reference rate is needed. To select the reference rate, all variables have been put for stylise tests, which include the tests for standard deviation, mean, skewness, kurtosis and tests for time series properties. Results indicate that Government of India 91-day treasury bill (G91) variable has a remarkably low standard deviation, kurtosis and skewness. Further, except U.S. Fed Fund rate, which is found to be stationary at the level, all other variables are stationary at their first difference. The reference rate is supposed to have causal relationship with other rates. For this reason, the 'Granger's Non-Causality Test' has been carried out in a bivariate framework for the identification of the reference rate. Results of the Granger non-causality test indicates that the Government of India Treasury Bill rate of 91-day is influencing almost all variables of Money Market, Credit Markets and Foreign Exchange Market. Hence, G91 can be treated as the standard reference rate for the present study of market integration.

8. DOMESTIC FINANCIAL INTEGRATION

After identifying the reference rate, tests of integration of domestic financial markets are carried out using (1) cross correlation matrix, (2) partial adjustment analysis and (3) co-integration technique.

8.1 Cross Correlation Matrix

The partial correlation matrix of selected rates and ratios shows the varying degree of co-movements of the different rates and ratios. The correlation matrix further indicates positive co-movements of 91-day Government of India Treasury bill rate (G91) with almost all variables of money market, foreign exchange market and short-term credit market. However, commercial banks deposit rate and lending rate, Price-Earning ratio of BSE sensitive index and return on capital are not having significant correlation with other variables. Hence, from the results, it cannot be generalised that domestic financial markets are strongly integrated.

8.2 Partial Adjustment Analysis

The variables, which are found to be highly correlated with 'G91', are only considered as dependent variables for partial adjustment analysis. The estimated results for each of the selected variables is given in Table 1.

TABLE 1: Comparative Analysis of Partial Adjustment Model (Independent Variable: G91)

Select Dependent Variable	Adjustment Coefficient (δ)	Impact Elasticity	Long run Elasticity
CPR	0.108	0.191	—
CMR	0.383	1.155*	3.01
CDR	0.949	–2.316	—
DRT	0.075	0.132	—
LRT	0.020	–0.083*	–4.15
FRW3	0.145	0.448	—
FRW6	0.094	0.348	—

* Indicates significant at 5% level.

Table 1 presents the comparative analysis results of partial adjustment analysis. The table reveals the following salient observations:

(i) As far as adjustment coefficient is concerned, Certificate Deposits Rate (CDR) has the highest value (0.949) followed by Call Money Rate (CMR) (0.383).

(ii) Impact elasticity is meaningfully significant only in case of CMR (1.155). In case of Lending Rate (LRT), it is significant, but, with perverted value of the coefficient (-0.083).

(iii) The long run elasticity is 3.01 for CMR and (-)4.15 for LRT.

An important observation can be made from the above analysis is that while CMR shows less degree of adjustment with itself, it is more responsive to the reference rate (G91). On the other hand, although CDR shows very high speed of adjustment process, it is not sensitive to reference rate.

From the above analysis, it can be inferred that financial integration is not significantly widespread according to Partial Adjustment Model.

8.3 Cointegration Technique

8.3.1 ***Money Market Integration***: Money market integration is analysed in bivariate and multivariate cointegrating framework. Before that, the order of integration of all variables under consideration have been checked and are found to be stationary at their first difference. The money market integration process is analysed by estimating the alignment of different instruments of this market. It is expected that instruments are integrated among themselves and there will be less arbitrage opportunities among them.

The results of cointegration for intra-money market are reported in Table 2. From the comparative analysis of the pairwise alignments of select variables following important observations are emerged:

(i) Number of cointegrating vector is one in all cases indicating unidirectional relationship. In this context, it is also seen that CPR follows in all cases, while CMR leads.

TABLE 2: Comparative Analysis of Cointegration Results of Intra-Money Market Integration

Variable Pair (Group)	Order of VAR	No. of Cont. Vector	Nature of Significance of Coefficient	
Dept. Indpt.			OLS	Cointegration
CPR & CMR	4	1	NS	S
CDR & CMR	1	1	S	S
CPR & CDR	1	1	S	S
CPR, CDR & CMR	6	1	CDR-S CMR-S	CMR-NS CDR-S

NS - Not Significant, S - Significant; Vectors at 5% level of significance; First variable is dependent variable.

(ii) The long run co-movements among select variables are evident.

(iii) All the long run relationships are statistically significant.

8.3.2 ***Integration of Money and Gilt Markets***: The participants in both money and Gilt markets are same and they arbitrage between these two markets. Also, the Reserve Bank of India intervenes in both markets to maintain liquidity in the economy. Therefore, it is expected that interest rates on different instruments in both the markets have long run relationship. To investigate this, alignment of various instruments of money and Gilt markets are considered in a cointegrating framework and the comparative analysis of the alignments of variables is provided in Table 3.

TABLE 3: Comparative Analysis of Cointegration Results of Money & Gilt Markets Integration

Variable Pair (Group)	Order of VAR	No. of Cont. Vector (CV)	Nature of Significance of Coefficient	
Dept. Indpt.			OLS	Cointegration
CPR, G91 & CDR	2	1	CDR-S G91-S	CDR-S G91-S
LRT & G91	1	0	S	—
DRT & G91	5	0	NS	—
CPR & G91	1	1	S	S
CDR & G91	1	1	S	S
CMR & G91	1	1	S	S

NS - Not Significant, S - Significant; Vectors at 5% level of significance; First variable is dependent variable.

The following observations can be inferred from Table 3:

(i) The number of cointegrating vector is one for four cases (CPR both multivariate and bivariate analysis, CDR and CMR).

(ii) In case of LRT and DRT, cointegrating vector is not found.

(iii) Long-run unidirectional relationship is present for the four cases.

(iv) In all four cases of cointegration, relationship is significant.

8.3.3 ***Integration of Money and Credit Markets*****:** Through the alignment of interest rates of different instruments of money market with the commercial bank lending rate and deposit rates, it is possible to know the integration of money and credit markets. In India, about 90 per cent of business activities in money market are controlled by commercial banks and they arbitrage their funds between the markets to make profits. Because of the arbitrage activities, it is expected that different instruments of the markets would follow same path and bring about integration in these two markets. Results of cointegration analysis between select pairs of variables in the two markets are presented in Table 4.

TABLE 4: Comparative Analysis of Cointegration Results of Money & Credit Markets Integration

Variable Pair (Group) Dept. Indpt.	Order of VAR	No. of Cont. Vector	Nature of Significance of Coefficient: OLS	Nature of Significance of Coefficient: Cointegration
LRT & DRT	5	1	NS	S
LRT & CMR	1	1	S	S
CDR & DRT	1	1*	S	NS

NS - Not Significant, S - Significant; Vectors at 5% level of significance.

* Only at 10% level of significance.

Table 4 provides a comparative analysis of the results of money and credit markets integration. It reveals the followings:

(i) Cointegrating vector in case of each pairs of variables is one. The long run relationship between the paired variables is, therefore, established. However, the same is at 10 per cent significance level in case of the pair CDR and DRT.

(ii) As far as the significance of relationship is concerned, in case of the pair LRT and CMR, it is significant, however, in case of the pair LRT and DRT, the relationship is not significant under OLS analysis. On the other hand, in case of the pair CDR and DRT, the test is not significant under cointegration approach.

8.3.4 *Integration of Money and Foreign Exchange Markets*: Financial markets are interdependent. It is the interest rates, which integrate financial markets. For foreign exchange market, the money market is most important. Forward points, *i.e.,* the spread between the spot and the forward exchange rate is perhaps the best indicator of close relationship between the two markets. Both in money and foreign exchange markets, banks and authorised financial institutions are the lenders and borrowers. They take part in both markets on behalf of customers and are able to make profits through arbitrage opportunities. Since interest rate differentials are the price for the foreign exchange contract, it is expected that there could be some inherent relationship between money market and foreign exchange forward market. The most important component of money market is the call money market and, therefore, one should focus attention to study the causality and integration between call money rate and foreign exchange forward rate. The cointegrating relationship between call money rate and three months forward premium is found to have a VAR of order one. It has a single cointegrating vector, indicating the long run relationship, which is significant both under OLS and cointegration approaches. The results of the Granger Non-Causality test conducted under bivariate framework imply that the variables cause each other.

8.3.5 *Integration of Money and Capital Markets*: The Certificate Deposit Rate (CDR) and Commercial Paper Rate (CPR) along with Return On Capital (ROC) and Price-Earning Ratio (PER) of 100-scrip Bombay Sensitive Index (BSE) are considered for the testing of capital market integration with money market. The comparative cointegration results

(Table 5) reveals that cointegration exists only in the case of CDR and PER pair. However, the test for the relationship is not significant both under OLS and cointegrating relationship.

TABLE 5: Comparative Analysis of Cointegration Results Pertaining to Money & Capital Markets Integration

Variable Pair (Group) Dept. Indpt.	Order of VAR	No. of Cont. Vector	Nature of Significance of Coefficient OLS	Cointegration
CDR & PER	1	1*	NS	NS
CPR & PER	2	0	NS	—

NS - Not Significant, S - Significant; Vectors at 5% level of significance.
* Only at 10% level of significance.

8.3.6 ***Integration of Foreign Exchange Markets***: Exchange rate volatility has been a subject of research since the collapse of the Bretton Woods system in 1973. The volatility has increased the exchange rate risk. As an insurance against this risk, the forward market for exchange rate has been developed. Foreign exchange market will be efficient, if current forward is just equal to its future spot. If spot and forward markets are integrated, then both markets are functionally dependent.

In India the foreign exchange market has become more active with the opening up of current account and partial liberalisation of the capital account. By integration of foreign exchange market, it means that the spot and forward markets are integrated. In theory, it is generally held that foreign exchange market is efficient, if current forward is equal to its future spot. If both the markets are integrated, then it would be a long run functional relationship between them and price of one market can be used to predict the price of other.

An analysis of alignment of the spot and forward markets have been carried out. The cointegrating relation between spot and forward rates (both 3 and 6 months) with a VAR order of four gives a single cointegrating vector, but, the implied long run relationship between the two is not significant. OLS estimate also does not provide any significant results.

9. INTERNATIONAL INTEGRATION

To study the international integration of domestic financial markets, the U.S.A. financial market has been considered as the representative of world financial markets. In this respect, US-treasury bill rate, US-Fed Fund rate and NASDAQ index have been considered to measure the degree of international integration of the Indian financial market. Domestic saving-investment correlation and the interest parity hypotheses have also been analysed.

In India, the process of reforms in trade, industry, banking and finance, international trade and capital inflows have increased considerably in recent years, yet in a discrete pattern. The trade-GDP ratio, which is generally considered as an indicator of open economy, after a rising trend from 1991-92 to 1995-96, is exhibiting somewhat declining trend thereafter. One of the encouraging indicators of international integration is the foreign capital inflow to India. Though, all emerging market economies have witnessed the rising inflows of foreign capital in 1990s, in India it has significantly contributed in the rising trend of stock indices and foreign exchange reserves.

9.1 Co-movement of Domestic and International Stock Indices

Another way to measure degree of financial openness is to gauge the co-movements of indices in the domestic stock markets and international stock markets. The correlation between domestic stock (BSE index) and NASDAQ is given in Table 6. As a result of large capital flows, especially portfolio investments since 1993-94, the sensitivity of the Indian stocks to developments in international stocks has increased. The impact was particularly strong in 1999-2000 as movements in the technology stocks in the NASDAQ had a significant bearing on the Indian stock markets. Many Indian GDRs/ADRs listed on the international stock markets during the period from 1993-94 to 1990-2000 traded either at discount or at premium. The value of correlation coefficient between BSE and NASDAQ was 0.762 in 1993, which got reduced to 0.013 in 1995 due to scam at BSE. In 1996 it again rose to 0.759. The value again declined to 0.204 in 1998 due to the liquidity problem and change in the settlement pattern. However, in 1999 it again increased to 0.751 and stood at 0.652 in 2003. The discrete movement of the correlation coefficient is an encouraging sign of international integration of domestic capital market.

TABLE 6: Correlation between BSE-Index and NASDAQ

Variable/ Year	1993	1994	1995	1996	1997	1998	1999	2000	2001	2002	2003
BSE ~ NASDAQ	0.762*	0.012	0.013	0.759*	0.628*	0.204	0.751*	0.723*	0.729*	0.671*	0.652*

* Significant at 5% level.

9.2 Correlation between Short-term Interest Rates and Forward Premia

In India, the very short-term interest rate is the inter-bank call money rate, which is an overnight rate. It is highly volatile in nature and very much affected by the development of foreign exchange market, which, in turn, is influenced by the international financial development. It is generally observed that the call money market and foreign exchange market moves in tandem. Players in both the markets are same. They arbitrage between the two markets to make profit. Therefore, if the domestic financial markets are integrated with the world financial markets then call money and forward premium will bear good correlation.

TABLE 7: Correlation Between Forward Premia and Call Money Rates

Variable/ Year	1993	1994	1995	1996	1997	1998	1999	2000	2001	2002	2003
CMR~ FRW3	0.95*	0.45*	0.41*	0.94*	0.52*	0.67*	0.32*	0.44*	0.51*	0.54*	0.67*
CMR~ FRW6	0.94*	0.39*	0.84*	0.98*	0.44*	0.55*	0.38*	0.35*	0.37*	0.42*	0.45*

*Significant at 5% level.

The correlation between call money rates and 'three-month' and 'six-month' forward premia are given in the Table 7. The correlation coefficient between 'three-month' forward premium and call money rate was 0.95 in 1993 which came down to 0.41 in 1995 and after that increased to 0.94 in 1996 and stood at 0.44 in 2000. In 2001 the correlation coefficient improved to 0.51 and stood at 0.67 in 2003. Similarly, the correlation coefficient between 'six-month' forward premia and call money rate was 0.94 in 1993, which got reduced to 0.39 in the subsequent year and then it increased to 0.98 in 1996. It again got reduced to 0.38 in 1999 and stood at 0.45 in 2003. Thus, there is no definite trend in the correlation between call money rates and forward premia. However, the significant correlation indicates co-movements of rates, which is an encouraging sign of market integration.

9.3 Saving-Investment Correlation

The financial liberalisation has opened the avenue for domestic industries to tap the global financial market and many industries have mopped up capital through GDRs/ADRs issue. Because of the liberalisation measures, it is expected that domestic investment would be independent of domestic saving. If this happens, then domestic capital market would be integrated with that of World capital market. Following the Feldstein and Horioka (1990) and Feldstein and Bacchetta (1991), an empirical analysis has been carried out to test the capital market integration.

TABLE 8: Empirical Estimation of Capital Market Integration [Dependent variable: Saving-Income Ratio (S/Y)]

Parameter	Cochrane-Orcutt [AR(2)]
Investment-Income Ratio (I/Y)	0.7465* (30.69)
Intercept	4.896* (8.3317)
R^{-2}	0.998
F(1.5)	89.66*
D-W	2.014

*Significant at 5% level.

Through the empirical analysis the coefficient of Investment-Income ratio (I/Y) is found to be significantly different from zero. This imply, domestic investment and domestic savings have significant connectivity. In other words, the capital inflows have not been able to integrate the domestic capital market with the world capital market. However, the fact that the coefficient of I/Y is found to be 0.75 is an indicator of some degree of ongoing integration of domestic capital market with the world capital market.

9.4 Interest Rate Parity Hypothesis

International Parity conditions provide criteria for measuring the degree of integration between different world markets. The Covered Interest Parity (CIP) theory postulates that spot and forward exchange rates quoted at the same instance in time, tend, in general, to diverge exactly in line with the short-term interest rate differential on identical assets across countries. The equilibrium condition implied by the hypothesis is expressed as:

Domestic interest rate (I) – Foreign interest rate (I*) = Forward Premia (FD)

The equation estimated to test for CIP is in the following form:

$$Y = \alpha + \beta \, FD + \upsilon$$

Where 'Y' is the interest rate differential between India and US, 'FD' is the forward premia between Indian rupee and US Dollar and 'υ' is the stochastic error term with zero mean and constant variance $(0,\sigma^2)$. For interest rate differential, Indian call money rates and US Fed Fund rates have been considered.

The CIP will hold if the coefficient of interest rate differential is unity and the intercept is zero. To test the joint hypothesis $(\alpha = 0; \beta = 1)$, 'Wald Test' of restrictions has been imposed on the parameters.

The Uncovered Interest Parity (UIP) hypothesis equates interest rates differential with expected change in spot rate. In other words, if the market is efficient then current forward rate, which reflects the interest rate differential, should be equal to the future spot rate. The equilibrium condition for UIP can be expressed as:

Interest rates differential = expected change in spot rate.

In conventional regression equation this relation can be written as:

$$Y = \alpha + \beta \, (\Delta S^e) + \upsilon$$

Where 'Y' is the interest rate differential and 'ΔS^e' is expected change in the spot rate. Since it is very difficult to know the expected depreciation, actual depreciation has been considered for the analysis. UIP hypothesis will hold if the coefficient of expected depreciation is one and intercept is zero. To test the joint hypothesis ($\alpha = 0$; $\beta = 1$), 'Wald Test' of restriction has been imposed on the parameters.

The Real Interest Parity (RIP), on the other hand, states that expected exchange rate depreciation equates with the real interest rates differential between countries under consideration. For arriving at RIP, in place of expected inflation, following the rational expectation, one period lag of actual inflation is considered. In equation form it can be written as:

$$Y^* = \alpha + \beta(\Delta DS^e) + \upsilon_t$$

Where Y* is the real interest rate differential between India and US and 'υ_t' is the stochastic error term with zero mean and constant variance. RIP hypothesis holds, if, coefficient of expected depreciation is one and intercept is zero ($\alpha = 0$, $\beta = 1$).

The variables under study, are tested for their stationary property using Augmented Dicky Fuller (ADF) Test and Phillips Perron Test and all variables are found to be stationary at their levels [I(0)]. Since all variables are I(0), Ordinary Least Squares (OLS) is used to estimate the equations.

The results of CIP, UIP and RIP hypotheses are presented in Tables 9, 10 and 11 respectively. Cochrane-Orcutt method [AR(2)] has been employed to correct the autocorrelation. Table 9 (CIP results) show that α and β are statistically significant. The results further indicate that the parameters estimated are statistically significant. However, the Wald test of restrictions (joint hypothesis) imposed on parameters ($\alpha = 0$; $\beta = 1$) rejected the CIP hypothesis.

Altogether similar results have emerged in case of UIP and RIP hypotheses (Table 10 and Table 11). In a nutshell, the interest rate parity hypotheses does not appear to hold good under Indian situation. Imperfect substitutions of assets, trade restrictions, control over capital flows and also high risk premia are some possible reasons for not holding of interest rate parity conditions in India.

TABLE 9: Results of the Empirical Estimation of CIP Hypothesis (Dependent Variable: Rupee-Dollar Forward Premia)

Parameter	Cochrane-Orcutt [AR(2)]
α	5.62*
	(3.55)
β	0.81*
	(6.56)
R^{-2}	0.82
DW	1.993
Wald Test	χ^2=218.2*

TABLE 10: Results of the Empirical Estimation of UIP Hypothesis (Dependent Variable: Interest Rate Differential)

Parameter	Cochrane-Orcutt [AR(2)]
α	4.8654*
	(3.0439)
β	-1.17944*
	(-3.1539)
R^{-2}	0.818
DW	2.0116
Wald Test	χ^2=17.576*

*Significant at 5% level.

TABLE 11: Results of the Empirical Estimation of RIP Hypothesis (Dependent Variable: Real Interest Rate Differential)

Parameter	Cochrane-Orcutt [AR(2)]
α	4.1512*
	(3.3086)
β	-2.8024*
	(-3.0368)
R^{-2}	0.3063
DW	2.0101
Wald Test	χ^2=24.944 *

*Significant at 5%.

9.5 Stock Market Integration

The correlation between NASDAQ and BSE is found to be significant at 5 per cent level. Therefore, it can be inferred that BSE is being influenced by the movements of NASDAQ. To analyse the point further, both ordinary least and cointegration technique have been used. There is no cointegrating vector between BSE and NASDAQ indices. Hence, there is no long run relationship between the two indices.

CONCLUSION

The financial and trade liberalisation measures undertaken since 1991 facilitated the process of integration of financial markets in India. The analyses revealed that despite partial financial integration, the economy has been consistently moving towards the greater degree of integration with the world financial market. The findings of the study clearly indicate that financial integration is not continuous, but a discrete phenomenon in the Indian context. Integration is a selective in nature, which can be witnessed in some sub-parts of different financial markets. A number of impediments in the forms of political risk, transaction costs, taxation, capital controls and capital market imperfections hamper complete integration of the domestic and world financial markets. With fast moving development taking place nationally and internationally in the financial scenario, there is an accentuation in the integration process.

The overnight domestic interest rates are being affected with the changes in the international financial market. There has been some evidence of integration of money and foreign exchange markets. There is a high degree of correlation between call money rates and foreign exchange forward premia, indicating their mutual dependence. Domestic capital market is not completely integrated with the world capital market. The saving-investment correlation test of Feldstein-Horioka, with a statistically significant value of 0.75 indicates that domestic capital market is not completely segregated from the international capital market. The domestic stock indices have significant correlation with the NASDAQ index. The absence of interest parity completely rules out the phenomenon of international financial integration of domestic financial markets. Since the current forward is not equal to the future spot, the Indian foreign exchange market is not efficient. However, the declining trends of deviations from the interest rate parity and excess returns indicate the growing process of integration of the domestic financial markets with that of world financial markets.

The macroeconomic implications of the ongoing process of integration cannot be relegated completely to the back burner. A noticeable feature of the crises of 1990s has been the transmission of financial market instability to countries with otherwise sound fundamentals. As a consequence, the possibility of a local crisis getting magnified into a global crisis in a very short time span has emerged. In view of this, a wide debate has been initiated regarding the issues involved in the anticipation, management and containment of the crisis for the benefit of all concerned.

Financial globalisation has become an inescapable reality. Both developed and developing countries have to manage it for sustained growth and sharp discontinuities. Indian economy has not been completely integrated with the rest of the world. Control on capital movements continue to check any sudden withdrawal of foreign capital. Short-term capital flows, like the 'hot money', which can be withdrawn at any time and, so, reversal of these may create panic in both foreign exchange market and in the stock market. Therefore, control on free mobility of capital is necessary for the stability of the financial sector. The authorities should either control the composition of inflows or restrict the outflows. As far as the composition of inflows is concerned, long-term investment, if possible, in the form of direct investment should only be allowed. Capital with maturity less than one year may be put into reserve deposit in order to restrict their outflows. Reserve percentage can be linked with the maturity of the foreign capital. This will effectively prevent the volatility both in stock and foreign exchange markets.

In a liberalised environment of capital flow, it will be difficult for the central bank to practice autonomous monetary policy and manage the exchange rate concurrently. This calls for, as is the case of other countries, re-designing of macroeconomic policymix in case of India. A managed floating exchange rate policy along with a discretionary monetary policy is desirable. There is also a need for greater autonomy of the central bank for more assured success.

Since 1993, India has been practising a liberally managed floating exchange rate, with a cautious approach to capital account convertibility. However, recent policy measure on 'margin trading' by removing the distinction between foreign direct investment and foreign institutional investment and by diverting banks' funds to equity market is a risky step. If not managed properly, it will generate high volatility in equity market and, thus, a havoc of capital flight.

The East Asian experience has highlighted the role played by financial fragility in amplifying currency crisis. Proper supervision and regulations are essential for financial markets to work in tandem with market discipline. The ongoing process of financial integration has provided opportunities and challenges to banks and other financial institutions in India. It has given some degree of operational freedom to them, particularly in the determination of interest rates and in raising capital from domestic and international markets. Domestic banks are likely to face stiff competition from foreign banks.

At the international level, the issue of safety nets programme and new institutional arrangements for sound banking system have evoked considerable discussions. However, safety nets should not be used to subsidise risk, because the measure may induce reckless lending by the banking system. As regards new institutional arrangement, discussions should cover a wide ground, including the establishment of Global Financial Regulator and Global Central Bank.

The Basel Committee on Banking Supervision has given a well defined guideline for supervision of banks. However, insurance sector, capital market, non-banking financial institutions and varieties of other unregulated financial institutions have been posing serious threat to financial systems of developing countries, particularly in case of India. It is probable that financial crisis in India may spring from either the co-operative banking structure or from the non-banking financial intermediaries, particularly the development banks, if timely reform/corrective measures are not initiated. Hence, it is necessary to put in place concerted measures with a sense of urgency to check the onset, magnitude and gravity of the crisis.

REFERENCES

Bascom, W.O., *The Economics of Financial Reforms in Developing Countries,* St. Martins Press, Inc., New York, 1994.

Bhoi, B.K. & Dhal, S.C., "Integration of Financial Market in India: An Empirical Evaluation" *RBI, Occasional Papers,* Vol. 10, No. 4, Dec. 1998.

Blyn, G., "Price Series Correlation as a Measure of Market Integration", *Indian Journal of Agricultural Economics,* Vol. 28, No. 2, 1983.

Branson, W., *Financial Capital Flows in the U.S. Balance of Payments,* North Holland, Amsterdam, 1998.

Cumby, R.E. and Obstfeld, M., "International Interest Rate and Price Level Linkages under Flexible Exchange Rates: A Review of Recent Evidence"; in Bilson, J.F.O. and Marston, R.C. (Eds.), *Exchange Rate Theory and Practice,* University of Chicago Press, NBER, Chicago, 1984.

Feldstein, Martin & Horioka, Charles, "Domestic Saving and International Capital Movements in the Short-run and the Long-run", *European Economic Review,* 21 (March/April), 1980.

Fisher, I., *The Theory of Interest,* Macmillan, New York, 1930.

Fleming, J.M., "Domestic Financial Policies Under Fixed and Floating Exchange Rates", *IMF Staff Papers,* Vol. 9, 1962.

Granger, C.W.J., "Development in the Study of Cointegrated Economic Variables", *Oxford Bulletin of Economics and Statistics,* 48, 3, 1986.

Harris, B., "There is Method in my Madness: or is it *vice versa,* Measuring Agricultural Product Performance", *Food Research Institute Studies,* 17, 2, 1979.

Jones, W.O., "The Structure of Staple food marketing in Nigeria as Revealed by price Analysis", *Food Research Institute Studies,* 2, 1968.

Joshi, H., "Liquidity Effects on the Term Structure of Government Securities Markets in India," *Occasional Paper, RBI,* No. 19, 1998.

Kenen, P.B., *A Model of the US Balance of Payments,* Lexington Books, New York, 1978.

Kwack, S. and Schink, G.R., "A Disaggregated Quarterly Model of the U.S. Trade and Capital Flows, Simulations and Test of Policy Effectiveness", in Lemma Senbet (1981), "The effects of international operations on the market value of the firm: Theory and Evidence" *Journal of Finance,* 36: 1975.

Mckinnon, R.I., *Money and Capital in Economic Development,* Brookings Institution, Washington DC, 1973.

Mishkin, F.S., "The Real Interest Rate: A Multicountry Empirical Study". *Canadian Journal of Economics,* Vol. 17, No. 2, 1984.

Monke, E. and Petzel, T., "Market Integration for Application for International Trade in Cotton", *American Journal of Agricultural Economics,* 66, 4, 1984.

Mundell, R.A., "Capital Mobility and Stabilisation Policy Under Fixed and Flexible Exchange Rates", *Canadian Journal of Economic and Political Science,* Vol. 29, 1963.

Nag, A.K. & Ghosh, S.K., "Yield Curve Analysis for Government Securities in India", *Economic & Political Weekly of India,* 35, 5, 2000.

Neal, L., "The Integration and Efficiency of the London and Amsterdam Stock Markets in the Eighteenth Century", *Journal of Economic History,* XLVII, 1, 1987.

Pattanaik, S., "REER : The Leading Indicator" *Occasional Paper, RBI,* No. 20, 1999.

Report on Currency and Finance, RBI, 1999-2000.

Report on Financial Sector Reforms, Chairman Narasimham, 1991.

Report of the Committee to Review the Working of the Monetary System, Chairman, S. Chakravarty, 1985.

Report on Recommendations on Money Market Reform, Vaghul Committee appointed by RBI, in 1986, submitted report in 1987.

Uri, N.B. & Riffin, E.J., "Geographic Markets, Causality and Railroad Deregulation", *Review of Economics and Statistics,* 67, 1985.

4

Impact of India's Economic Reforms on Poverty: Critical Issues and Challenges

DEBESH ROY

INTRODUCTION

A high incidence of poverty in India with an estimated 260 million people lacking access to even the minimum consumption basket in 2001 causes concern and consternation. While poverty eradication has been one of the major objectives of the five-year plans, the Tenth Plan (2002-07) document asserts that the eradication of poverty is integral to humanity's quest for sustainable development, and is vital for the attainment of international goals (Government of India, 2002: 293).

Strongly influenced by socialist ideology the post-Independence Indian leaders and economists initiated the Five-Year Plans, with a focus on public sector investment in heavy industry and infrastructure. Thanks to a regulated economy, draconian laws like the Monopolies and Restrictive Trade Practices (MRTP) Act, widespread inefficiency in public sector undertakings, and poor governance, the average annual growth rate of real GDP of the country hovered around a measly 3.6 per cent during the first four Plans. Since the Fifth Plan the average annual growth rate accelerated and peaked at 6.8 per cent during the Eighth Plan, the period of launching the economic reform agenda. The growth rate, however, slipped down to 5.6 per cent during the Ninth Plan. The Tenth Plan has projected an annual average growth rate of GDP of 8 per cent during the Plan period.

The programme of economic policy reforms in India initiated in July 1991 comprised measures for attaining macro-economic stabilization and structural reforms in order to put the Indian economy on a higher growth path (Sachs, *et al.*, 1999). While the 1980s witnessed rather limited deregulation and halting liberalization of only a few aspects of the pre-existing control regime, by contrast the reforms of the 1990s in the industrial, trade, and investment regimes among others, were much wider and deeper (*ibid.*).

The impact of economic reforms on the poor has been a subject of intense debate in India. The pro-reform group argues that the reforms will help the poor by encouraging rapid and efficient growth. This would involve labour intensive and employment-generating growth, which would in turn have a positive impact on the problem of poverty. The critics, however, claim that this process will take time, and would even remain beyond the reach of a vast majority of the poor. Some sections may even be hurt as certain kinds of products and processes are displaced by structural changes brought about by the reforms. India's structural reforms programme sought to deal with these problems by combining structural reforms with strong poverty alleviation programmes to ensure an adequate flow of benefits to the poor even in the short term (Ahluwalia, 1999: 73).

Against this background, this paper attempts to provide an overview of poverty and genesis and progress of economic reforms. An attempt is also made to examine the impact of economic reforms on the poor and policy issues and challenges on the task of poverty alleviation.

POVERTY IN INDIA — AN OVERVIEW

The official measure of poverty in India is based on the concept of income-poverty. Based on a calorie norm, income-poverty estimates the income that would be needed to provide each individual a maximum of 2400 calories of food intake per day in rural areas, and 2100 calories per day in urban areas.

Table 1 shows that the decline in poverty ratio (Head Count Ratio) in India and even a sharper decline in rural

TABLE 1: Estimates of Incidence of Poverty in India

Year	Poverty ratio (%)			Number of poor (million)				
	Rural	Urban	Combined	Rural	% share	Urban	% share	Combined
1973-74	56.4	49.0	54.9	261.3	81.3	60.0	18.7	321.3
1977-78	53.1	45.2	51.3	264.3	80.4	64.6	19.6	328.9
1983	45.7	40.8	44.5	252.0	78.0	70.9	22.0	322.9
1987-88	39.1	38.2	38.9	231.9	75.5	75.2	24.5	307.1
1993-94	37.3	32.4	36.0	244.0	76.2	76.3	23.8	320.3
1999-00	27.1	23.6	26.1	193.2	74.2	67.1	25.8	260.3
2007*	21.1	15.1	19.3	170.5	77.5	49.6	22.5	220.1

*Projection.

Source: Tenth Five Year Plan, Vol. 1, Planning Commission, Government of India.

poverty during the period 1973-74 to 1999-2000. Significant declines were also registered in terms of other aspects. But the share of urban poor increased from 19.7 per cent to 25.8 per cent because of the policy of a direct attack on rural poverty through various anti-poverty programmes implemented during the last three decades. Further, the steady increase in the number of urban poor during 1973-74 to 1993-94 could partly be explained by the rural-urban migration. The Tenth Plan projected a decline in poverty to 19.3 per cent (220.1 million people) in 2007, with rural poverty expected to decline to 21.1% (170.5 million people) and urban poverty is expected to reach 15.1 per cent (49.6 million people).

Rural poverty in a year is governed principally by the work opportunities generated by the contemporary and previous year's agricultural harvest situation, on the one hand, and by the supply and the market price of foodgrains, on the other (Tendulkar, 1998: 291). In contrast to the rural population there has been no major target group-oriented direct anti-poverty programmes for the urban poor. Agricultural harvest conditions had an indirect impact on urban poverty, via their effect on prices of foodgrains (*ibid.*).

A wide disparity in poverty across Indian states and their uneven progress in poverty reduction characterize poverty in

India. In most instances better-off states remained relatively affluent and reduced poverty, while poorer states remained poor and made less progress in poverty reduction. There are, however, cases where poorer states made major progress in poverty reduction and growth (World Bank, 2000: 12).

A state-wise/region-wise analysis of poverty during the period 1983 to 1999-2000 shows some interesting results. For the purpose of analysis the Indian states have been divided into six categories, *viz.* Southern States, Western States, Northern States, Eastern States, North-Eastern States and BIMARU States[1] (Table 2). While poverty has mainly concentrated in the BIMARU States (Bihar, Madhya Pradesh, Rajasthan, and Uttar Pradesh), Orissa and North-Eastern States, the Northern, Southern and Western States have reduced poverty substantially, mainly due to effective implementation of anti-poverty programmes (*e.g.* Maharashtra), increase in agricultural production and productivity (*e.g.* Haryana and Punjab), good governance (*e.g.* Goa), successful human development efforts (*e.g.* Kerala), and faster economic reforms (*e.g.* Andhra Pradesh, Karnataka, Tamil Nadu, Maharashtra and Gujarat).

The BIMARU States, which are laggards in the reform process, account for more than half of India's poor. Rajasthan is the only BIMARU State to buck the trend by achieving a poverty ratio much lower than the all-India figure (26.1 per cent).

The Northern States of Punjab, Haryana, Himachal Pradesh, Jammu and Kashmir, National Capital Region of Delhi, and the Union Territory of Chandigarh, despite some regional variation, registered declines in poverty ratio during this period.

The four Southern states of Andhra Pradesh, Karnataka, Kerala, and Tamil Nadu experienced steady decline in poverty ratio. Incidentally, the States of Andhra Pradesh, Karnataka, and Tamil Nadu are frontrunners in the market reform process, while Kerala is the undisputed leader in human development.

The Western States of Goa, Gujarat, and Maharashtra experienced steady decline in poverty. Goa with a poverty ratio of just 4.40 per cent shows how good governance, market reforms and positive social sector policies can work wonders

TABLE 2: Number and Percentage of Population below Poverty Line

(Number in million)

States/UT	1983		1993-94		1999-00	
	No. of persons	Poverty ratio	No. of persons	Poverty ratio	No. of persons	Poverty ratio
Northern States/UT						
Delhi	1.84	26.22	1.55	14.69	1.15	8.23
Chandigarh	0.12	23.79	0.08	11.35	0.05	5.75
Haryana	2.96	21.37	4.39	25.05	1.73	14.07
Himachal Pradesh	0.74	16.40	1.59	28.44	0.51	8.74
Jammu & Kashmir	1.56	24.24	2.09	25.17	0.35	3.48
Punjab	2.86	16.18	2.51	11.77	1.45	6.16
Southern States						
Andhra Pradesh	16.46	28.91	15.40	22.19	11.90	15.77
Karnataka	14.98	38.24	15.65	33.16	10.44	20.04
Kerala	10.68	40.42	7.64	25.43	4.10	12.72
Tamil Nadu	26.01	40.03	20.21	35.03	13.05	21.12
Eastern States						
Orissa	18.13	65.29	16.06	48.56	16.91	47.15
West Bengal	31.87	54.85	25.46	35.66	21.35	27.02
Western States						
Goa	0.22	18.90	0.19	14.92	0.07	4.40
Gujarat	11.79	32.79	10.52	24.21	6.79	14.07
Maharashtra	29.09	43.44	30.52	36.86	22.80	25.02
BIMARU States						
Bihar*	46.21	62.22	49.34	54.96	42.56	42.60
M.P.*	27.80	49.78	29.85	42.52	29.85	37.43
Rajasthan	12.68	34.46	12.85	27.41	8.18	15.28
U.P.*	55.67	47.07	60.45	40.85	52.99	31.15
North Eastern States						
Arunachal Pradesh	0.28	40.88	0.37	39.35	0.40	33.47
Assam	7.77	40.47	9.64	40.86	9.46	36.09
Manipur	0.57	37.02	0.68	33.78	0.72	28.54
Meghalaya	0.56	38.81	0.74	37.92	0.82	33.87
Mizoram	0.20	36.00	0.19	25.66	0.18	19.47
Nagaland	0.35	36.00	0.50	37.92	0.55	32.67
Sikkim	0.14	39.71	0.18	41.43	0.21	36.55
Tripura	0.90	40.03	1.18	39.01	1.30	34.44
All India	**322.90**	**44.48**	**320.30**	**35.97**	**260.10**	**26.10**

* Undivided States.

Source: National Human Development Report 2001, Planning Commission, Government of India.

in the removal of poverty. Gujarat and Maharashtra, the most industrially advanced states in the country, significantly implemented the market reforms process.

Orissa suffers from severe poverty, with the highest poverty ratio in the country, in spite of a steady decline from 65.29 per cent in 1983 to 47.15 per cent in 1993-94 and further to 47.15 per cent in 1999-2000. The KBK (Kalahandi, Bolangir, and Koraput) region of the State, which is home to the largest concentration of people living in abject poverty in the country, has suffered from severe and frequent bouts of famine. While the godowns of the Food Corporation of India were overflowing with stocks of foodgrains, the poor tribal population of this region starved to death. West Bengal, which had historically one of the highest poverty ratios in the country at 54.85 per cent (in 1983), showed remarkable progress through land reforms and rural development programmes spearheaded by strong Panchayati Raj Institutions (PRIs) by reducing poverty to 27.02 per cent in 1999-2000.

The North-Eastern States, with the exception of Mizoram, experienced near stagnation or at best slow progress in poverty alleviation. The poverty ratio in Assam marginally increased from 40.47 per cent in 1983 to 40.86 per cent 1993-94, before declining to 36.09 per cent. Development has taken a back seat in the region due to years of neglect by the Central Government and lack of sincere efforts by the State governments. Mizoram, with its commendable track record of human development has experienced substantial decline in poverty.

The large cross-state differential in poverty reduction partly reflects lower growth in the poorer states. Most states that began the 1970s with relatively low per capita GDP had slower growth in GDP and its three main components, *viz.* agriculture, industry, and services, than the middle and high-income states. The poor states also generally have the worst human resource indicators. Infrastructure is a major constraint in poor states. The differentials in private GDP growth and public investment in infrastructure and human capital partly reflect weak legal and regulatory framework for business and problems of governance, law and order, and weak institutional capacity more generally. Finally, the lagging states, despite allocations of central funds that favoured them in per capita terms because of their low per capita incomes, suffered from fiscal problems. This was particularly the case in the 1990s, because their lack of fiscal adjustment and increased debt service payments coincided with a decline in overall central grants and loans to the states and rise in interest costs. These fiscal problems forced the states to slash their capital and human resource spending as a percentage of GDP (World Bank, 2000: 18).

Income poverty, defined as a basic minimum calorie intake, captures a limited perspective of what poverty really connotes. Human poverty is more severe than income-poverty — it is a denial of choices and opportunities for living a tolerable life (UNDP, 1997). Human deprivation includes, lack of access to education, housing and sanitation, malnutrition, unjust employment of children, bonded labour, environmental pollution, social exclusion etc. A multi-dimensional, people-centred concept is required which transcends income and consumption to include other aspects of human life (Chelliah and Sudarshan, 1999: 131). According to Dréze and Sen (1989: 183), there are two contrasting approaches to poverty alleviation. One approach, *i.e.* the strategy of 'growth-mediated security' is to promote economic growth, which would not only enable the population to take advantage of the potentialities released by greater general affluence but would also provide an improved basis for public support. The alternative approach, called 'support-led security', consists of resorting to direct public support in fields such as employment provision, income redistribution, health care, education, and social assistance so that destitution may be removed without waiting for an improvement in the general level of affluence.

While evidence suggests that income poverty in India declined steadily during the last two decades, the same cannot be directly attributable to the economic reform process. Further, considering the uncertainty in the estimation of income poverty, it is useful to move away from the narrow focus of Head Count Ratios, and to consider a broader range of social indicators. Looking at the broader evidence of social indicators in the 1990s, a somewhat different picture emerges, with areas of accelerated progress as well as indicators of slowdown in some fields (Dréze and Sen, 2002).

THE GENESIS AND PROGRESS OF ECONOMIC REFORMS IN INDIA

During 1980s and 1990s most developing countries initiated economic reforms with widely varying scope and pace. In China, for example, the 'household responsibility' replaced communal farming, and created new incentives for rural households to produce, invest and innovate. These reforms were promoted neither by macroeconomic crisis nor by ideological epiphany; rather they reflected a growing realization that China's agricultural potential was not being fulfilled (World Bank, 2001: 62). In other countries macroeconomic crises provided the catalyst for reform. The Mexican debt crisis of the 1980s was followed by the introduction of wide ranging economic reforms. In the former Soviet Union and Eastern Europe, the political transition precipitated a dramatic progress towards markets that succeeded immensely in some countries, but failed in others (*ibid.*).

In July 1991 severe balance of payments problems, high inflationary expectations and acute fiscal crisis, triggered an economic disaster. This was caused by persistent mistakes in economic policy that accumulated through the 1980s. Fiscal deficits, met by borrowing at home, mounted steadily. This was coupled by current account deficits in the balance of payment. It led to borrowing abroad which grew steadily larger (Bhaduri and Nayyar, 1996: 22).

In 1990-91, the Gross Fiscal Deficit (GFD) of Government of India accounted for 8.4 per cent of GDP, and annual rate of inflation peaked at nearly 17 per cent. During the 1980s, the growth rate was accelerated by borrowings but without any drastic restructuring of the economy (Sachs *et al.*, 1999). In 1990-91 increased political risk, overly expansionary macroeconomic policies, and a sharp decline in remittances from abroad in the wake of the Gulf War, led to outflow of short-term capital, putting extreme pressure on India's foreign exchange reserves. This was the proximate cause of India's market liberalization measures in 1991 (*ibid.*). The initial phase of reforms led to focus on macroeconomic stabilization.

Simultaneously, reforms of industrial policy, trade and exchange rate policies, and foreign investment policy were initiated, along with tax reforms, financial sector reforms, and public sector reforms (Sachs *et al.*, 1999).

Reforms significantly reduced Government's involvement in economic activity in many developing countries. Domestic markets became more open to international trade and capital flows. Privatization of state enterprises along with market determined prices, output, and allocation of resources have taken place. Most of these reforms reflected the so-called Washington Consensus, which laid out the following ten policy priorities that were adopted in different combinations by many countries (World Bank, 2001: 62, 63):

1. Fiscal discipline.
2. Reduction of public expenditure toward education, health and infrastructure investment.
3. Tax-reforms broadening the tax base and cutting marginal tax rates.
4. Interest rates that are market determined and positive (but moderate) in real terms.
5. Competitive exchange rates.
6. Trade liberalization — replacement of quantitative restrictions with low and uniform tariffs.
7. Openness to Foreign Direct Investment.
8. Privatization of state enterprises.
9. Deregulation — abolishment of regulations that impede entry or restrict competition, except for those justified on safety, environmental and consumer protection grounds, and prudential oversight of financial institutions.
10. Legal security to property rights.

The main thrust of reforms in India has been to move the economy to a higher growth path; to build the mechanism for inducing greater efficiency and competitiveness in all spheres of economic activities; and to gain capability for dealing with the immense shortcomings accumulated over the years in social sectors, such as education and health.

Structural reforms in India focused on decontrol of private investment, opening the economy to foreign trade and foreign investment and financial sector reforms. Market oriented reforms were supplemented by efforts to strengthen various anti-poverty programmes reflecting a widely shared perception that liberalization by itself would not provide adequate flow of benefits to the poorest sections of the population at least in the short run (Ahluwalia, 1999: 43).

Prior to the initiation of the reform process, the industrial sector in India was stifled by industrial licensing policy, in terms of which Government of India's permission was needed for investment in new units (beyond a relatively low threshold) as well as for substantial expansion of capacity in existing units. This resulted in widespread inefficiency and stagnation of the industrial sector. Delicensing and abolition of the MRTP Act created the right environment for rapid industrial growth, by private sector investment. Industries, which were earlier dominated by the public sector, *viz.* steel, telecom services and equipment, electricity generation, petroleum exploration, development and refining etc. have been opened up for private domestic as well as foreign investment. The accent on greater efficiency is expected to result in rapid economic growth, through improvement in productivity of the inputs of production.

Globalization by opening the economy to trade and investment formed part of structural reforms in India. Removal of Quantitative Restrictions and lowering of tariffs accompanied opening up of the economy. Further, India declared full current account convertibility in 1994. As a result, several steps were taken to liberalize exchange restrictions on current account transactions. Accordingly, the Foreign Exchange Regulation Act (FERA), 1973 was repealed and replaced by a more modern Foreign Exchange Management Act (FEMA) (Ahluwalia, 1999: 52).

Foreign Direct Investment (FDI) augments investible capital and leads to increase in output. However, a far more important impact of FDI is through externalities, leading to higher efficiency and productivity. FDI serves to increase competition in markets by bringing in new technology, and foster skill acquisition amongst domestic labour. FDI by international corporations is also utilized as a platform for global production chains, which would pave the way for strong export growth (Government of India, 2003: 146).

India has followed a cautious approach to public sector reforms. Radical solutions, such as outright privatization of commercially viable units, were eschewed to begin with, in favour of a more cautious approach. However, there has been an increasing consensus on the merits of privatization, as a means for increasing efficiency and productivity. The privatization process began in 1991-92, with the sale of minority stakes in some Public Sector Undertakings (PSUs). From 1999-2000 onwards, the focus shifted to strategic sales to develop physical and social infrastructure. As in China, the sale proceeds from disinvestments of PSUs[2] could be used for the development of social infrastructure.

It has been recognized that faster economic growth would require major investments in infrastructure, with a focus on private sector investment supplementing public sector efforts. Accordingly, private (including foreign) investment has been encouraged in power generation, telecom services, ports, and roads. While many private sector infrastructure projects have taken off successfully, the significance of infrastructure for sustained agriculture and rural development is yet to fully sink in (Sharma, 2000).

In recent decades, the focus of industrial policy has increasingly emphasized the importance of competition as a tool for disciplining firms, and fostering allocative efficiency. In order to improve competition, and thus contain the distortions caused by monopoly power, the Competition Act, 2002 was enacted. It aims at promoting competition through prohibition of anti-competitive practices, abuse of dominance and through regulation of companies beyond a particular size (Government of India, 2003: 149).

Structural reforms aim at reallocating real resources in the economy and this process needs to be lubricated by an efficient financial system. Accordingly, financial sector reforms have become an integral part of structural reforms. Financial sector reforms in India included a concerted effort to reform banking, insurance and capital market institutions. Based on the recommendations of the Committee on the Financial System (Narasimham Committee I, 1991), banking sector reforms were initiated in 1992. The first stage of reforms focused on interest rate liberalization, improvement in prudential norms and standards, strengthening supervision, and increasing competition in the banking sector. The Committee on Banking Sector Reforms (Narasimham Committee II, 1998) set the agenda for second stage of banking sector reforms. The banking sector reforms has stressed:

(a) Interest rate deregulation and a move towards soft interest rate regime;

(b) Adoption of prudential norms and standards relating to capital adequacy, income recognition, asset classification, and provisioning, as per Basle norms;

(c) Strengthening supervision of banks and evaluation of banks' performance on the basis of prudential standards;

(d) Increased competition in the banking system, by providing licences to new private banks, and allowing expansion of the operation of foreign banks;

(e) Technological upgradation;

(f) Increasing operational efficiency of banks.

An area where reforms have not yet gained momentum is the fiscal policy. There is an urgent need to address the problem of high level of combined fiscal deficit of the Centre and the States. In this connection the Fiscal Responsibility Act, 2003 was enacted to address the issues relating to fiscal consolidation and removal of fiscal deficit within a reasonable time frame. Fiscal reforms call for a two-pronged approach, *viz.* (a) restructuring of government expenditure by restraining inessential expenditure, while increasing expenditure in important areas; (b) tax reforms and strengthening of tax administration, to increase buoyancy in tax revenue. These efforts may be supplemented by much bolder efforts at disinvestment of public sector undertakings, which would help generate greater revenue and reduce fiscal deficit. The revenue generated could also be allocated to the social sector.

Despite an increased awareness, the labour market

continues to be marked by distortions and structural rigidities. India's labour laws, which apply to all industrial units employing more than 100 persons, make it difficult for firms to either shed excess labour or close down unviable units. Labour rigidities also make it difficult for Indian companies to undertake the much needed restructuring (Ahluwalia, 1999: 61). There is an urgent need to increase productivity in PSUs by pruning down surplus workers, who may be retrained and redeployed in sectors, which face a shortage of labour. While such a measure may lead to temporary loss of jobs resulting in social strife, it would be pragmatic to provide social security assistance to the displaced workers during the period of frictional unemployment, as a temporary measure. Globalization requires that Indian industry achieve efficiency gains to be internationally competitive. Greater flexibility in the labour market will be an important prerequisite to attain this goal.

The Tenth Plan has set an ambitious target of 8 per cent average annual growth rate of real GDP. This requires removal of infrastructural bottlenecks with massive investments both in the public and private sector. Public investment in infrastructure depends crucially upon the ability to raise resources in the public sector and this in turn depends upon the ability to levy user charges. Reforms of power sector tariff, introduction of road user charges, and rationalization of railway fares are necessary (Ahluwalia, 1999: 78, 79). Public initiative in infrastructure development must be supplemented by a vigorous effort to attract private investment.

While reforms did not acquire the desired pace, they nevertheless, moved in the right direction. The liberalization programme led to considerable expansion of exports in some sectors and a substantial improvement in the balance of payments, foreign exchange reserves, and a stronger Rupee *vis-à-vis* the US Dollar. It also led to a vibrant international response, involving renewed interest in the possibilities of the Indian economy (Dréze and Sen, 2002: 302).

However, India's development performance during the 1990s remained quite moderate. The average annual growth rate of real GDP during the pre-reforms period (1981-82 to

1990-91) and the reforms period (1991-92 to 2001-02) remained stagnant at 5.64 per cent [Table 3(a)]. The mid-1990s (1992-93 to 1996-97) experienced robust growth rate averaging 6.69 per cent, with the highest growth rate at 7.84 per cent achieved during 1996-97 (Table 3). Subsequently, the growth rate slowed down averaging 5.46 per cent during the five-year period 1997-98 to 2001-02. Similarly, annual growth rate of per capita GDP rose marginally from 3.22 per cent during 1981-82 to 1990-91, to 3.56 per cent during 1991-92 to 2001-02. During the first five years of reforms (1992-93 to 1996-97) per capita GDP stood at 4.54 per cent. But it declined to 3.6 per cent during the next five years of reforms (1997-98 to 2001-02) [Table 3(a)]. However, from an international perspective India's growth rate of GDP during the reform period has been satisfactory.

The central issue, however, is not the overall growth rate of the economy. Rather, it is a question of achieving widely shared development, of a kind that has not really happened in the 1990s (Dréze and Sen, 2002: 307). Indeed there are many reasons for concern about India's growth pattern in the 1990s (1991-92 to 2001-02), including stagnation and even deceleration in the growth rate of agricultural and allied activities at 2.92 per cent as against 3.84 per cent during the pre-reforms period (1981-82 to 1990-91) [Table 3(a)]. The dismal growth performance of some of the poorer states (*e.g.* Bihar and Uttar Pradesh) is another reason for concern. Further, there does not appear to have been a transformation in the living conditions of the poor.

THE IMPACT OF ECONOMIC REFORMS ON THE POOR

Markets matter for the poor because poor people rely on formal and informal markets to sell their labour and labour products, to finance investment, and to insure against risks, well-functioning markets are important in generating growth and expanding opportunities for poor people. Accordingly, market-friendly reforms have been promoted by international donors and by developing country governments, especially those democratically elected (World Bank, 2001: 61).

Successful reforms frequently impose costs on the poor, who are vulnerable to shocks. Under such circumstances the

TABLE 3: Gross Domestic Product at Factor Cost by Industry of Origin in India

(At 1993-94 prices) (Rs. billion)

Year	Agriculture and allied activities	% growth	% share in GDP	Industry	% growth	% share in GDP	Trade, transport, storage and communication	% growth	% share in GDP
1971-72	1401	-1.75	46.81	606	2.71	20.25	472	2.39	15.77
1972-73	1337	-4.57	44.82	627	3.47	21.02	483	2.33	15.82
1973-74	1430	6.96	45.85	634	1.12	20.33	503	4.14	16.13
1974-75	1412	-1.26	44.74	642	1.26	20.35	535	6.36	16.96
1975-76	1593	12.82	46.32	681	6.07	19.80	583	8.97	16.95
1976-77	1508	-5.33	43.31	744	9.25	21.37	610	4.63	17.52
1977-78	1654	9.68	44.20	798	7.26	21.33	649	6.39	17.34
1978-79	1692	2.30	42.86	862	3.48	21.83	702	8.17	17.78
1979-80	1487	-12.12	39.73	833	-3.48	22.25	699	-0.43	18.67
1980-81	1678	12.84	41.83	866	3.96	21.59	738	8.17	18.40
1981-82	1773	5.66	41.71	930	7.39	21.88	784	6.23	18.44
1982-83	1773	0.00	40.47	957	2.90	21.84	820	4.59	18.72
1983-84	1935	9.14	41.02	1040	8.67	22.05	860	4.88	18.23
1984-85	1964	1.50	39.91	1105	6.25	22.45	904	5.12	18.37
1985-86	1984	1.02	38.60	1157	4.71	22.51	976	7.96	18.99
1986-87	1987	0.15	37.05	1228	6.14	22.90	1033	5.84	19.26
1987-88	1967	-1.00	35.33	1314	7.00	23.60	1087	5.23	19.52
1988-89	2271	15.45	36.92	1427	8.60	23.20	1152	5.98	18.73
1989-90	2314	1.89	35.26	1580	10.72	24.07	1237	7.38	18.84
1990-91	2420	4.58	34.93	1697	7.41	24.49	1298	4.93	18.73
1991-92	2393	-1.11	34.09	1680	-1.00	23.94	1331	2.54	18.96
1992-93	2522	5.39	34.18	1752	4.29	23.75	1405	5.56	19.04
1993-94	2621	3.93	33.55	1851	5.65	23.69	1505	7.12	19.26
1994-95	2760	5.30	32.94	2041	10.26	24.36	1661	10.37	19.82
1995-96	2751	-0.33	30.58	2291	12.25	25.47	1882	13.31	20.92
1996-97	2995	8.87	30.87	2468	7.73	25.44	2029	7.81	20.92
1997-98	2950	-1.50	29.02	2561	3.77	25.19	2188	7.84	21.52
1998-99	3125	5.93	28.86	2560	-0.04	23.64	2358	7.77	23.44
1999-00	3143	0.57	27.37	2791	9.02	24.30	2558	8.48	22.27
2000-01	3138	-0.16	26.18	2987	7.02	24.92	2733	6.84	22.80
2001-02	3303	5.26	26.10	3093	3.55	24.44	2972	7.18	23.49

TABLE 3 (Contd.)

(At 1993-94 prices) (Rs. billion)

Year	Financing, insurance real estate and business services	% growth	% share in GDP	Public administration, defence and other services	% growth	% share in GDP	GDP at factor cost	% growth	Annual growth rate (%) of Per capita net national product
1971-72	185	5.11	6.18	331	4.42	11.06	2993	1.01	-1.70
1972-73	192	3.78	6.44	342	3.32	11.46	2983	-0.33	-3.10
1973-74	197	2.60	6.32	351	2.63	11.25	3119	4.56	2.50
1974-75	196	-0.51	6.21	367	4.56	11.63	3155	1.15	-1.00
1975-76	210	7.14	6.11	380	3.54	11.05	3439	9.00	7.00
1976-77	226	7.62	6.49	391	2.89	11.23	3482	1.25	-1.20
1977-78	237	4.87	6.33	401	2.56	10.72	3742	7.47	5.30
1978-79	254	7.17	6.43	419	4.49	10.61	3948	5.51	3.30
1979-80	257	1.18	6.87	449	7.16	12.00	3743	-5.19	-8.30
1980-81	262	1.95	6.53	468	4.23	11.67	4011	7.16	5.10
1981-82	283	8.02	6.66	480	2.56	11.29	4251	5.98	3.80
1982-83	313	10.60	7.14	518	7.92	11.82	4381	3.06	0.00
1983-84	344	9.90	7.29	538	3.86	11.41	4717	7.67	5.40
1984-85	373	8.43	7.58	575	6.88	11.68	4921	4.32	1.70
1985-86	411	10.19	8.00	613	6.61	11.93	5140	4.45	2.10
1986-87	458	11.44	8.54	656	7.01	12.23	5363	4.34	1.80
1987-88	496	8.30	8.91	703	7.16	12.63	5568	3.82	1.20
1988-89	553	11.49	8.99	748	6.40	12.16	6151	10.47	8.30
1989-90	622	12.48	9.48	810	8.29	12.34	6563	6.70	4.60
1990-91	670	7.72	9.67	844	4.20	12.18	6929	5.58	3.30
1991-92	750	11.94	10.69	865	2.49	12.32	7019	1.30	-1.50
1992-93	794	5.87	10.76	905	4.62	12.27	7378	5.11	3.10
1993-94	901	13.48	11.53	936	3.43	11.98	7813	5.90	3.40
1994-95	951	5.55	11.35	967	3.31	11.54	8380	7.26	4.90
1995-96	1028	8.10	11.43	1043	7.86	11.59	8996	7.35	5.20
1996-97	1100	7.00	11.34	1108	6.23	11.42	9701	7.84	6.10
1997-98	1228	11.64	12.08	1238	11.73	12.18	10166	4.79	2.60
1998-99	1319	7.41	12.18	1367	10.42	12.63	10827	6.50	4.40
1999-00	1459	10.61	12.70	1534	12.22	13.36	11484	6.07	4.30
2000-01	1509	3.43	12.59	1619	5.54	13.51	11987	4.38	2.40
2001-02	1577	4.51	12.46	1710	5.62	13.51	12654	5.56	4.30

Source: Economic Survey 2002-03, Government of India.

TABLE 3(a): Sectoral Average Percentage Growth of GDP

Period	Agri-culture & Allied	Industry	Services (Trade, Transport, Communi-cation)	Financing, insurance, real estate	GDP	Per capita real National income
1971-72 to 1980-81	1.96	3.51	5.11	4.09	3.16	0.79
1981-82 to 1990-91	3.84	6.98	5.81	9.86	5.64	3.22
1991-92 to 2001-02	2.92	5.68	7.71	8.14	5.64	3.56
1992-93 to 1996-97	3.68	8.04	8.83	8.66	6.69	4.54
1997-98 to 2001-02	2.02	4.66	7.62	7.52	5.46	3.60

Source: Economic Survey 2002-03, Government of India.

governments should provide the much-needed social infrastructure to improve the living conditions of the poor. While the general perception is that reforms have led to faster economic growth, at least in the medium term, there are few instances of failed reforms. Failure of reforms may be attributable to lack of supporting institutions and infrastructure.

Market oriented reforms impact differently on various segments of society. The particular vulnerability of the poor people demands a careful assessment of the likely impact on poverty and the implementation of appropriate compensating policies (World Bank, 2001: 62).

Even when markets function in an imperfect world physical access to markets is difficult for poor people living in remote areas. Regulatory barriers often stifle economic activity in sectors and regions where the poor people are likely to seek jobs. Investment in infrastructure, lighter regulatory burdens, and innovative approaches to improving access to financial markets can, therefore, do much to ensure that the benefits of markets are shared by poor people (World Bank, 2001: 62).

Empirical studies have revealed that countries, which have adopted pro-market reforms, have achieved faster economic growth *vis-à-vis* countries where such policies are absent. Results of studies for Latin America found a significant growth impact of reforms. Similar studies of the transition economies of the Soviet Union, where success in implementing market reforms varied widely, found that countries that implemented reforms forcefully and early, achieved stronger growth than reform laggards (World Bank, 1996). A study of India finds that the states that implemented reforms saw faster growth and stronger improvements in education and primary health care than those that did not (Bajpai and Sachs, 1999).

Market friendly reforms have generally delivered lower inflation and higher growth, both powerful forces for reducing income poverty. But lack of supporting institutions, mistakes in sequencing reforms, and the capture of reform process by powerful individuals or groups lie at the bottom of most failed reforms (World Bank, 2001: 64).

Even where market friendly reforms succeeded in delivering growth, the effects on the income of the poor varied. This reflects both initial inequalities in income and opportunity, and the effects of reforms on growth and inequality. Further, cross-country evidence suggests that macroeconomic reforms on average did not significantly alter income distribution (World Bank, 2001).

Growth helps to reduce poverty because of the following reasons: (a) it creates jobs that 'pull up' the poor into gainful employment by providing more economic opportunity; (b) it provides the revenues with which we can build more health facilities for the poor; and (c) it creates the incentives that enable the poor to access these facilities and also for the advancement of progressive social agenda generally (Bhagwati, 2001).

Dréze and Sen (2002) have argued that economic growth can be extremely helpful in removing poverty. This is both because the poor can directly share in the increased wealth and income generated by economic growth, and also because the overall increase in national prosperity can help in the financing of public services (including health and education), which in turn can be particularly useful for the poor and deprived.

The average annual growth rate of real GDP of the country hovered around a measly 3.6 per cent during the first four Plans, but accelerated during the subsequent Plans and peaked at 6.8 per cent during the Eighth Plan (1992-97). The Ninth Plan period, however, experienced a decline in the average annual growth of real GDP to 5.6 per cent. India suffered a severe setback during the year 2002-03, when the growth rate of GDP plunged to 4.3 per cent due to droughts across states. However, buoyed by a favourable monsoon during the year 2003-04 India attained the position of the second fastest growing economy in the world, with its GDP growth rate clocking 8.2 per cent.[3] But the over-dependence of the Indian economy on the monsoons even after over a decade of the implementation of economic reforms, causes concern. This was despite the fact that the share of agriculture in India's GDP has declined substantially from 56.1 per cent in the 1950s to 36.4 per cent in the 1980s and further to 22.1 per cent in 2002-03.[4] Obviously, the poor state of infrastructure constrained faster growth in the industrial sector. Sustainable GDP growth is attainable only when substantial investment in infrastructure, industry (with more emphasis on manufacturing industry), agriculture, and human resources takes place. Equally important, good governance in industry and public services needs to be practised.

The growth rate of real GDP averaged 3.16 per cent during the period 1971-72 to 1980-81 [Table 3(a)]. During the subsequent period 1981-82 to 1990-91, and the reform period 1991-92 to 2001-02, the average growth rate remained constant at 5.64 per cent. On the other hand, poverty ratio in India declined steadily from 54.9 per cent in 1973-74 to 44.5 per cent in 1983 and further to 36 per cent in 1993-94 and 26.1 per cent in 1999-2000 (Table 1). The higher growth rates during the 1980s and 1990s over the 1970s have clearly been accompanied by lower poverty ratios. However on this basis alone it cannot be conclusively stated that reforms had a positive impact on poverty.

The average annual growth rate of per capita income increased from 0.79 per cent during the period 1971-72 to 1980-81 to 3.22 per cent during the period 1981-82 to 1990-91. During the reform period of the 1990s, the growth rate increased marginally to 3.56 per cent [Table 3(a)]. This certainly raises questions about any substantial impact of economic reforms on poverty.

Majority of the poor in India lives in rural areas. However, the percentage of rural poor to total number of poor in the country declined from 81.3 per cent in 1973-74 to 74.3 per cent in 1999-2000 (Table 1). The number of rural poor, which initially increased from 261.3 million in 1973-74 to 264.3 million in 1977-78, declined steadily since then, to reach 193.2 million in 1999-2000. This is also reflected in the rural poverty ratio, which declined from 56.4 per cent in 1973-74 to 27.1 per cent in 1999-2000. Urban poverty declined from 49 per cent to 23.6 per cent during the same period. But the number of urban poor increased steadily from 60 million in 1973-74 to 76.3 million in 1993-94, before declining to 67.1 million in 1999-2000. Urban poverty could be an extension of rural poverty due to migration of surplus agricultural labour to urban areas for employment, generally in the unorganized sector.

On *a priori* grounds, given the very close administrative, financial and organizational links of public expenditure and policies with the organized sector, the direct impact of reform-related policies would be immediately felt by the urban organized sector with second order effects on the urban unorganized sector and still weaker effects on the rural population (Tendulkar, 1998). The time lag in impact is also expected to be the shortest for the urban organized sector and the longest for the rural segment.

Despite the sharp decline in the share of agriculture and allied activities in GDP (Table 3), the rural population India still depends mainly on agriculture for their livelihood. Further, the average growth rate of GDP from agriculture and allied activities, which stood at 1.96 per cent and 3.84 per cent during the periods 1971-72 to 1980-81 and 1981-82 to 1990-91, respectively, decreased to 2.92 per cent during the reforms period 1991-92 to 2001-02 [Table 3(a)] because of reduced impetus for productivity increases in Punjab, Haryana, Andhra Pradesh and western Uttar Pradesh, dwindled and limited public investment in agricultural infrastructure (World Bank, 2003). Slow agricultural growth is of concern less because of its contribution to India's overall output or food security concerns, and more because of the sector's importance in the country's economic, social and political fabric. The sector still provides employment to a large share of India's population, and even larger share of the poor (*ibid.*).

The share of industry in GDP increased, though not substantially, from 20.25 per cent in 1971-72 to 24.44 per cent in 2001-02. The average growth rate of GDP of industry increased from 3.51 per cent during 1971-72 to 1980-81, to 6.98 per cent during 1981-82 to 1990-91. The same, however, declined to 5.68 per cent during the reform period 1991-92 to 2001-02. A high average growth rate of GDP (6.69 per cent) during the first half of the reform years 1990s (1992-93 to 1996-97) coincided with a high average growth rate of industrial GDP at 8.04 per cent [Table 3(a)]. A slower average growth rate of GDP during the period 1997-98 to 2001-02 at 5.46 coincided with an even slower growth rate in industrial GDP at 4.66 per cent. While the former period reflected the urgency of reforms, the latter experienced complacency and a lack of clear direction in the reform process. As demand failed to expand as rapidly as expected and facing greater competition from imports, the industrial sector was left with excess capacity. Simultaneously, the domestic policy environment did not support productivity increases (World Bank, 2003).

Growth of the services sector has been strong and broad-based. The average annual growth rate of trade, transport, and communications sector increased marginally from 5.11 per cent during the period 1971-72 to 1980-81, to 5.81 per cent during 1981-82 to 1990-91, and substantially to 7.71 per cent during the reforms period 1991-92 to 2001-02 [Table 3(a)]. The period 1992-93 to 1996-97 witnessed a growth rate of 8.83 per cent. The subsequent period (1997-98 to 2001-02), however, experienced a slower growth rate at 7.62 per cent. The average annual growth rate of the financial sector increased from 4.09 per cent during the period 1971-72 to 1980-81, to 9.86 per cent during 1981-82 to 1990-91, but declined to 8.14 per cent during the period of reforms. However, the growth rate in this sector was higher than that of agricultural and industrial sectors. Rapid expansion of information technology was one of the reasons behind the high growth rate of the services sector.

An analysis of growth of factor income suggests that reforms benefited the organized sector and more specifically the industrial and services sectors rather than the unorganized sector (represented mainly by the agricultural sector). While the share of factor income from agriculture in the organized sector declined from 2.70 per cent in 1994-95 to 2.19 per cent in 1999-2000, the share of factor income from industry declined from 34.79 per cent to 28.25 per cent, the same in respect of the services sector increased from 62.51 per cent to 69.56 per cent during the period under review [Table 4(a)]. The average annual growth rate of factor income in the organized sector during the period 1993-94 to 1999-2000 stood at 17.02 per cent [Table 4(a)], as against 14.54 per cent in the unorganized sector [Table 4(b)]. In the organized sector factor income from the services sector grew at an average annual rate of 19.18 per cent, as against 13.17 per cent in case of agriculture and 13.02 per cent in case of industry. In the unorganized sector factor income from industry grew at an average annual rate of 17.58 per cent, followed by 16.27 per cent in the services sector and 11.24 per cent in agriculture [Tale 4(b)]. Further, the share of factor income from the organized sector in total factor income increased from 65.26 per cent in 1993-94 to 68.13 per cent in 1999-2000, while that of the unorganized sector declined from 34.74 per cent to 31.87 per cent [Table 4(c)]. Income in the organized sector thus grew faster than that of the unorganized sector, and income from industry and services sectors grew faster than income from agriculture.

As the poor spend nearly 40 per cent of their income on cereals, the well-being of the poor in India is directly related to foodgrain prices (Kotwal and Ramaswami, 1999). Not surprisingly, the poverty ratio has been positively correlated with foodgrain prices. Studies on rural poverty in India show a strong negative association between poverty ratio and agricultural growth.

The 1990s witnessed a decline in the growth rate of real agricultural wages from over 5 per cent per annum in the 1980s to 2.5 per cent. Given the close and inverse association between real agricultural wages and rural poverty, this pattern is consistent with the belief that poverty has continued to decline in the 1990s but perhaps at a slower rate than in the 1980s. Regional disparities are also discernable in the growth rate in real wages. Findings by Dréze and Sen (2002) reveal that real wages have grown quite fast in the Western and Southern states, especially Gujarat, Tamil Nadu and Kerala — more than 5 per cent in each case, but rather slowly in much

TABLE 4(a): Factor Income: Growth of Compensation to Employees in the Organized Sector (OS)

Year	Agriculture & Allied % growth	% share in OS	Industry % growth	% share in OS	Services % growth	% share in OS	Total CE (OS) % growth
1994-95	12.58	2.70	13.24	34.79	14.19	62.51	13.81
1995-96	34.51	1.58	25.12	35.00	23.51	62.08	24.37
1996-97	12.95	2.97	4.16	32.82	14.90	64.21	11.09
1997-98	-0.39	2.50	13.21	31.37	21.99	66.13	18.45
1998-99	14.71	2.39	11.50	29.22	23.81	68.39	19.72
1999-00	4.68	2.19	10.90	28.25	16.66	69.56	14.69
Avg.	13.17		13.02		19.18		17.02

Source: National Income Statistics, Centre for Monitoring Indian Economy, Jan. 2003.

TABLE 4(b): Factor Income: Growth of Compensation to Employees in the Unorganized Sector (UOS)

Year	Agriculture & Allied % growth	% share in UOS	Industry % growth	% share in UOS	Services % growth	% share in UOS	Total CE (UOS) % growth
1994-95	27.52	46.37	16.74	30.80	24.53	22.83	23.34
1995-96	11.59	45.43	13.31	30.63	19.39	23.93	13.90
1996-97	12.79	44.55	16.67	31.07	17.19	24.38	15.03
1997-98	10.86	42.57	27.77	34.22	10.46	23.21	16.02
1998-99	0.48	40.52	17.83	36.69	15.50	24.39	9.90
1999-00	4.20	37.19	13.17	38.08	10.53	24.73	9.03
Avg.	11.24		17.58		16.27		14.54

Source: National Income Statistics, Centre for Monitoring Indian Economy, Jan. 2003.

TABLE 4(c): Factor Income: Compensation to Employees (Amount in Rs. billion)

Year	Organized Sector	Share of OS income	Unorganized Sector	Share of UOS income	Total CE
1994-95	1752.55	63.41	1011.10	36.59	2763.65
1995-96	2179.60	65.43	1151.66	34.57	3331.26
1996-97	2421.23	64.63	1324.80	35.37	3746.03
1997-98	2867.85	65.11	1537.01	34.89	4404.86
1998-99	3433.46	67.03	1689.17	32.97	5122.63
1999-00	3937.78	68.13	1841.78	31.87	5779.56

Source: National Income Statistics, Centre for Monitoring Indian Economy, Jan. 2003.

of the northern and eastern regions, especially in the poorest states (*e.g.* 0.3 per cent in Bihar and 0.7 per cent in Orissa).

The share of agriculture and allied activities in India's GDP has been declining steadily from 41.83 per cent in 1980-81 to 26.1 per cent in 2001-02 (Table 3). However, about 75 per cent of the country's poor live in rural areas, and a majority of them depend on agriculture as a major source of livelihood. In view of the high rates of poverty among agricultural households the large concentration of labour engaged in agriculture, and their low productivity, the National Agricultural Policy and the Tenth Plan accorded high priority on raising agricultural productivity, as a means of achieving rapid agricultural growth and to reduce poverty. Growth of rural non-farm sector has also gained importance. Promotion of both agricultural and non-farm sector growth is necessary because of backward and forward linkages (World Bank, 2003: 64). Promotion of rural non-farm sector (RNFS) growth requires improved access to basic infrastructure (roads, markets, electricity, water) and services (market information, credit, education). In opening greater employment opportunities in RNFS, this could create demand for agricultural labour, contributing to higher agricultural wages and incomes (*ibid.*).

There is a growing realization that the goals set for the agricultural sector under the Tenth Five Year Plan might be difficult to attain unless major reform initiatives are carried out in this sector. In the context of viable and sustainable development of the sector, the efficient management of land and water resources assumes critical importance. The conservation of land and water resources through watershed development in ecologically fragile areas is intrinsic to sustainable development in agriculture. The country's irrigation potential is 139.89 million hectares, against which the cumulative irrigation potential created is estimated at 94.7 million hectares. Programmes like Accelerated Irrigation Benefits and Rural Infrastructure Development Fund (RIDF) have been facilitating the development of available potential. An area endowed with a good network of irrigation, roads and power will yield high returns to agricultural investment. Animal husbandry has become an important sub-sector contributing nearly one-fourth of GDP of the agriculture sector. Research and

Development efforts should focus on bringing about further improvement in the production potential. Further food and agro-processing sector involving value addition should be a thrust area.

Trade liberalization in the agricultural sector in the wake of the 'Agreement on Agriculture' under the WTO, is expected to improve the scope for increasing the exports of non-traditional agricultural commodities. The Ministry of Commerce, Government of India, is promoting the establishment of Agri-Export Zones in collaboration with state governments to boost agricultural exports.

An important indicator of the impact of reforms on poverty is the growth in employment. As per the results of the quinquennial survey of National Sample Survey Organization (NSSO) on Employment and Unemployment (55th Round, 1999-2000) the rates cf growth of employment in India, on Current Daily Status (CDS) basis declined from 2.7 per cent per annum during 1983-1994, to 1.07 per cent per annum during 1994-2000 (Table 5). The decline in the rate of growth of employment during the 1990s was associated with a comparatively higher growth rate in GDP, indicating a decline in labour intensity of production.

The decline in the overall growth rate of unemployment during 1993-94 to 1999-2000 was largely attributable to near stagnation in agriculture. As a result, the share of agriculture in total employment substantially dropped from 60.4 per cent in 1993-94 to 56.7 per cent in 1999-2000 (Table 6). During the period under review the share of industry increased from 15.83 per cent to 17.56 per cent, and that of the services sector increased from 23.78 per cent to 25.7 per cent. These results corroborate the hypothesis that market reforms benefited the industrial and services sectors more than the agricultural sector. Accordingly, its impact on poverty has been less than desired.

In conformity with the past trend the NSSO Survey reveals that the share of casual labour in total employment increased. Only a small percentage (8 to 9 per cent) of the total workforce of the country is employed in the organized sector. While employment growth in the private organized sector significantly

TABLE 5: Macro-scenario on Employment and Unemployment (CDS basis)

	(Million)			Growth per annum (%)	
	1983	1993-94	1999-00	1983 to 1993-94	1993-94 to 1999-00
All India					
Population	718.2	894.01	1003.97	2.00	1.95
Labour force	261.33	335.97	363.33	2.43	1.31
Workforce	239.57	315.84	336.75	2.70	1.07
Unemployment rate (%)	(8.30)	(5.99)	(7.32)		
No. of unemployed	21.76	20.13	26.58	-0.80	4.74
Rural					
Population	546.61	658.83	727.50	1.79	1.67
Labour force	204.18	255.38	270.39	2.15	0.96
Workforce	187.92	241.04	250.89	2.40	0.67
Unemployment rate (%)	(7.96)	(5.61)	(7.21)		
No. of unemployed	16.26	14.34	19.50	-1.19	5.26
Urban					
Population	171.59	234.98	276.47	3.04	2.74
Labour force	57.15	80.60	92.95	3.33	2.40
Workforce	51.64	74.80	85.84	3.59	2.32
Unemployment rate (%)	(9.64)	(7.19)	(7.65)		
No. of unemployed	5.51	5.80	7.11	0.49	3.45

Source: Economic Survey 2002-03, Government of India.

TABLE 6: Sectoral Employment Growth (CDS basis)

Sector	Employment (in million)			
	1983	1987-88	1993-94	1999-2000
Agriculture	151.35	163.82	190.72	190.94
Industry	37.43	47.85	49.99	59.15
Services	50.78	60.72	75.11	86.65
All Sectors	239.56	272.39	315.82	336.74
Sector	Annual growth (%)			
	1983 to 1997-98	1987-88 to 1993-94		1993-94 to 1999-00
Agriculture	1.77	2.57		0.02
Industry	6.48	2.01		0.58
Services	4.10	3.75		3.64
All Sectors	2.89	2.50		1.07

Source: Economic Survey 2002-03, Government of India.

improved during the 1990s, the growth of employment in the public sector was negligible. Since the public sector accounts for more than two-thirds of the total organized sector employment, there was a slowdown in the overall growth in organized sector employment (Government of India, 2003: 214).

POVERTY ALLEVIATION: POLICY ISSUES AND CHALLENGES

Anti-Poverty Programmes

Poverty alleviation has been one of the guiding principles of the planning process in India. The most widespread anti-poverty programmes are the ones that seek to transfer assets and skills to the people for self-employment, coupled with public works programmes that enable people to cope with transient poverty.

The Integrated Rural Development Programme (IRDP) was the first attempt in India to directly attack poverty. Introduced in 1978-79, this programme provided assistance to rural poor in the form of subsidy and bank credit for productive employment opportunities through successive plan periods. Subsequently, Training of Rural Youth for Self-Employment (TRYSEM), Development of Women and Children in Rural Areas (DWCRA), Supply of Improved Toolkits to Rural Artisans (SITRA), and Ganga Kalyan Yojana (GKY) were introduced as sub-programmes of IRDP to take care of the specific needs of the rural population. The Mid Term Appraisal of the Ninth Five-Year Plan had observed that these sub-programmes "presented a matrix of multiple programmes without desired linkages". The IRDP suffered from sub-critical investments, lack of bank credit, overcrowding in certain projects and lack of market linkages. The programme was basically subsidy driven and ignored the process of social intermediation necessary for the success of self-employment programmes. Further a one-time provision of credit without follow up action and a lack of a continuing relationship between borrowers and bankers undermined the programme's objectives (Government of India, 2002). Moreover, there was the widespread problem of wrong identification of beneficiaries, and consequent leakages.

On 1st April 1999 the IRDP and allied programmes were

merged into a single programme *viz.*, Swaranjayanti Gram Swarozgar Programme (SGSY). The SGSY was conceived as a holistic programme of micro enterprise development in rural areas with emphasis on organizing the rural poor into SHGs, capacity building, planning of activity clusters, infrastructure support, technology, credit and marketing linkages.

The implementation of SGSY between 1999-2000 and 2001-02 has highlighted many deficiencies. The District Rural Development Agencies (DRDA) responsible for administering the programme lacked the requisite skills in social mobilization. Linkages with NGOs, which could have facilitated this process, were also not in place. Further Government of India's release of funds was substantially lower than the allocation as the field offices were not in a position to organize SHGs. Credit mobilization also suffered in the process. With proper implementation of the SGSY programme, the inadequacies of formal credit institutions could be overcome by combining the strengths of commercial banks with the intermediation capabilities of the NGOs to effectively link the poor with the commercial banking channels. This would be a cost-effective alternative for providing credit to the poor as banks would be able to reach a large number of small borrowers with low transaction cost. The risk of default on loans would be lower due to group pressure and the groups would also monitor the end-use of credit.

The Tenth Plan document (Government of India, 2002) maintains that it has been the Government's endeavour to leverage funds under different self-employment programmes to enable rural poor to diversify into non-agricultural activities. The inadequate availability of micro-infrastructure relevant to service or trade has been a major constraint in rapid development of rural non-farm sector. Marketing strategy is an integral part of every self-employment programme venture. There is a need to develop market intelligence. Rural *haats* or village markets have to be set up to position the products of SHGs.

Self-employment programmes are likely to have an uneven regional spread, succeeding in areas that have a tradition of artisanship, developed roads and rail infrastructure, banking facilities and a skilled human base. The negative relationship between the incidence of rural poverty and land access is well established. The landless face the greatest risk of poverty. Access to even small pieces of land which may not be sufficient for providing income to a family for subsistence can significantly reduce poverty and food insecurity by providing an essential component in a diversified livelihood system (Government of India, 2002).

Subsidy has hampered the promotion of self-employment programmes. The experience of NABARD's SHG-Bank Linkage Programme shows that the poor are capable and also willing to pay for the credit and other financial services rendered by NGOs and banks without depending on the government for subsidy. The Tenth Plan, therefore, would direct financial resources for providing infrastructure and other support facilities, which increase the returns to households and reduce their risks.

Wage employment programmes, another important component of the anti-poverty strategy, not only provide employment opportunities during the lean agricultural seasons but also in times of floods, droughts and other natural calamities. They create rural infrastructure, which supports further economic activity. They also put an upward pressure on market wage rates. The National Rural Employment Programme (NREP) and Rural Landless Employment Guarantee Programme (RLEGP) were started in Sixth and Seventh Five-Year Plans. They were merged in 1989 into Jawahar Rozgar Yojana (JRY). The JRY was revamped on 1 April 1999 as Jawahar Gram Samriddhi Yojana (JGSY) to create rural economic infrastructure together with employment generation.

JGSY, Employment Assurance Scheme (EAS) and Food for Work Programme (FWP), all of which aimed at the creation of employment opportunities in rural areas, were revamped and merged under the Sampoorna Gramin Rozgar Yojana (SGRY) scheme in 2001 to generate wage employment, creation of durable economic infrastructure in rural areas and provision of food and nutrition security to the poor. Though the creation of community assets has important spin-offs for rural poverty and development, the impact of the programmes on employment and income has been limited. During the Ninth

Five-Year Plan period there was a considerable reduction in terms of allocation as well as employment generation under the various wage employment programmes.

Land reforms were implemented immediately after India's Independence. The abolition of intermediaries in spite of its many well-documented shortcomings and ineffective implementation in certain parts of the country covered nearly 40 per cent of the cultivated area. However, progress in other components of land reforms *viz.*, implementation of land ceiling laws, security of tenure to tenants and consolidation of land holdings, was woefully inadequate. Land reforms had been relegated to the background in the 1990s. More recently, initiatives of state governments related to liberalization of land laws in order to promote large-scale corporate farming. There is indeed a need for effective implementation of the existing land ceiling laws. Farmers owning land below the ceiling limit may be provided a guarantee that their land would not be taken away. The fixation of rent could be left to the market forces.

Human Development

Education is a critical input for investment in human capital. As against a goal of 6 per cent of GDP, the total expenditure in education in India was 3.99 per cent of GDP in 2001-02. There has, however, been a significant improvement in literacy. Over the years, literacy rates substantially improved (Table 7). Male-female gap in literacy reduced from 24.84 per cent in 1991 to 21.70 per cent.

TABLE 7: Literacy Rates in India

Census Year	Males	Females	Persons	Male-female gap in literacy rate
1951	27.16	8.86	18.33	18.30
1961	40.40	15.35	28.30	25.05
1971	45.96	21.97	34.45	23.98
1981	56.38	29.76	43.57	26.62
1991	64.13	39.29	52.21	24.84
2001	75.85	54.16	65.38	21.70

Source: Economic Survey 2002-03, Government of India.

Within the education sector, elementary education has been given the highest priority in terms of sub-sectoral allocation and number of schemes launched by the Government of India to meet the needs of the educationally disadvantaged, *viz.* Operation Blackboard, District Primary Education Programme, Sarva Shiksha Abhiyan, and Alternative and Innovative Education.

Children of poor families are less likely to be enrolled in schools. The poverty gap in enrolment is large — the enrolment rate is 25 percentage points lower for the poorest households than for the richest households. Further, the dropout for the poorest households is about four times that of the richest ones. A major deterrent to school enrolment among the poor is its high cost (World Bank, 2000: 23). With the enactment of the Constitutional (93rd Amendment) Bill, 2002, free and compulsory elementary education has been made a fundamental right.

The problem of child labour is a major social concern. The estimated number of working children in the country as per the 55th Round of NSSO Survey (1999-2000) is 10.4 million. Children continue to be employed in the unorganized sector. The policy of the Government of India is to ban the employment of children below the age of 14 years in factories, mines and hazardous employment and regulate the working conditions of children in other areas of employment. Incidentally, high child labour population is found both in developed as well as backward states.

While the health facilities in the country have improved over the years, there is a long way to go, particularly among the poor. Improvement in the health status of the population is a major thrust area under the social development programmes being implemented in the country. This could be achieved through improvement in access to and utilization of health services in the country with special focus on under-served and underprivileged segments of the population. Technological advances and improvement in access to health care technologies have resulted in a substantial improvement in health indices of the population and a steep decline in mortality. However, the extent of access to and utilization of health care has varied substantially between states.

India has a high percentage of malnutrition and some segments of the population have among the highest levels of malnutrition in the world. There has been only modest decline in the levels of malnutrition of children in the last two decades. Presently, one half of the children below the age of five years in the country are moderately or severely malnourished; 30 per cent of the newborn babies are significantly under weight and nearly 60 per cent of women are anaemic.

The reduction in infant mortality slowed during the 1990s because of high levels of disease and malnutrition, and poor sanitation and water supply, especially in the poorer states (Table 8).

Safe drinking water and improved sanitation play a major role in the overall well-being of the people, with a significant bearing on infant mortality rate, death rate, longevity, and productivity. The poor, both in rural and urban areas bear a disproportionately high burden of the non-availability of water, as well as its poor quality. The reduction in poverty has typically been faster in regions with better-developed social opportunities. There is a clear connection between initial social achievements on the one hand, and subsequent reduction of income poverty, on the other. The experience of the 1990s shows that states with better level of social preparedness (particularly in the Southern and Western states) have done well, while much of the northern region remained mired in poverty. India's development experience in the 1990s recognizes the complementarity between economic progress and social opportunities. India has done reasonably well in the former, but not so in the latter. The continued neglect of the social sector has seriously compromised the gains that might otherwise have been derived from the country's reasonably high economic growth.

While there have been adverse effects of market oriented reforms on social policy in India, the impact has been limited partly because of relatively unsuccessful attempts to improve fiscal discipline (Dréze and Sen, 2002). Thus, ironically the fiscal profligacy of the 1990s has made it easier to sustain social expenditure.

TABLE 8: State-wise Infant Mortality Rate

	1981	2001
Northern States/UT		
Delhi	54	51
Chandigarh	48	32
Haryana	52	69
Himachal Pradesh	82	64
Jammu & Kashmir	N.A.	45
Punjab	74	54
Southern States		
Andhra Pradesh	55	66
Karnataka	74	58
Kerala	42	16
Tamil Nadu	54	53
Eastern States		
Orissa	125	98
West Bengal	62	53
Western States		
Goa	51	36
Gujarat	78	64
Maharashtra	74	49
BIMARU States		
Bihar#	75	67
Madhya Pradesh#	133	97
Rajasthan	87	83
Uttar Pradesh#	99	85
North Eastern States		
Arunachal Pradesh	91	44
Assam	92	78
Manipur	28	25
Meghalaya	80	52
Mizoram	53	23
Nagaland	51	N.A.
Sikkim	60	52
Tripura	82	49
All India	77	71

Undivided States.

Source: Economic Survey 2002-03, Government of India.

India is ranked 127th out of 175 countries in terms of UNDP's Human Development Indicator (HDI) and is classified in the group of Medium Human Development with HDI of 0.590 in 2001 (Table 9).

TABLE 9: Human Development Index Trends in Selected Countries

HDI Rank		1980	1990	1995	2001
	High Human Development				
1	Norway	0.876	0.900	0.924	0.944
7	United States	0.883	0.911	0.923	0.937
9	Japan	0.875	0.906	0.920	0.932
	Medium Human Development				
58	Malaysia	0.658	0.721	0.759	0.790
65	Brazil	0.678	0.712	0.738	0.777
99	Sri Lanka	0.644	0.692	0.715	0.730
104	China	0.554	0.624	0.679	0.721
112	Indonesia	0.576	0.619	0.659	0.682
127	India	0.443	0.519	0.553	0.590
139	Bangladesh	0.352	0.414	0.443	0.502
	Low Human Development				
143	Nepal	0.326	0.413	0.451	0.499
144	Pakistan	0.370	0.440	0.472	0.499

Source: Human Development Report, 2003, UNDP.

The National Human Development Report (Planning Commission, Government of India, 2001) placed Kerala at the top among states, with HDI of 0.638 in 2001. The prosperous states and the states which have been frontrunners in the economic reforms programme *viz.*, Punjab, Tamil Nadu and Maharashtra had HDI of 0.537, 0.531 and 0.523 respectively. Orissa on the other hand ranked way below with HDI of 0.404. Thus, it may be argued that reforms have benefited states, which have accorded high priority to human development.

India has some lessons to learn from the Chinese experience in human and economic development. China has demonstrated that properly supplemented, a thriving market economy can help a great deal to lift the masses out of poverty and transform their living conditions (Dréze and Sen, 2002: 140). Further, China's experience brings out the complementarity between two essential bases of expansion of social opportunity, *viz.* (a) supportive public intervention, especially in the fields of education, health care, social security, and land reforms; and (b) the market mechanism — an essential part of effective trade and production arrangements. Moreover, the market mechanism has been used in China to create additional channels of social and economic opportunities, without attempting to rely on the market itself as a surrogate social system on its own (*ibid.*).

Effectiveness of the Food Security System

Poverty is the principal cause of hunger. Paradoxically there are surplus food grain stocks in the country, while a large section of India's population continues to be underfed and undernourished. The surplus food grains emanates from the fact that the government is committed to unrealistically high 'minimum support prices' (MSP) for food grains. This has boosted production, lowered consumer demand and forced the government to buy the difference in order to sustain these high prices (Dréze and Sen, 2002: 337). Further, the food grain distribution machinery in the country is woefully inadequate. The achievement of food security is, therefore, of prime importance in the country. The principal reason for hunger is that the poor have inadequate real income to buy food. Loss of agricultural production due to unfavourable weather conditions lead to loss of income for the poor. Further disguised unemployment and lack of alternative employment opportunities also lead to fall in real income of the rural poor.

The strategy to overcome chronic food insecurity includes short-term intervention to raise the purchasing power of the poor through the endowment of land and non-land assets with the help of programmes, which generate employment. India is one of the few countries that have experimented with a broad spectrum of food security. It has made substantial progress in terms of overcoming transient food insecurity through public procurement and distribution of food grains, employment programmes etc. However, in spite of a significant reduction in the incidence of poverty from 54.9 per cent in 1973-74 to 26.1 per cent in 1999-2000, chronic food insecurity persists with a large proportion of population living below the poverty line.

The long-term solution to food insecurity is economic development that can provide productive employment to all. Once every one has adequate income, the food system will provide food at a reasonable price to all. In the short run the public distribution system (PDS) should provide food security. The period 1978-1991 was marked by the growth of comfortable buffer stocks, and this provided the basis for the large-scale expansion of PDS as well as Food for Work type employment programmes. During the 1970s and 1980s PDS was viewed as a component of the strategy to alleviate poverty (Swaminathan, 2000). Apart from a substantial fall in food grains distributed through PDS during the 1990s, prices of PDS food grains increased disproportionately.

Swaminathan (2000) has explained that evidence on the consumption of food, on calorie intake, and on nutritional outcomes clearly establishes that chronic hunger persists on a mass scale in India. The persistence of hunger and malnutrition, and of vulnerability to hunger and malnutrition, on such a mass scale is the principal justification for strengthening PDS.

There are large regional differences in the scale and operation of PDS. The four southern states of Andhra Pradesh, Karnataka, Kerala and Tamil Nadu accounted for about one half of total PDS off take of food grains in the country (in 1995). These states were followed by West Bengal. However, the BIMARU states together accounted for only 10 per cent of total off take (Swaminathan, 2000). There is a positive correlation between per capita off take and the incidence of poverty. Further, in the states with high coverage and an effective distribution network (*e.g.* Andhra Pradesh and Kerala), the poor had greater access to PDS. In states with inefficient and ineffective network (*e.g.* Bihar and Uttar Pradesh), PDS reached neither the poor nor the rich.

There has been a widespread decline in per capita off

take of food grains during the initial years of economic reforms between 1991 and 1995. During this period per capita off take of food grains fell in fourteen states. There was a reverse in the trend between the period 1995 and 1998, when per capita off take rose in ten states. Nevertheless, PDS has provided some safeguards against worsening of inequalities of consumption across states. Over the last three decades, although cereal consumption per capita declined, inter-state variations in cereal consumption and in calorie intake have declined (Swaminathan, 2000).

PDS had been widely criticised for its failure to serve the population below the poverty line, its urban bias and negligible coverage in the states with the highest concentration of the rural poor. Consequently, targeted PDS (TPDS) was introduced in 1997. The system follows a two-tier subsidized pricing structure for BPL and APL (above poverty line) families. Under the TPDS special cards are issued to BPL families and food grains are sold to them at highly subsidized prices. The most striking feature of TPDS has been a shift from universal coverage to a target approach. It was argued that universal coverage was an extravagance that a poor country like India can ill-afford. The reform period has favoured cutting down of subsidies. Further, the monthly entitlement for the poor has been fixed at the meagre level of 10 kg per household. In other words, TPDS ensures poor households the pitiful quantity of about 2 to 3 kgs per person per month (Swaminathan, 2000).

It has been argued that, with tight targeting as under TPDS, errors in measurement can mean disqualification for genuinely poor persons. Further the use of time-specific cut-off makes little sense when there is significant income mobility even in the lower income deciles (Swaminathan, 2000). There must, therefore, be a mechanism to continuously identify upward and downward mobility of families, as there is a risk of decline in income for families marginally above the poverty line.

In order to make TPDS more focused and targeted towards the poor population the Antyodaya Anna Yojana (AAY) was launched in December 2000. The AAY targets 15 million poorest of the poor families out of a total of 65.2 million BPL families covered under TPDS. These identified families are currently being provided 35 kg food grains per family per month at highly subsidized prices.

The importance of food security has been widely recognized during the reforms period, and limited progress, has been achieved in this area. The formulation and implementation of a long term Grains Policy, improvement in the procurement and distribution network, free from apathetic and corrupt government officials, would bring about food security in the country.

Banking with the Poor

The Committee on Banking Sector Reforms (1998) recognized the imperative need to maintain adequate flow of credit to agriculture and small industrial sectors. The Committee also recognized the need of the small and marginal farmers as well as micro entrepreneurs requiring small loans, which has to be met to make them competitive and efficient.

The thrust of the formal banking sector has been on productive activities, whereas the rural poor need credit mainly for financing income-consumption gap or tiding over occasional crises and emergencies. However, the formal sector took the initiative to develop a supplementary credit delivery mechanism by encouraging NGOs to act as facilitators. It is being increasingly recognized that micro-credit institutions would play an important role in rural development. Studies have revealed that wherever SHGs are active, ably supported by NGOs and banks, there is a distinct and perceptible improvement in the economic status and the quality of life of the members. The intermediation of SHGs has considerably reduced the time spent by bank personnel on identification of borrowers, documentation, follow-up and recoveries.

The concept of micro finance has come to the fore in: (a) freeing the credit market of its myriad dysfunctionalities that arise mainly from political interference, imprudent financial policies and systemic deficiencies; and (b) replacing state sponsored directed credit programmes for poverty alleviation, which are seen as inherently non-viable because of high dose of subsidy by private initiatives.

The linkage between SHGs and banks is an effective instrument to provide banking facilities to the poor, without subsidies and Government support. The repayment record under the linkage programmes has been very good. Banking policy should facilitate the evolution of cost effective systems for banking for the poor, with satisfactory linkages; and support scaling up of such efforts resulting in expanded outreach as well as quality of loan assets.

No weapon can be more potent for an attack on poverty and human deprivation than building human capital among the deprived, through sustainable development initiatives. This principle is central to the SHG-Bank Linkage programme in India, which endorses the basic human feeling of self-worth at its core. The programme also aims to empower the poor, especially women, with a view to promoting sustainable economic development and social upliftment. NABARD, in partnership with regional rural banks, rural branches of commercial banks, cooperatives banks, and select NGOs, developed this strategy to enable the banking system to transcend the confines of an already existing savings and credit delivery mechanism, which was neither cost-effective for the banks, nor user-friendly for the poor. The SHG-Bank Linkage Programme, involving about 31,000 rural outlets of more than 500 banks, with an advance portfolio of Rs. 2000 crore in micro-finance lending to SHGs, has blossomed into the fastest growing and the most cost-effective micro-finance initiative in the world, enabling 11.6 million poor families to access sustainable financial services from the banking system, through a network of over 7,17,000 SHGs (NABARD, 2003). NABARD has set a target of reaching banking services to one-third of the very poor of the country *i.e.* a population of about 100 million rural poor through one million SHGs by the year 2007-08.

The Reserve Bank of India advised banks in February 2000 to mainstream micro-credit and extend the outreach of micro credit providers. Micro-credit extended either directly or through any intermediary is reckoned as part of banks' priority sector lending. Banks are now free to prescribe their own lending norms. Micro-credit would form an integral part of their corporate credit plan and would be reviewed at the highest level every quarter. In view of its potential in the alleviation of poverty, banks have been advised to make all out efforts for provision of micro-credit. Micro-finance can definitely prove to be an effective vehicle in attacking poverty (Sharma, 2004).

CONCLUSION

Economic reforms are expected to lead to rapid economic growth, which in turn would increase economic opportunities and employment leading to an increase in per capita income and the removal of poverty. India achieved impressive growth of GDP during the first half of the 1990s. However, a slowdown in the growth rate in the late 1990s coincided with a lack of direction in the reform process. The much-needed second-generation reform has been delayed mainly due to a lack of political will.

It has been observed that the reduction in poverty has typically been faster in states with more developed social opportunities. The experience of the 1990s shows that states with better level of social preparedness (particularly in the Southern and Western states) fared well, while the BIMARU states, Orissa and the North East remained mired in poverty. The former states have also been frontrunners in implementing economic reforms. India's development experience in the 1990s recognizes the complementarity between economic progress and social opportunities.

The Tenth Plan targeted an average annual GDP growth rate of 8 per cent. At an aggregate level, any acceleration in growth requires some combination of an increase in gross domestic capital formation and an increase in efficiency of resource use. The feasibility of sustaining an annual growth rate of 8 per cent during the Tenth Plan would depend upon improvements in efficiency in agriculture, industry, and service sectors by accelerating structural reforms and development of infrastructure.

Fiscal consolidation requires a two-pronged strategy of augmenting revenues and restraining expenditure, with a view to substantially reducing the current level of fiscal deficit of 10 per cent (combined for the Centre and States). Disinvestment of public sector undertakings can reduce fiscal deficit, unlock the productive potential inherent in the pubic sector undertakings and enhance social infrastructure.

Reforms in India emphasized a continuing commitment to traditional programmes for poverty alleviation. These included direct support of consumption of the poor by subsidized sale of food grains through wage employment programmes in public works projects, especially in rural areas, and a number of self-employment programmes involving provision of a combination of capital subsidy, credit, and technological assistance to set up micro enterprises in both rural and urban areas. However, pro-market reforms did not lead to more efficient anti-poverty programmes.

India's human development experience has been unsatisfactory. There is an urgent need for rapid reforms in education, health, food and nutrition, sanitation, safe drinking water facilities, etc. for the purpose of accelerating economic growth, and removal of poverty. A lesson from the Chinese experience is that the success of reforms in achieving faster economic growth and reduction in poverty levels, to largely depends on development of social infrastructure.

Accumulation of large quantities of food stocks has posed a serious challenge to the food management policy of the government. Despite FCI godowns overflowing with food grains, a substantial number of people do not get even the basic minimum requirements of food. Replacement of universal PDS by TPDS has created some anomalies. PDS should cover BPL families as well as those APL families that are marginally above the poverty line. There must be a mechanism to continuously identify upward and downward mobility of families, as there is a risk of decline in income for families marginally above the poverty line. Further, the monthly family quota of food grains should be increased to adequate levels.

Access to financial assets is a prerequisite for economic well-being. In this respect reforms in rural banking is expected to play a catalytic role in the acceleration of rural development. The formal banking institutions can serve the poor in an efficient and cost effective manner by promoting micro finance through the SHG-Bank Linkage Programme. This programme has proved that the poor are bankable. It has also offered a viable business opportunity for the banks by serving a large section of the society, which was earlier denied access to the formal banking channels. Micro finance innovations can prove to be fruitful in attacking both income and human poverty.

The benefits of reforms must reach the poor. The *e-choupal*[5] project of ITC Ltd. has proved that economic reforms can benefit the rural poor by innovative use of information technology. Implementation of second-generation economic reforms, a second Green Revolution, a holistic approach towards economic development, and above all a pro-reforms political climate would be critical in achieving sustainable economic growth and removal of poverty. Such a broad-based inclusive strategy would pave the way for India to become a developed nation by the year 2020.

NOTES

1. The analysis of BIMARU states includes the states of Chhatisgarh, Jharkhand and Uttaranchal, which were earlier parts of Madhya Pradesh, Bihar and Uttar Pradesh, respectively.
2. As in China the focus should be on privatization of profit making PSUs, which would fetch more returns, compared to other PSUs. Hence, more resources could be released for the development of social infrastructure.
3. The fastest growing economy in the world, China achieved a GDP growth rate of 9.8 per cent during 2003-04.
4. See Table 2.5 of Report on Currency and Finance, 2002-03, Reserve Bank of India (p. 7).
5. *e-choupal* uses information technology to provide data/information to farmers/artisans on weather conditions, markets, inputs, technology, etc.

REFERENCES

Ahluwalia, Montek S. (1999), 'India's Economic Reforms: An Appraisal', in Jeffrey D. Sachs, A. Varshney and N. Bajpai (eds.) *India in the Era of Economic Reforms,* OUP, New Delhi.

Bajpai, N. and Jeffrey D. Sachs (1999), 'The Progress of Policy Reform and Variations in Performance at the Sub-National Level in India', Development Discussion Paper 730, Harvard Institute of International Development, Cambridge, Mass.

Bhaduri, A. and D. Nayyar (1996), *The Intelligent Person's Guide to Liberalization,* Penguin Books India (P) Ltd.

Bhagwati, J. (2001), 'Growth, Poverty and Reforms' in *Economic and Political Weekly* Vol. XXXVI No. 10, March 10-16, 2001, Mumbai.

Chelliah, R.J. and R. Sudarshan (eds.) (1999), *Income Poverty and Beyond: Human Development in India,* Social Science Press, New Delhi.

Drèze, J. and Amartya Sen (1989), *Hunger and Public Action,* Oxford: Clarendon Press.

——— (2002), *India: Development and Participation,* OUP, New Delhi.

Government of India (2001), *National Human Development Report,* Planning Commission, New Delhi.

——— (2002), *Tenth Five Year Plan 2002-2007,* Planning Commission, New Delhi.

——— (2003), *Economic Survey 2002-2003,* Ministry of Finance and Company Affairs, Economic Division, New Delhi.

Kotwal, A. and B. Ramaswami (1999), 'Economic Reforms in Agriculture and Rural Growth', in Jeffrey D. Sachs, A. Varshney and N. Bajpai (eds.), *India in the Era of Economic Reforms,* OUP, New Delhi.

NABARD (2003), *Progress of SHG-Bank Linkage in India 2002-2003.*

Reserve Bank of India (1991), *Report of the Committee on the Financial System.*

_____(1998), *Report of the Committee on Banking Sector Reforms.*

——— (2003), *Report on Currency and Finance 2002-03.*

——— (2004), *Annual Policy Statement 2004-05.*

Sachs, Jeffrey D., A. Varshney and N. Bajpai (eds.) (1999), 'Introduction' in *India in the Era of Economic Reforms,* OUP, New Delhi.

Sharma, Manoranjan (2000), 'Sustainable Agricultural and Rural Development: The Case for Infrastructure' in *Rural Prosperity & Agriculture — Policies, & Strategies Infrastructure & Institutional Support* (ed.) R.C. Choudhary and R.P. Singh, NIRD, Hyderabad.

——— (2004), 'Resuscitating Rural Financial Institutions in India: Catalytic Role of Micro Finance'. Paper presented at the Sixth Conference on Money and Finance organized by IGIDR, Mumbai.

Swaminathan, Madhura (2000), *Weakening Welfare: The Public Distribution of Food in India,* LeftWord Books, New Delhi.

Tendulkar, S.D. (1998), 'Indian Economic Policy Reforms and Poverty: An Assessment' in I.J. Ahluwalia and I.M.D. Little (eds.), *India's Economic Development: Essays for Manmohan Singh,* OUP, New Delhi.

UNDP (1997), *Human Development Report, 1997,* OUP, New York.

——— (2003), *Human Development Report, 2003,* OUP, New York.

World Bank (1996), *World Development Report, 1996.*

——— (2000), *India: Reducing Poverty, Accelerating Development,* OUP, New Delhi.

——— (2001), *World Development Report, 2000/2001: Attacking Poverty,* OUP, New York.

——— (2003), *India: Sustaining Reform, Reducing Poverty,* A World Bank Development Policy Review.

5

RURAL FINANCE: ISSUES AND PERSPECTIVES

P. SATISH

1. Introduction

Rural finance is at a crossroads. It currently suffers from a dichotomy in purpose and direction. In view of increasing concerns about the food situation as a result of world population growth and accelerated world food demand especially among low-income, large population countries, the need for substantial new investment in agriculture is clear (FAO, 1996). On the other hand, it is obvious that the number of donor-supported agricultural credit programmes have declined and there is little evidence, in many countries, that commercial financial intermediaries are compensating for the reduction in supply of loanable funds to agricultural production, processing, and marketing. However on a positive angle there has been a growing interest, around the developing world and economies in transition, in the promotion of rural financial deepening. International development agencies, governments of developing countries, and professionals and academics interested in agriculture, rural poverty, and financial development have focused increasing attention on the thin flows of agricultural credit as well as on the narrow delivery of diverse types of financial services to the rural population of these countries. Moreover attention has gradually shifted, from the earlier exclusive emphasis on credit, towards a growing recognition of the importance of different types of financial services, including deposit services, payment instruments, remittances and in general, mechanisms to manage liquidity and cope with risk.

2. Agricultural Credit – Traditional Perspectives

2.1 The critique of the traditional perspectives in agricultural credit, including the role of the state was first crystallized in the USAID's Spring Review of Small Farmer Credit Programmes[1] in 1973. The Ohio School[2] further pioneered thinking in the area on issues such as the role of credit in development process, the role of the state and state owned institutions, the idea of targeting loans to specific sectors and the need for state intervention (Von Pischke, Adams and Donald, 1983). The traditional perspective on agricultural credit envisages active government role in rural financial markets and leans heavily toward direct interventions. It dates back to the 1950s, when Keynesian economic thinking was inspiring successful interventions at macroeconomic level. Over the last forty years policy makers identified a host of problems in rural financial markets. There was an attempt to resolve these problems through targeting, providing subsidies, and applying governmental controls. It was hoped that these measures would stimulate growth and reduce rural poverty (Yaron, Benjamin and Piprek, 1997).

2.2 Government involvement in the management and implementation of rural financial system has proven expensive and inefficient. Often state controlled rural finance institutions are viewed as tools for distributing political benefits to constituents. Governments have in the past used and continue to use these institutions to target specific rural groups for income transfer. Subsidized credit programmes which are part of state intervention in rural financial markets undermine the institutional sustainability of financial institutions, distort rural finance markets and discourage savings mobilization and fail to develop market driven sources of funding. Such credit programmes that do not include repayment capacity as part of loan analysis impoverish their borrowers and destroy the lending operations of the institutions (Branch, Ito and Slover, 2002).

2.3 Farm credit institutions accumulated losses due to loan defaults, and applied inadequate credit technologies, while excessive inflation eroded their capital bases. Also, inflexible objectives within an inappropriate policy and legal framework and lack of institutional autonomy contributed to poor financial performance. More specifically, institutional viability was often neglected; risk management measures were missing or inadequate; credit was provided at concessionary interest rates, mostly to larger farm enterprises; loans were wrongly and unprofitably allocated or misused; standard credit programmes were not suited to the heterogeneous needs of small farmers; subsidized interest rates blocked the emergence of vigorous rural financial markets, fostered loan repayment indiscipline, prevented banks from covering costs, and discouraged local savings mobilization (FAO and GTZ, 1998).

2.4 State agricultural development banks were characterized by inefficiencies, high operating costs, losses and decapitalisation. These banks were highly inefficient, supply driven and had weak non-market driven management. Experience indicates that these institutions required repeated recapitalisation and ultimately a large number of institutions failed, especially in Africa and Latin America. Still where these banks have failed, private sector institutions have not stepped in to fill the vacuum created. A foremost example in this regard is that of Banco Agrario del Peru (BAP). BAP was established and operated in line with the traditional agricultural credit paradigm, compatible with subsidies and government directed operations. With the onset of financial sector liberalization in Peru BAP collapsed. However its collapse left a void in servicing small farmers and rural households (Coffey, 1998). The microfinance revolution that came to the fore during 1980s and 1990s had largely been an urban phenomenon in most parts of Africa and Latin America. Even where it had entered the rural areas, as in parts of Asia, it confined itself essentially to rural microenterprises. As such mainstream agricultural finance remained outside the pale of microfinance.

2.5 With private sector not entering the rural finance area and microfinance confining itself basically to microenterprise financing, the focus has again shifted to state owned agricultural development banks and the need to restructure and retool them to meet the demand for rural finance. These banks have certain inherent strengths. Often state owned development banks possess large branch network for rural financial intermediation and have staff that is especially familiar with agricultural enterprises (Zeller, 2003).

3. Rural Finance System in India

3.1 In India the institutionalization of rural finance started with the establishment of credit cooperatives following the enactment of Cooperative Societies Act in 1904. After independence, the efforts to develop rural credit were intensified following the recommendations of All India Rural Credit Survey Committee of 1954. The entry of the traditional commercial banks into rural finance commenced with the nationalization of Imperial Bank of India and its conversion to State Bank of India in 1955. In 1969, the review undertaken by the All India Rural Credit Review Committee found that the cooperatives had not reached up to the expectations in mobilizing deposits and dispensing credit at national level. The Committee therefore, felt that the efforts of the cooperatives had to be supplemented and recommended the adoption of multi-agency approach to provide credit to rural areas with a role for Commercial Banks. The nationalization of Commercial Banks in 1969 was a major step which facilitated rapid expansion of the banking system to the rural areas. With the nationalization of the banks special responsibility of stepping up advances for agriculture and allied activities was given to them. In 1970 the Lead Bank Scheme was introduced in which each district in the country was assigned to one commercial bank to coordinate the efforts of financial institutions in meeting the credit needs of the rural economy.

3.2 **Rural Credit Cooperatives**: Unlike many developing countries, India has an extensive and well-organized rural banking system. In the cooperative sector there is a network of 92,219 Primary Agriculture Cooperative Societies (PACS) at the base level which are federated into 369 District Central Cooperative Banks (DCCBs) and affiliated to 30 State Cooperative Banks (SCBs). The DCCBs themselves have a network of 13,635 branches. This cooperative banking sector was originally catering exclusively to short-term crop production credit for the farmers but since the last decade they are gradually diversifying into other agricultural and non-agricultural investments. In the cooperative sector there are also 20 State Cooperative Agriculture and Rural Development Banks (ARDBs) and 739 Primary Agriculture and Rural Development Banks (PARDBs) which are technically not banks but disburse credit for investment activities in agriculture through their network of 2001 branches. Bereft of deposits from public, these banks are mainly dependent on refinance resources for their lendings to agriculture from National Bank for Agriculture and Rural Development (NABARD), an apex refinance institution for agriculture and rural credit, owned by Government of India and RBI.

Institutional Arrangements for Rural Finance

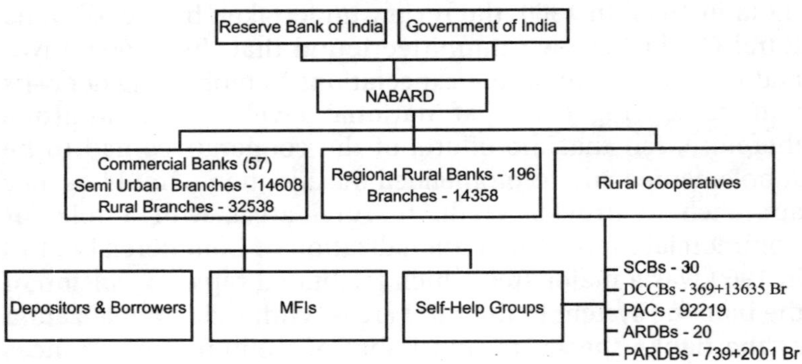

3.3 **Regional Rural Banks**: In mid-1970s it was felt that the operations of Commercial Banks were not compatible with rural environment and involved high costs. In addition there was a view that the commercial banking system had a cultural barrier in dealing with the rural masses. On the other hand the cooperative institutions which had their roots in the rural areas were not having sufficient resources to meet the credit demand, as their deposit base was inadequate. The cooperatives did not also have the professional competence in banking. It was, therefore, thought that India being a vast country with diverse physical, regional, social and economic features no single pattern of financial institutions could handle the task of credit dispensation. Thus, the Regional Rural Banks were visualized as hybrid banks incorporating the technical competence and the professional approach of the commercial banking system with the local field level knowledge and low cost structure of the cooperative banking system. These banks were conceived as a network of institutions for dispensing rural credit especially to the weaker sections of the society. Hence, the issues of outreach and credit were most fundamental to the concept of Regional Rural Banks (RRBs). The Regional Rural Banks have been established under the RRBs Act 1976. An RRB is owned by the Central Government, State Government and sponsoring Commercial Bank in the ratio of 50, 15 and 35. Sponsoring Commercial Bank provides the technical support to the RRB as well as the key personnel including the Chairman and senior officers like General Managers. Each RRB is basically a small bank covering 1 to 4 districts in a State and having a branch network, which varies from 8 to 238. But the mean branch size of RRB is about 60 branches. Today there are 196 RRBs in India with a total branch network of 14,358.

3.4 **Commercial Banks**: The commercial banking system has a major role in rural finance system in India, with a total share of 57.9 per cent of rural credit flow. A total of 27 public sector banks and 30 private sector banks have 32,538 rural and 14,608 semi-urban branches whose portfolio is predominantly in agriculture and allied sectors.

The regulation and supervision of the banking system rests with the Reserve Bank of India (RBI) — the Central Bank of the country which is also the monetary authority.

4. Rural Finance System — Focus and Reforms

4.1 Till mid-nineties, the entire rural finance system was characterized by lack of operational freedom due to all pervasive governmental intervention as well as control on all aspects of the functioning of the institutions by the Central Bank of the country — the Reserve Bank of India (RBI). While in the period mid-1950s to mid-1970s, the main concern of the government was on increasing food production, during mid-1970s the focus shifted to poverty alleviation through subsidized credit. The predominant aim of policy makers during the period 1950s to 1980s was to extend the outreach of the rural finance system and to increase the level of credit flow to agriculture and for poverty alleviation programmes. The issues relating to the development of a sound banking system or rural financial market involving, proper loan appraisal, recovery and recycling, resource and savings mobilisation, and sustainable viability of the operations were lost sight of. The outcome of these policies was a rural finance system with poor resource base, high transaction costs, low or negative margins, mounting bad debts and continuous losses. By 1994-95 India had reached a stage where financial needs of rural population could not be met without a complete overhaul of the existing system or creation of an entirely new system.

4.2 It was in a scenario where the options before the Government and the RBI in the financial sector were limited, that the Government of India initiated financial sector and banking sector reforms from 1991-92 onwards (RBI, 1991). But the situation in the rural finance sector was hardly conducive to an effective credit delivery system, especially in the context of emerging competitive environment in the wake of the financial sector reforms. There was an imperative need for the rural financial institutions (RFIs) to be sensitive to concept of cost effectiveness, commercial orientation and professionalism. To bring about such sensitivity a total diagnosis of the ills afflicting these institutions was necessary. It was recognized that any programme evolved after such diagnosis should encompass the 'critical minimum effort' that will attack simultaneously all the crucial factors that impinge upon the viable functioning of these banks. The remedy to these problems was ultimately in allowing these institutions to function truly as financial intermediaries based on market forces rather than, compelling them into the role of mere conduits of directed credit. The institutions should therefore be left free to determine the terms and pace of their resource mobilisation, lending and investment operations. This implies that the system should allow the institutions to devise their own policies for mobilization of resources and deployment thereof on the most profitable lines.

5. Development Action Planning

5.1 Keeping this philosophy as the cornerstone, in 1994-95, the apex institution for rural finance — National Bank for Agriculture and Rural Development (NABARD) had initiated the process of drawing up of Development Action Plans (DAP) for each of the rural finance institutions (RFIs). This initiative represents a paradigm shift from institutional development that is top-down to bottom-up and self-targeting. It was also a tool for building RFIs' self-esteem, accountability and services that are relevant to their customers. The basic philosophy of the DAP was to prepare institution specific action plans taking into account their strengths and weaknesses, diagnosing the past and looking into the future, anticipating the course of events and preparing coping strategies, implementation of which would improve their viability. In order to assess the viability status of the institution, a thorough analysis of the various aspects — such as financial, organizational, systems and procedures and human resource development — having bearing on the viability of the credit institutions was envisaged. On the basis of such an analysis, the factors that affect the viability of the banks were identified and specific remedial measures were chalked out. The DAPs contained realistic projections for growth in the operations of the institutions based on their optimal performance, potential available in the area of operation and their capacity to exploit such potential (NABARD, 1995).

5.2 Further, the impact of accumulated losses and loan losses and other unrealizable assets were also estimated on a realistic basis through this exercise. This was an important component of the entire exercise, which had to be kept in view while devising the package of time bound measures for enabling the institutions to become viable. The institutions in losses were attuned to achieve current viability and later sustainable viability. Current viability denoted the ability of the institution to meet the cost of management and the risk cost out of the gross financial margin available and be in a position to earn reasonable profit. Sustainable viability indicates the ability of the institution to completely wipe out all accumulated losses and to provide for bad debts/assets adequately and start afresh on a clean balance sheet. A distinctive feature of the preparation of DAP is the break-even analysis which projected the business levels which the institutions have to aim for if they have to achieve current viability. It was also realized that the DAPs have to be backed up by a certain level of performance obligation on part of all the stakeholders concerned. Accordingly, in the year 1994-95 the Finance Minister of the Government of India in his budget speech indicated that all the institutions concerned would enter into Memoranda of Understanding (MoU) with the major stakeholders to ensure that these DAPs are implemented in a time bound manner. Their performance obligations were specifically pinned down through the MoUs.

5.3 The DAP exercise was also facilitated by deregulation in the banking sector. From 1994 onwards, Reserve Bank of India gradually deregulated the deposit and lending interest rates — first for the Cooperative Banks and later for RRBs and Commercial Banks. While broad sectoral targets for agriculture and other priority sectors were retained, specific directions of credit flow were withdrawn. The emphasis on subsidized credit programmes also disappeared. Banks have been given autonomy to devise and market their saving and credit products. These elements in the liberalization process enabled the banks to recast their lending and savings programmes to take care of the profitability aspect. It would also be pertinent to mention that till the early 1990s the banking sector in India was not in tune with the internationally accepted prudential norms. These practices — capital adequacy norms, exposure limits, asset classification, provisioning norms, accounting rules, valuation norms etc. as per the Basle recommendations were implemented gradually for Commercial Banks, RRBs and Cooperative Banks starting from 1992 onwards. The Reserve Bank of India also introduced greater levels of transparency and standards of disclosure. A positive externality of the reform process has been the building up of the institutional architecture in terms of markets and creation of enabling environment through technological and legal infrastructure and improving the managerial competence.

6. Viability of Rural Banking

6.1 The Development Action Planning should also be viewed in theoretical context of issue of viability of rural banking as such. A financial institution is viable when its assets exceed the liabilities excluding share capital and reserve fund. A related concept in viability is that a financial institution is currently viable if it can generate surplus over its expenses. Agriculture Credit Review Committee (ACRC) describes profitability as a function of the spread available to the banks between the rates of income and expenses (RBI, 1989). The spread in turn depends upon —

(a) the cost of raising resources comprising deposits and borrowings (the lower the cost, higher will be the spread);

(b) the income earned on the investment and loans made out of the resources (the higher the income, higher will be the spread).

6.2 Additionally, profitability is also a function of the internal efficiency of the bank and the volume of business handled (higher the efficiency and larger the volume, the higher will be the profitability). A major theoretical proposition in the study of viability of banking relates to the level of transaction costs. Financial institutions must cover the administrative costs (essentially salaries and establishment expenditure), taxes, the cost of capital and losses from default. They do so by charging an interest on the loan.

6.3 The viability of a financial institution can also be looked at from the point of view of interest rate to be charged. Hulme and Mosley (1996) have pointed out that the break-even condition for any financial institution over a period of time is simply that net income must be at least equal to total expenditure. In other words:

[(Income from loan portfolio + other income)] 0 [Cost of borrowing (principal and interest)+other expenditures]

In symbols:

$$(\mapsto j+r)\sphericalangle(1-pj)xj+Y0(\updownarrow j+i+aj)xj+Z$$

where —

xj = size of each loan

i = interest rate on borrowings and deposits.

aj = administrative cost per unit of principal

r = lending interest rate

pj = expected default rate on loan j, *i.e.* expected losses due to non-repayment of principal and interest on loan j.

$\mapsto$ j,$\updownarrow$ j = share of principal of each loan that has to be paid back

per time period to the lender ($\mapsto$) or by the lender ($\updownarrow$)

Y = non-loan income (fees etc.)

Z = non-loan expenditure

The default rate (p), the level of administrative cost (a) and the share of principal that has to be repaid per time period ($\mapsto$, $\updownarrow$) may be expressed as averages for the entire loan portfolio.

Further to simplify, if we assume that the share of principal that has to be paid back by borrower and lender each period is the same ($\updownarrow$ = $\mapsto$) and non-loan income and expenditure are the same (Z = Y), then the break-even formula reduces to

$$r^* = \frac{i + a + \mapsto p}{1 - p}$$

which expresses the break-even condition in the form of an interest rate. This implies that the break-even level of interest rate for a financial institution is a function of all the above variables *viz.* cost of deposit and borrowings, administrative cost, rate of default, share of principal to be repaid (to the lender or by the lender), non-loan incomes and expenditures. It could be seen that the default rate assumes a great significance. Higher the default rate, higher the break-even interest rate that has to be charged.

6.4 In the final analysis, it may be noted that the viability of any unit of banking including rural banking is a function of generating sufficient spreads and margins to cover the transaction costs and the risk costs. However, transaction cost itself is a function of volume of working funds. For a given amount of operating expenditure, higher the volume of working funds the lower the transaction costs and *vice versa.* The risk cost is a function of default rate or overdue rate. The lower the overdues, lower will be the risk cost. In the long run, to be viable, the institutions have to either raise interest rates on lending or reduce cost of funds or reduce transaction costs or improve loan recoveries (Satish and Gopalakrishna, 1997).

7. Studies in Viability

7.1 Commercial Banks and RRBs: A study commissioned by World Bank (World Bank, 1995) and undertaken by a private consultancy organisation has gone into profitability of rural financial institutions especially of commercial banks as well as RRBs. The analysis of profitability for these institutions is given in Table 1.

TABLE 1: Profitability of Rural Commercial Banks and Regional Rural Banks

(Percentages)

As a Percentage of Average Working Funds	Commercial Bank Overall	Commercial Bank Rural	RRB Overall	Commercial Bank Sample	RRB Sample
Interest Income	11.4	11.5	7.4	13.9	8.1
Interest expenditure	7.8	7.5	6.6	8.6	7.8
Interest spread	3.6	4.0	0.8	5.3	0.3
Non-Interest Income	0.3	0.2	0.3	0.2	0.3
Operating Income	3.9	4.2	1.1	5.5	0.6
Operating Expenses	2.2	2.0	6.0	2.3	5.0
Gross Profit	1.7	2.2	-4.9	3.2	-4.4
Provisions	–	–	2.7	–	–
Net Profit	1.7	2.2	-7.6	3.2	-4.4

From this it is seen that a rural branch of a Commercial Bank is in net profit whereas the RRB is in a net loss. This is mainly on account of a comparatively lesser operating income for the RRB as well as a greater percentage of operating expenses. This study also estimated a minimum lending rate required at 16.69 per cent to 17.6 per cent for a commercial bank branch and 19.5 per cent for an RRB branch. From the Table above it may be seen that the areas where RRB can attempt reduction in the lending rate is in operating costs, as well as decrease in the loan loss provisions. This study has suggested that a complete deregulation of interest rates on rural loans by all institutions would ensure that they cover the cost of funds (including a healthy return on equity), cost of operation, and cost of bad debts. Higher interest rates should be accompanied by reduced transaction costs.

It also suggests that rural operations of commercial banks

can be self-sustaining if loan appraisal and repayment follow-up systems are tightened to reduce loan losses to within 2 per cent of the outstanding. This would require significant changes in internal procedures and practices and mechanisms that enhance or thwart access to credit within the bank along with a strategic focus on this segment of the market. Minimum macro policy changes that are likely to underlie such changes include much higher levels of bank autonomy and effective legal remedy for non-repayment. This, along with a complete deregulation in the rates of interest would be making the managements interested in taking financial services to the rural segment in a financially sustainable manner.

7.2 A Macro Level Study — Cooperative Credit Institutions and RRBs

7.2.1 In this context a study of the overall assets and liabilities of rural financial institutions *i.e.* SCBs, CCBs, ARDBs, PARDBs, PACs and RRBs and their costs and returns is necessary. This study based on the macro level proportions of the assets and liabilities of rural financial institutions reveals an interesting analysis. These proportions as on 31 March 1995 have been taken from published data of NABARD, NAFSCOB[3] and NCARDBF.[4] Highly deviant figures have been evened out. The prevailing rates of interest have been applied to all the indices. Where there were too many slabs of interest rates, averaging out, without affecting the overall proportions and rates has been carried out.

7.2.2 The margin between the total cost of liabilities and the total return on assets based on the above analysis for various rural financial institutions is given in Table 4.

It may be observed that for all RFIs there is a positive margin, though it ranges from a low of 1.52 per cent for ARDB (Unitary Structure) to a high of 4.40 per cent for RRBs. Within this margin, the cost of management of the institution has to be met and the risk cost of the advances has to be taken care of. Of course, to an extent the risk cost is taken care of in the non-earning assets proportions in Table 3. It would be futile to dwell upon the question whether these margins would be sufficient to meet the transactions costs and risk costs of all the RFIs due to two reasons. Firstly any financial

TABLE 2: Liabilities

	Owned Funds	Demand Deposits		Term Deposits			Borrowings					Total
		Current	Savings	T1	T2	T3	B1	B2	B3	B4	B5	
SCB	9.61	10.20	19.70	11.20	8.13	8.04	13.40	6.99	7.68	5.02	–	100
r/i	0.00	0.00	5.00	6.50	11.50	12.50	5.00	6.50	9.50	12.00	–	6.35
DCCB	8.81	6.12	23.10	11.20	12.10	11.10	13.20	7.89	3.28	2.93	–	100
r/i	0.00	0.00	5.00	8.50	11.50	12.50	7.00	8.50	11.50	14.00	–	7.33
PACS	17.79	0.52	7.25	7.10	2.23	–	32.10	21.10	11.90	–	–	100
r/i	0.00	0.00	5.00	11.00	12.50	–	9.00	10.50	13.50	–	–	8.13
ARDB(U)	11.76	–	–	1.41	–	–	4.73	9.12	11.10	7.92	11.20	100
r/i	0.00	–	–	11.00	–	–	6.50	9.50	10.00	12.00	13.80	7.73
ARDB(F)	11.76	–	–	1.41	–	–	4.73	9.12	11.10	7.92	11.20	100
r/i	0.00	–	–	11.00	–	–	6.50	9.50	10.00	12.00	13.80	7.73
PARDB	11.02	–	–	1.71	–	–	51.70	11.20	13.00	11.10	–	100
r/i	0.00	–	–	11.00	–	–	8.50	11.50	14.00	16.00	–	9.48
RRB	2.02	4.38	35.70	14.30	15.40	10.00	8.81	1.12	0.94	5.09	2.05	100
r/i	0.00	0.00	4.50	8.50	11.50	12.50	6.50	7.50	8.50	9.50	12.00	7.33

Note: r/i = interest rate.

TABLE 3: Assets

	Cash and Bank Balance	Non-earning assets	Investments				Advances						Total
			I1	I2	I3	I4	A1	A2	A3	A4	A5	A6	
SCB	4.80	2.61	5.42	5.35	9.09	5.06	29.90	17.12	6.70	7.20	4.42	2.30	100
r/i	0.00	0.00	10.00	12.00	14.00	16.00	7.00	8.50	11.50	14.00	16.00	18.00	9.72
DCCB	8.60	3.97	7.75	9.63	4.64	2.42	27.20	9.51	8.27	8.20	7.25	2.53	100
r/i	0.00	0.00	10.00	12.00	14.00	16.00	9.00	10.50	13.50	16.00	18.00	20.00	10.66
PACS	7.52	12.18	4.12	2.73	–	–	41.21	20.15	6.03	4.54	1.52	–	100
r/i	0.00	0.00	0.00	12.00	–	–	12.00	14.00	16.00	18.00	20.00	–	10.66
ARDB(U)	8.92	5.42	4.70	6.80	–	–	40.30	21.30	7.75	3.03	1.68	–	100
r/i	0.00	0.00	0.00	0.00	–	–	12.00	14.00	16.00	18.00	20.00	–	10.76
ARDB(F)	8.92	5.42	4.70	6.80	–	–	46.50	12.71	9.62	3.24	2.05	–	100
r/i	0.00	0.00	0.00	0.00	–	–	10.00	12.00	14.00	16.00	19.00	–	9.25
PARDB	6.00	4.00	–	–	–	–	50.70	22.40	11.48	4.25	1.06	–	100
r/i	0.00	0.00	–	–	–	–	12.00	14.00	16.00	18.00	20.00	–	12.05
RRB	8.37	4.58	6.51	12.35	12.28	7.99	23.00	12.05	9.60	2.24	1.03	–	100
r/i	0.00	0.00	10.00	12.00	14.00	16.00	12.00	14.00	16.00	18.00	20.00	–	11.72

TABLE 4: Margin Between Total Cost of Liabilities and Total Return on Assets for Various Rural Financial Institutions

SCB	3.38
DCCB	3.32
PACS	2.05
ARDB(F)	3.04
ARDB(U)	1.52
PARDB	2.57
RRB	4.40

institution — whether rural or non-rural is not interested in transactions cost *per se* on advances, but on the cost of management as a whole, which includes not only transaction costs on advances but also the cost of servicing of deposits and other activities. Secondly at the present level of expansion and diversification of financial services, it would be worthwhile to focus on the non-asset based income of banking institutions.

7.2.3 The margin between the costs and returns is a function of volume of business. As such even a minimum positive margin can meet the cost of management, provided there exists the requisite level of business in that institution. As the macro level proportions of assets and liabilities are feasible proportions for each of the rural financial institution and these proportions are able to generate margins at the prevailing rates of interest on resource mobilisation as well as resource deployment, it may be observed that all the rural financial institutions are intrinsically viable. Non-viability is a result of non-performance rather than of the structural deficiency in the rural credit system. Institutions which are at present unviable have scope for turning-around and becoming viable. The possible solution which is indeed available to these institutions is the adjustment of their assets and liabilities proportions (Satish and Gopalakrishna, 1997).

7.2.4 It is amply clear that there is nothing intrinsically non-viable about rural banking operations or rural financial institutions as such. Except for the views or discussions which have emerged from the ACRC none of the propositions regarding non-viability of rural banking operations have been based on detailed well-studied grounds. A basis for some of the viewpoints on the non-viability of rural banking have also been based on a viewpoint at the international level that the past approach to rural credit institutions is ill-founded and has led to non-viability of RFIs. A generalised analysis of specialised farm credit institutions the world over could be the basis for this viewpoint. This analysis views the impact of one-sided intervention in rural financial markets which can have a series of unfavourable consequences like poor distribution of loans, low repayment discipline and political interference (Von Pischke, 1980).

However in making this analysis applicable to Indian situation it has to be realised that Indian RFIs are structurally and operationally not very different from commercial banking institutions and at present, in the Indian financial systems, there is no philosophy of directed interest rates.

7.2.5 Further the definition of ACRC of measuring viability through net margin in lending also has certain inherent shortcomings. The viability is of an institution rather than of any single service like loaning (Desai and Namboodiri, 1996). The institution not only loans but also borrows and mobilises deposits, besides providing other services. Many of these operations are joint and complementary. As such, transaction costs are common to all services. Their allocation to lending is artificial, arbitrary and fraught with assumptions that can prove to be misleading. A better alternative would be to look at the total asset/liability positions of the institutions or the units and their costs and returns as compared to the cost of management of the institutions. This type of analysis would throw up a better picture of the actual level of viability of banking institutions or its units.

7.2.6 With the development of banking operations in the rural areas and the consequent broadening and deepening of the banking services, greater levels of incomes or revenues can be non-interest based *i.e.* non-asset based or non-fund based incomes. Any suggestion to improve of viability of rural banking operations should ensure that the non-asset based income also substantially increases in that institution adding to the profitable operations of that unit.

7.2.7 The viability of banking institutions is also a function of the volume of operations rather than of only the margins available. The existence of scale economies in RFIs reveals that their average transaction/administrative costs (*i.e.* per Rs. 100 of business volume) are declining and/or constant (Desai and Mellor, 1993). This implies that these institutions would improve their viability through expansion of business volume rather than the increase in their gross margin as suggested by ACRC (Desai and Namboodiri, 1996). With the increase in the volume of business, with the cost of management remaining the same the unit of banking can indeed be viable. So aiming for an increased volume of business operations of banking institutions especially rural banking institutions or units would be a major plan of action for the units which are at present non-viable. This fact is borne out even by the observations of ACRC that the quantitative expansion and qualitative improvement in the business would lead to economies of scale increasingly thereby resulting in lower per unit cost of management and consequently higher margins and profitability (RBI, 1989).

7.2.8 The discussions also reveal that viability is mainly related to business related factors *viz.* low level of deposits and unbalanced mix, low level of advances and non-profitable composition, and also inefficient management of cash and bank balances. So any strategy to make rural banking operations viable should address the above business issues. As far as rural branches of commercial banks are concerned a major area which requires attention is the transfer pricing mechanism. A transfer pricing mechanism which aims at corporate goals of mobilising low cost resources from rural and semi urban centres rather than on the actual measurement of the profitability of the operations of the branch is in no way a correct measure to calculate the viability or non-viability of rural branches of commercial banks. It is also to be realised that one of the important reasons for non-viability of rural banking operations is the loan losses or risk costs which are linked to the operational aspects of the business of the institution rather than to the structure as such (Satish and Gopalakrishna, 1997).

7.3 DAP — Micro Study of a DCCB and an RRB

7.3.1 In the background of the reforms in the financial sector and the process of liberalization, the DAP exercise was utilized by many institutions to recast their systems and procedures, lending and deposit taking programmes, strategies of recovery and human resource management practices to emerge profitable while at the same time not neglecting the outreach aspect of their credit programmes. Though the results of the revitalization and turnaround exercises have been mixed, a larger number of institutions, both in case of District Central Cooperative Banks and the Regional Rural Banks, have turned around successfully emerging profitable while continuing to remain as major purveyors of agricultural credit. By 2001-02, 246 out of the 369 District Central Cooperative Banks and 167 of the 196 Regional Rural Banks emerged profitable.

The case studies of two institutions in North-West India, of a District Central Cooperative Bank and a Regional Rural Bank which have successfully turned around using the instrumentality of the DAP as a basis, are discussed below:

7.3.2 ***Sangrur Central Cooperative Bank***

Before Restructuring

At the start of the process of restructuring, the bank was basically a single product bank — the product being the short-term crop loan, which was disbursed through the societies. There were negligible banking operations at the branches and it did not focus much on savings. The bank made a loss of Rs. 9.66 millions during the year 1993-94 and made a nominal profit of Rs. 0.14 millions in 1994-95 but still had accumulated losses of Rs. 23.5 millions. With the DAP as its plan of action the bank focused on the areas on which it had to concentrate for turning around in the shortest possible time. The basic thrust was on increasing the levels of business, reducing the cost of resources as well as operations and increasing the recovery of loans. Table 5 gives the financial indicators of the bank for the year 1994-95 and for the three-year period from 2000-01 to 2002-03.

7.3.3 ***Credit and Savings***: In addition to the existing short-term crop loan, the bank introduced and popularized the Kisan Credit Card (KCC) which gave credit flexibility to the

TABLE 5: Sangrur Central Cooperative Bank

Sl. No.		1994-95	2000-01	2001-02	2002-03
Outreach Indicators					
1.	No. of borrowers**	50,366	77,912	93,870	114,234
2.	Outstanding loan portfolio*	755	2048	2414	3473
3.	No. of depositors**	68,375	135,373	153,833	162,216
4.	Outstanding deposit portfolio*	547	1636	1846	2079
5.	Loans to Total Assets	61.60	69.83	62	82.62
Sustainability Indicators					
6.	Financial Margin (Difference between average cost of funds and average yield on assets)	2.67	3.64	3.97	4.02
7.	Cost of Management (Operating Costs to Average assets)	2.60	3.60	3.10	2.48
8.	Return on assets	0.01	0.17	1.02	1.14
9.	Return on Net worth	0.10	2.94	20.77	28.81
10.	Loan recovery percentage	89	93	93	95
11.	NPA Ratio (Ratio of Non-Performing Assets to Total Loans Outstanding)	12.48	4.84	4.76	3.70
12.	Profit / Loss*	0.14	0.04	30	46
13.	Owned Funds* (Share Capital + Reserves)	76	141	146	158

* in million Indian Rupees; ** in numbers; all other figures are in percentages.

farmers. The bank also devised an omnibus credit limit for medium and bigger farmers known as the Revolving Cash Credit. Based on the collateral available with the farmer in form of land, a credit limit was fixed, of which a part is covered for investment purposes and another for consumption needs. The bank hitherto known only as a short-term financing bank, diversified into term credit in agriculture and non-farm sector. The motto of the Credit Department of the Bank is — show us any economic activity, our Bank has a scheme or will have a scheme to finance it. This underlines the fact that the credit products of the bank were a result of its quick responses to the changing economic and occupation profile of the people in its area of operations. The bank realized that it has to focus more on mopping up of rural savings to improve its clientele as well as its own resource base and one of the schemes introduced for that purpose was the Deposit linked Insurance Scheme. The bank had been showing a consistent growth in deposits, having posted a growth of 12.60 in 2002-03, which was more than the average deposit growth rate of Commercial Banks in the district.

7.3.4 ***Outreach and Sustainability***: In 1994-95 the bank had a client base of 50,336 borrowers and 68,375 depositors. Now it caters to 114,234 loan accounts and 162,216 deposit accounts. The borrower client base of the bank now constitutes 44 per cent of the rural families in the district. Thus the growth in the breadth of its outreach is unparalleled among the banking institutions not only in the district but elsewhere too. The extension of its outreach had also been facilitated by decentralisation and delegation of powers. In the year 1994-95, the cost of management of the bank was 2.60 per cent, this increased to 3.60 per cent in 2000-01 and it started declining, falling to 2.48 per cent in 2002-03. The financial margin was 2.67 per cent in the year 1994-95. It increased to 3.64 per cent in 2000-01 and further to 4.02 per cent in 2002-03. The Return on Assets, which was 0.01 per cent in 1994-95 increased to 0.17 per cent in 2000-01 and further to 1.14 per cent in 2002-03. The bank started on its profit run from 1994-95 onwards with a modest profit of Rs. 0.14 million. But this was interrupted in 1996-97 when it suffered a loss of Rs. 43.46 million, as it had to make huge provisions due to the application of prudential norms to cooperative banks in India. Again it made a loss of Rs. 7.56 million in the year 1999-2000 as it had to pay heavy amounts as back-pay to the employees and contribute to their pension funds. But from the year 2000-01 onwards the growth in profits has been steady and with a profit of Rs. 46 millions during 2002-03 it has wiped out its accumulated losses and reached its set goal of sustainable viability (Satish, 2003).

7.3.5 ***Gurgaon Gramin Bank***

Before Restructuring

Till 1994-95, the Regional Rural Banks operated under highly restrictive environment where even the smallest of the administrative decision-making, what to speak of policy matters was beyond their purview. Chaffing under these conditions the banks were under continuous losses, with high level of loan overdues and low returns on advances. In 1994-95 Gurgaon Gramin Bank was in a precarious shape financially with negative net margin of 0.88 per cent, a low loan recovery of 51 per cent and accumulated losses of Rs. 67.4 millions. This bank has also utilized the Development Action Planning process to chalk out a programme for achieving sustainable viability without loosing its focus on the outreach. Table 6 gives the financial parameters of the bank for the year 1994-95 and for the three-year period from 2000-01 to 2002-03.

TABLE 6: Gurgaon Gramin Bank

Sl. No.		1994-95	2000-01	2001-02	2002-03
Outreach Indicators					
1.	No. of borrowers**	119,697	89,684	100,152	114,763
2.	Outstanding loan portfolio*	986	2395	2468	2493
3.	No. of depositors**	522,994	525,879	528,865	546,328
4.	Outstanding deposit portfolio*	2205	5382	5811	6027
5.	Loans to Total Assets	40.44	35.16	32.44	31.39
Sustainability Indicators					
6.	Financial Margin (Difference between average cost of funds and average yield on assets)	2.71	5.35	5.68	4.70
7.	Cost of Management (Operating Costs to Average assets)	3.18	2.32	2.45	2.45
8.	Return on assets	(–) 0.83	3.26	4.03	4.09
9.	Return on Net worth	(–) 36.15	31.24	29.09	24.22
10.	Loan recovery percentage	51	86	86	88
11.	NPA Ratio (Ratio of Non-Performing Assets to Total Loans Outstanding)	38.41	9.47	7.52	5.63
12.	Profit / Loss*	(–) 20	221	303	324
13.	Owned Funds* (Share Capital + Reserves)	55.87	707	999	1323

* in million Indian Rupees; ** in numbers; all other figures are in percentages.

7.3.6 ***Credit and Savings***: A part of the operational area of the bank nearer to the National Capital New Delhi was getting urbanized and industrialized with number of private sector firms opening their plants and offices there. The bank looked at this phenomenon as an opportunity and devised a scheme for pay roll lending where it entered into tie-up arrangements with the corporate entities for extending loans to their employees. It was successful in this sector in comparison to other banks as it was the first bank to recognize the opening up of an opportunity and was able to negotiate in a skilful manner with these industries. The Bank was able to beat off challenges in this segment even from private sector and foreign banks due to its strong customer service credentials and quick decision-making abilities on loaning due to the local presence of the management. Another area where the bank has given a strong thrust was of short-term crop loans. Other than the industrialized and urbanized region adjacent to the National Capital, the operational area of the bank was predominantly agricultural. The crop loans constituted just 23.27 per cent of the total disbursements of the bank in the year 1995-96. The bank was able to increase the crop loan disbursements as it identified 24 branches as having abundant potential as intensive agricultural development branches and Branch Managers had been delegated the powers to sanction/increase the loans as per the farmers' requirements. This bank also introduced and popularised the Kisan Credit Card. It introduced a payroll linked loan product for rural schoolteachers and a pension linked loan scheme for army and other pensioners. Gurgaon Gramin Bank is also a very prominent RRB in the North-Western India to venture into microfinance. Through the microfinance route the bank is reaching nearly 20,000 borrowers. Through this method the bank was able to maintain its loan clientele even though there was a huge contraction in the number of loan accounts due to the cleansing of the Balance Sheet of bad loans. The bank's focus was on mobilizing low cost deposits so that low cost resources are available to it. Accordingly, the bank devised user friendly deposit schemes to tap such low cost deposits. Along with the formulation of the deposit schemes the bank ensured excellent and personalized customer service in comparison to the Commercial Banks in the same area.

7.3.7 ***Outreach and Sustainability***: In 1994-95, the bank had a client base of 119,697 borrowers and 522,995 depositors. Today it caters to 114,763 loan accounts and 546,328 deposit accounts. The loan portfolio of 1994-95 may be showing a big number, but a larger portion of that was a dead portfolio that needed to be cleansed out. While the outreach in terms of numbers has shown a steep decline immediately after the reform process, it started growing gradually from the year 1999-2000 onwards. At the same time the outreach deepened in terms of the average loan portfolio. The average amount per loan has increased from Rs. 8,237 in 1994-95 to Rs. 21,723 in 2002-03. The spread of the qualitative loan portfolio after 1994-95 was also positively impacted by the delegation and decentralization. This delegation of powers had also infused a sense of accountability to ensure that loan appraisal and monitoring is proper. The number of loan accounts per branch of the bank is 602, whereas the per branch loan accounts for commercial banks in the area of operation of this RRB is 546. The cost of management of the bank was 3.18 per cent in 1994-95, it declined to 2.32 per cent in 2000-01 and there was a marginal increase to 2.45 per cent in 2002-03. The financial margin was 2.71 per cent in 1994-95, it increased to 5.35 per cent in 2001-02 but had a slight decline to 4.70 per cent in 2002-03 on account of a steep fall in returns from investments. The Return on Assets which was a negative 0.83 per cent in 1994-95 increased to 3.26 per cent in 2000-01 and further to 4.09 per cent in 2002-03. The bank, which was making losses, started showing a profit from the year 1996-97 onwards. In the year 1997-98 itself it wiped out all its accumulated losses and embarked on the highway of sustainable viability. In 2001-02 it made the highest profit among all RRBs in India (Satish, 2003).

7.3.8 ***Two Case Studies: A Summary***: These two case studies reveal that to step up the outreach of rural finance the route of reinvigorating and retooling the existing institutional variants through a series of policy interventions is a better option than to set up totally new institutions which may be a costly and time consuming affair. As it may be noticed the institutions involved did not undergo major structural changes in the organisation or ownership. The most important change has been the greater freedom of operation and less of controls on the business aspects of these banks. The banks were given freedom to devise innovative products and also to set up strategies to market these products through which they were able to achieve the twin objectives of sustainability and outreach. As far as subsidy dependence is concerned, the Regional Rural Bank received additional share capital infusion and an amount for cleansing of its Balance Sheet. The Cooperative Bank did not receive any financial assistance, rather it reverse subsidizes the State Government. The only concession which the Government of India allows these banks is exemption from payment of income tax. Both the banks were able to achieve the breakthrough within the limited space available to them for maneuvering and coping up with several constraints (Satish, 2004).

8. Rural Finance — South East Asian Experience

8.1 Three rural finance institutions which have been widely studied for their success in addressing the twin concerns of outreach and sustainability are all state owned institutions — Bank Rakyat Indonesia (BRI) in Indonesia, Bank Pertanian Malaysia (BPM) in Malaysia and Bank for Agriculture and Agricultural Cooperatives (BAAC) in Thailand. The performance indicators of these three banks as given in the Table 7 are a reflection of the fact they have been successful in extending their outreach in rural finance and maintaining the institutional sustainability while they continued to exist as government owned institutions.

8.2 **Indonesia**: Bank Rakyat Indonesia-Unit Desa — Autonomy and Accountability BRI came into existence in 1950 by the merger of two state owned banks. The unit desas (village level retail windows) of BRI were established in 1973 to implement the BIMAS[5], an extension linked agricultural credit programme of the government. However due to lack of autonomy and absence of financial accountability at the unit level and low interest rates on loans and deposits BIMAS Credit Programme ended in a failure, jeopardizing the existence of the BRI-Unit Desa system itself. In June 1983 the Government of Indonesia removed controls on interest rates for both deposits and advances, withdrew ceilings on loans and prioritized savings mobilisation. These changes provided an

TABLE 7: Performance Indicators of BRI-Unit Desa, BPM and BAAC

Sl. No.		BRI-Unit Desa (2002)	BPM (2002)	BAAC (2002-03)
Outreach Indicators				
1.	No. of branches involved in agricultural lending	650 (4302 unit Desas)	150 (3000 mobile units)	664 (889 field offices)
2.	No. of rural borrowers (millions)	2.73	0.36	3.69
3.	Outstanding loan portfolio to agriculture (US $ millions)	1343	580	5446
4.	Average outstanding agri loan size as % of GDP per capita	72.34	46.7	74.9
5.	No. of Deposit accounts (millions)	27.28	1.73	9.23
6.	Outstanding deposit portfolio (US $ millions)	2626	625	6035
Sustainability Indicators				
7.	Outstanding rural loans per loan officer	350-400	550-650	450-550
8.	Loan arrears in agri/rural lending (%)	4.69	1.29	3.15
9.	Loan administration expenses as % of average outstanding loan portfolio	5.7	3.86	3.34
10.	Financial income as % of average outstanding loan portfolio	11.9	9.65	8.4

opportunity for BRI's management to explore new products and services and completely revamp the unit desa operations. The structure and organization of the system was also changed with more autonomy and accountability (Robinson, 1992).

Starting in 1984, the unit desas introduced the lending scheme of KUPEDES[6], which catered to the working capital as well as term credit needs of its clients. With the higher interest rates screening out the rent seeking wealthier farmers and the attractive flexible terms KUPEDES became so popular that within one year, by December 1984, the units made 639,000 loans totaling US $ 166 million (Patten and Rosengard, 1991). On the savings side while the existing scheme TABANAS[7] was marketed aggressively, the new savings product of SIMPEDES[8] was introduced in 1984. This scheme, which catered to the needs of rural savers in Indonesia, emerged as a cheap source of funds that effectively reduced the dependence of unit desas on the largesse of the government. The bold steps of reform effort yielded dramatic results. By 1986, the unit desa system of BRI turned from chronic loss-maker into a profit making entity, continuing to expand its client coverage; a performance that has been maintained until today.

8.3 Malaysia: Bank Pertanian Malaysia — Reorientation of Business Model

8.3.1 Bank Pertanian Malaysia (BPM) was established as an agricultural development bank by the government in 1969 primarily to route credit to rural borrowers. In the first two decades of its operations it posited indifferent performance as a passive farmers' bank with low resource base and dependent on government grants for its loan operations as well was administrative expenses. Due to low margins and poor recovery, as at the end of 1990, the bank's accumulated losses had risen to US $ 95.33 million. The customer base of the bank had shrunk to 295,000 from a high of 650,000 in 1981.

8.3.2 With a new management team, and freedom of operation from the government, which initiated a limited financial sector reform, BPM started turning around from 1991 onwards. There was a complete transformation of lending systems and procedures and new loan products were introduced to meet the needs of its clientele, especially in agriculture. These include Pinjaman Tanaman-crop loan for the production of paddy, fruits, vegetables, coconut, rubber and cocoa, Pinjaman Ternakan for animal husbandry including livestock and poultry and the Gratitude Loan which enables working people to support their parents' farms. The bank also started emphasizing on savings mobilisation that was hitherto neglected as government funds were routed through the bank. A wide range of innovative savings schemes were introduced which enabled the bank to mop up low cost resources. Patriot 2020, Patriot Ummah, Patriot Muda, Patriot Tani and Patriot Remaja are some of the popular deposit products of BPM (Vincent and Ing, 1994).

8.3.4 BPM was also successful in taking rural banking to the doorsteps of the clients. Its 3,000 mobile units armed with laptops reach even the remote areas, including locations in Sarawak and Sabah. With proper positioning and pricing of its loan and deposit products and steady expansion of its clientele, BPM has not looked back after 1992 in sustainability even while it maintains a completely agriculture based loan portfolio.

8.4 Thailand: Bank for Agriculture and Agricultural Cooperatives: the Group Approach

8.4.1 Bank for Agriculture and Agricultural Cooperatives (BAAC) was founded in 1966 as a government owned bank with a mandate of supporting agricultural development. BAAC's outreach and self-sustainability rank it among the world's leading agricultural development banks (Yaron, 1992). It has continuously expanded its outreach and in 2003 it covered 3.69 million farm household borrowers on an increasingly self-sustainable basis, thus serving 44 per cent of all farm households in the country. Three quarters of the borrowers access loans through joint liability groups (JLGs). In 2003 BAAC disbursed loans to 228,000 JLGs throughout the country. JLG loans accounted for 92 per cent of the total number of BAAC loans. The size of the groups ranges from 5 to 30 members averaging 15. While the bank targets low-income small farm households, it also lends to middle and higher income farmers. But more than two-thirds of its clients are located in the poorest regions of the country.

8.4.2 Apart from credit services BAAC provides savings deposit facilities and a range of complementary services, including marketing facilities. Little attention was paid to savings mobilisation until the mid-1980s, when the access to low cost funds from government and the central bank was cut. Expansion in the savings volumes enabled the bank to reduce dependence on government and external funding. BAAC has a strong client orientation and provides demand led financial services. Continuous adjustments and development of new credit technologies were crucial in reducing loan administration costs and in improving loan repayment performance. Much to its merit BAAC has managed to achieve strong financial performance despite the fact that it administers a number of government mandated concessionary lending programmes (Klein, Meyer, *et al.*, 1999).

9. Summary

9.1 The criticism of traditional interventions in rural finance is basically valid, especially regarding subsidies in rural finance at borrower level, subsidized interest rates, directed credit programmes, targeting credit to certain sectors and classes, neglect of savings, and mismanagement of state-owned agricultural credit institutions. Despite the seemingly negative role of these interventions, the case studies of the turnaround process in two Indian rural banks as well as the South-east Asian experiences prove that there still exists a considerable role for the state in rural financial markets. The above experiences illustrate that state owned banks could achieve the goal of sustainable outreach in rural finance so long as they operate under the sound financial sector best practice principles (Satish, 2004).

9.2 **Markets Failing the Poor**: Institutions catering to the credit needs of agriculture and rural sector are necessary because financial markets fail the poor. These markets fail the poor — whether farmers or microentrepreneurs due to the following reasons:

1. No lender is willing or permitted to pass on the extra costs associated with lending to customers.
2. No insurer is willing to compensate for borrowers' and lenders' risk aversion by offering insurance against non-payment due to natural calamities.
3. Potential borrowers are unwilling to borrow because of risk aversion, even if the expected value of their profits outweighs the expected costs of their investments.
4. Social and private values of costs and benefits diverge because of externalities. (Hulme and Mosley, 1996)

9.3 **Success and Public Management:** The fact that credit markets fail the poor underscores the importance of interventions in rural financial markets. These interventions could take any shape, not necessarily direct. A broader role for rural finance is the need of the day. Rural finance should encompass credit, savings, and insurance, and improve allocation of assets and income generation. But technologies have to be worked out to reduce transaction costs and risk costs in rural finance. There exists enough empirical data across the countries on how best to do it. Profit and success in business is not necessarily incompatible with public ownership if management is given the right incentives.

The review of macroeconomic and financial sector policy framework has shown that the state plays an important role in enabling an environment in which financial institutions can prosper, thus increasing financial deepening and access to financial services. The well documented failures of the past were based on supply-led approach, which pushed credit to low and sometimes even negative real interest rates, instead of promoting the formation of eventually sustainable financial institutions.

9.4 **Imperfect Markets — Ground for Positive Interventions:** The neoclassical view that financial market liberalization alone will lead to the formation of rural financial institutions that serve the poor has been (and must continue to be) seriously questioned in view of recent theoretical and empirical work. Because of the imperfections in intertemporal markets, institutional innovation and formation cannot emerge through market forces alone. A liberalized formal financial market may be a necessary condition for the creation of a spontaneous supply of financial services to the target group, but in itself it is not sufficient to achieve this effect. Consequently there is a need for intervention and technical assistance, even if financial repression has been abolished (Krahnen and Schmidt, 1994).

9.5 **Government Support — Institution building only**: There are numerous examples where governments, donors and non-governmental organizations have been involved in establishing, assisting and managing rural financial institutions.... The intervention was often instrumental in establishing the institutions. This reinforces the argument for providing resources to rural financial institutions during the initial stage of their development. Clearly, public assistance...should focus on institution building, not on subsidizing interest rates (Gurgand, Pederson and Yaron, 1994).

9.6 **Freedom of Operations**: The two turnaround case studies[9] reveal that to step up the outreach of rural finance the route of revitalising and retooling the existing institutional variants through a series of policy interventions is a better option than to set up totally new institutions which may be a costly and time consuming affair. As it may be noticed, the institutions involved did not undergo major structural changes in the organization or ownership. The most important change has been the greater freedom of operation and less of controls on the business aspects of these banks. The banks were given freedom to devise innovative products and also to set up strategies to market these products through which they were able to achieve the twin objectives of sustainability and outreach.

9.7 **Service to the Poor — At market determined terms:** As far the development of new and innovative products by banks is concerned, it is essential that these banks, especially rural banks have to take care of the twin aspects of outreach and profitability. Banks will be able to have an outreach for their products if their products and services are designed keeping in view the needs of the clientele. This is possible if the rural banks have an ear to the ground and try to assess the needs of the people in the area of operation. But at the same time each product has an impact on the profitability of the bank. Ultimately it is the product mix that decides the margins and profit of the banks. Every bank therefore attempts to have a mix in the deposits and advances so that the variety offers liquidity and return and wherein the tradeoff between the two is minimum. The product innovations done by rural banks and cooperative banks had an impressive effect on the viability and increased the business volumes. These products have come about due to the concern that the banks had for their own viability, the concern to provide adequate financial services to their clientele and their capacity to innovate. These banks have once again proved the fact that financial services to rural and poorer clients can be provided at a market determined terms and conditions and in doing so the banks can continue to take care of their viability issues.

10. Revitalisation of Rural Finance — An Agenda for Developing World

The lessons are clear — governments have a critical role to play in development of financial services and financial institutions for the rural and semi-urban sector. It is also clear that the revitalization of the state owned rural financial institutions is possible without a wholesale structural and ownership change. The further analyses of the case studies as well as the theoretical and empirical work in the field indicate that the following could be the broad policy framework with regard to the revitalization of rural financial services throughout the developing world:

10.1 **Volume Growth**: The factors governing viability in rural banking operations are not totally out of control as there is no inherent in-built non-viability about these operations. Institutions have to aim at increasing the levels of business both on asset as well as on the liability side. The greater the volume of working funds the lesser would be the per unit cost of management. They have also to aim at recasting the composition of the assets as well as liabilities of the institution or the unit keeping in view the yield associated with each item of asset and the cost associated with each item of liability. This has to be worked out by each unit and each institution keeping in view its own strengths, weaknesses and the potential and scope available in its area of operations.

10.2 **Legal Reforms**: The capital base of the case study cooperative bank is woefully inadequate with a capital adequacy ratio of 5.71, which does not meet the prudential norms of banking. But to increase the capital base a change in the cooperative statute is necessary, as under the existing laws non-constituents cannot hold the capital in cooperatives. Increasing the share capital or the own funds of the rural banking institutions so that longer term funds of lesser cost are available to the institutions to reduce the asset/liability mismatch when financing of long-term loans is taken up by the institution. Further, the Cooperative Bank still has to function within the administrative control of the State Government, which does not have a professional understanding of banking. The state government's control over the cooperative banks poses difficulties for the enforcement of prudential regulation and supervision by the Reserve Bank of India and NABARD. So legal reforms in the cooperative banking sector is an area that requires attention of the governments, not only in India, but throughout the developing world.

10.3 **Freedom in HRD Policies**: Another area of concern for the rural and cooperative banks is of manpower. With the rapid transformation taking place in the banking arena there is a need for well qualified, professional and trained staff in these institutions. In the period of next six years these institutions would witness an exodus of staff on account of retirements. No plan to recruit and position staff to take of future needs seems to be in place. The owners — the governments — do not seem to have given much serious thought to it. The banks should be free to evolve and implement their own policies on personnel, including recruitment, lay-off, promotion policies, training, incentive systems etc.

10.4 **Technological Orientation**: New technologies especially in the field of ICT provide significant scope for adoption of innovations in bank automation, electronic data processing and development of new products. But in this field these banks are yet to catch up with commercial banks. The level of computerization in the cooperative banks is still in a preliminary stage. These banks are hampered due to lack of operational freedom from the administrative machinery of the state government. However the RRBs are being guided and assisted technically by their sponsor banks for switching over to completely computerized banking environments. Rural and cooperative banks throughout the world are in need of a technology revolution.

10.5 **Making Agriculture a Remunerative Activity:** A policy of pushing agricultural credit should be supported by a policy to make agricultural activities themselves remunerative by an appropriate set of mechanisms and instruments, including investments in basic rural infrastructure like roads, electricity, communications and irrigation. The state has also a role in promotion of viable technologies through research and in promotion of support services like input supply, extension, marketing, information and training.

10.6 **Role of State in Policy Support**: The state has a role in formulating a policy which supports effective financial intermediation, reduces financial transaction costs and increases the access of farmers to financial services, facilitates the enforcement of collateral mechanisms and develops a proper regulatory and supervisory framework for different types of financial institutions.

10.7 **Minimal State Intervention**: The intervention of the state in rural financial institutions has to be minimal and indirect. A sense of autonomy coupled with accountability is the best way to ensure performance. This too should be in realm of the central banks rather than the State. The State should not impose indiscriminate loan targets on these institutions and also allow them the freedom to charge market determined interest rates. Instead of mandating to lend to agriculture and microenterprises the State should create an environment in which such lending becomes a business proposition to financial institutions. Under such conditions both private and state-owned financial institutions would take to rural lending willingly. Wholesale remission of debts, insistence on subsidized interest rates and statements discouraging loan repayments can vitiate this environment.

10.8 **Doing away with Micro-management**: The State has to withdraw from the direct control and micro management of the rural financial institutions without prescribing policies, programmes and targets, and create an enabling environment for these institutions to function with the requisite operational freedom. Wherever needed the governments should withdraw from these institutions and broad base their ownership. Private sector, including successful banking and financial institutions should be allowed to participate in the ownership of these institutions replacing the government. Governments should desist from the urge to control and direct these institutions. The regulatory concerns can be better addressed by the central banks.

The result of this policy framework would not be less of financial services to the rural sector, but the reverse — and a transition to healthy rural finance system in a manner which is both time and cost effective.

NOTES

1. The Spring Review of Small Farmer Credit Programmes was brought out by USAID in 1973. "This study produced a number of volumes on farm credit in a number of countries, which took up about two feet of shelf space. An impartial sampling of this incredible documentation

would have led to caution, in that so many schemes were defective in sustainability, outreach or both", comments J.D. Von Pischke on the Review in his theme paper 'The Evolution of Institutional Issues in Rural Finance Outreach, Risk Management and Sustainability' presented at "Paving the Way Forward for Rural Finance: An International Conference on Best Practices", Washington DC, 2-4 June, 2003.

2. The term Ohio School is generally used to refer to the group of agricultural economists at the Ohio State University, Columbus, who gave the intellectual underpinning to the ideas against the traditional approach to agricultural credit. The group included Dale W. Adams, Douglas H. Graham, J.D. Von Pischke, Richard L. Meyer, Robert C. Vogel, Claudio Gonzalez-Vega, Gordon Donald, Carlos E. Cuevas.
3. NAFSCOB: National Federation of State Cooperative Banks.
4. NCARDBF: National Cooperative Agriculture and Rural Development Banks Federation.
5. BIMAS: Bimbingan Massal (mass guidance).
6. KUPEDES: Kredit Umum Pedesaan (loan product for rural credit).
7. TABANAS: Tabangan Nasional (national savings).
8. SIMPEDES: Simpanan Pedesaan (savings of rural community).
9. The case studies are based on the visits undertaken by the author to the banks at various points of time and his interactions with cross sections of the functionaries and clientele of these banks as also from the data collected and analysed from the following published documents:
   - Annual Reports, Balance Sheets and Financial Statements of the Banks: of Gurgaon Gramin Bank for the years 1994-95; 1995-96; 2000-01; 2001-02 and 2002-03; of Sangrur Central Cooperative Bank for the years 1994-95; 1995-96; 2000-01; 2001-02 and 2002-03; of National Bank for Agriculture and Rural Development (NABARD) for the years 1994-95; 1995-96; 2000-01; 2001-02 and 2002-03; of Bank Rakyat Indonesia for 2002; of Bank Pertanian Malaysia for 2002; of BAAC for 2002-03.
   - 'Review of Working of Regional Rural Banks' for the years 1994-95; 1995-96; 2000-01; 2001-02 and 2002-03 (published by NABARD).
   - Development Action Plans — Memoranda of Understanding of Gurgaon Gramin Bank and Sangrur Central Cooperative Bank for the years 1994-95; 2000-01; 2001-02 and 2002-03.
   - Annual Reports of NAFSCOB and NCARDBF for the year 1994-95.
   - Financial Statements of Cooperative Banks (ST Structure) for the year 1994-95 (published by NABARD).
   - Financial Statements of Cooperative Banks (LT Structure) for the year 1994-95 (published by NABARD).

REFERENCES

Branch, Brian, Lucy Ito and Curtis Slover (2002): Concept Paper for "Paving the Way Forward for Rural Finance: An International Conference on Best Practices", BASIS/CRSP and World Council of Credit Unions, Madison, WI.

Coffey, Elizabeth (1998): 'Agricultural Finance: Getting Policies Right', Food and Agriculture Organization, Rome.

Desai, Bhupat, M. and Mellor, John, W. (1993): Institutional Finance for Agricultural Development: An Analytical Survey of Critical Issues, IFPRI, Washington DC.

Desai, Bhupat, M. and Namboodiri, N.V. (1996): 'Whither Rural Financial Institutions ?' *Economic and Political Weekly*, August 3, pp. 2083-93.

FAO (1996): Report of the World Food Summit, Part-I, Food and Agriculture Organization, Rome.

FAO and GTZ (1998): 'Agricultural Finance Revisited: Why?' Food and Agriculture Organization, Rome.

Gurgand, Marc, Glen Pederson and Jacob Yaron (1994): 'Outreach and Sustainability of six RFIs in Sub-Saharan Africa', The World Bank, Washington DC.

Hulme, David and Paul Mosley (1996): 'Finance against Poverty', Routledge, London.

Klein, Brigitte, Richard Meyer, Alfred Hannig, Jill Burnett and Michael Fiebig (1999): 'Better Practices in Agricultural Lending', Food and Agriculture Organization, Rome.

Krahnen, J.P. and R.H. Schmidt (1994): 'Development finance as institution building: A new approach to poverty oriented banking', West View Press, Boulder, CO.

NABARD (1995): 'Annual Report, 1994-95', National Bank for Agriculture and Rural Development, Mumbai.

Patten, Richard, H. and Jay, K. Rosengard (1991): 'Progress with Profits: The Development of Rural Banking in Indonesia', International Center for Economic Growth, ICS Press, San Francisco, CA.

RBI (1989): 'Report of the Agriculture Credit Review Committee', (Chairman, A.M. Khusro), Reserve Bank of India, Bombay.

RBI (1991): 'Report of the Committee on the Financial System', (Chairman, M. Narasimham), Reserve Bank of India, Bombay.

Robinson, Marguerite (1992): 'Rural Financial Intermediation: Lessons from Indonesia (Part One), Development Discussion Paper 434, Harvard Institute of International Development, Cambridge, MA.

Satish, P. and C.K. Gopalakrishna (1997): 'Viability of Rural Banking', *Economic and Political Weekly*, October 18, pp. 2711-16.

Satish, P. (2003): 'Rediscovering Rural Finance by Retooling the Existing

Institutions', Paper presented at "Paving the Way Forward for Rural Finance: An International Conference on Best Practices", Washington DC, 2-4 June.

Satish, P. (2004): 'Rural Finance: Role of State and State-owned institutions', *Economic and Political Weekly*, March 20, pp. 1321-30.

Vincent, Geraldine and Tan Bee Ing (1994): 'BPM's Innovative Schemes', *Corporate World*, Kuala Lumpur, Malaysia.

Von Pischke, J.D. (1980): "The Pitfalls of Specialised Farm Credit Institutions" *Development Digest*, Volume 18, No. 3 (July), pp. 79-91.

Von Pischke, J.D., Dale W. Adams and Gordon Donald, Ed. (1983): 'Rural Financial Markets in Developing Countries' Economic Development Institute, The World Bank — The John Hopkins University Press, Baltimore, MD.

World Bank (1995): "Report on Financial Services for Rural Poor and Women in India: Access and Sustainability", New Delhi.

Yaron, Jacob (1992): 'Successful Rural Finance Institutions', World Bank Discussion Paper 150, Washington DC.

Yaron, Jacob, Mc Donald P. Benjamin Jr and Gerda L. Piprek (1997): 'Rural Credit-Issues, Designs and Best Practices' The World Bank, Washington DC.

Zeller, Manfred (2003): 'Models of Rural Financial Institutions', Theme Paper presented at "Paving the Way Forward for Rural Finance: An International Conference on Best Practices", Washington DC, 2-4 June.

6

Rural Non-Farm Sector in India: Issues and Evidence

MANORANJAN SHARMA

PERSPECTIVE

In the history of economic growth, particularly since the onset of the industrial revolution, the development of capitalism enhanced material standards of living. The market is alone considered as the prime economic force to achieve improved standards of living through the profit motive based on Adam Smith's 'invisible hand' — the human motives of greed and self-interest. But the economic system failed to meet the welfare of all individuals and thus accentuated the social gap. Although social arrangements are not primarily determined by inherent economic structure or industrial set up, these structures have to be consistent with economic realities.

The Ricardian Theory of Comparative Advantage emphasised the role of natural resource endowments and factor proportions resulting in geographical concentration of industry and thus aggravated economic inequalities. This led to the emergence of a clear pattern of regional development in the late nineteenth and early twentieth centuries. In contrast, the second half of nineteenth century marked a departure against the natural resource endowment thought of regional development and the advent of modern transport and communication facilitated greater mobility of factors of production. This induced widespread diffusion and dispersal of industries across sectors/regions. In the literature on development in general and the transformation of less developed economies/regions in particular, a basic sense of continuity pervades the history of economic thought. This continuity is reflected in the fact that the Classical School of developmental economists from Karl Marx to W.A. Lewis stressed the significance of a major shift in labour from rural areas to urban industrial centres for accelerated economic growth. It was demonstrated that in an underdeveloped economy, a large section of the population live in the subsistence sector characterised by unlimited supply of labour with negligible, zero or even negative productivity.

However, with advancements in knowledge and technology, the neo-classical economists implicitly contended that rural sector could be transformed into industrial centres for faster economic development. It has been increasingly realised that the yawning chasm between the developed and the less developed regions need not necessarily be immutable. This found clear manifestation in Schumacher's thesis 'small is beautiful'. As President John F. Kennedy succinctly pointed out in his historic Inaugural Address delivered on January 20, 1961 "to those people in the huts and villages of half the globe struggling to break the bonds of mass misery, we pledge our best efforts to help them help themselves, for whatever period is required — not because..., but because it is right. *If a free society cannot help the many who are poor, it cannot save the few who are rich"* (italics mine). Rural non-farm sector (RNFS) could, therefore, help to bridge, to a limited extent, the dualistic pattern of economic development. In view of the criticality of RNFS in accelerating 'growth' and ensuring 'equity', RNFS has become a potent force in transforming social, economic and political life.

A global *tour d' horizon* brings out that the informal sector is marked by diverse employment, organisation of production and linkages with the formal sector. Since RNFS in LDCs lacks a formal and hierarchical structure, we need to situate changes in industrial structure and their implications on small enterprises and employment in a multi-disciplinary framework. The role of RNFS in extricating developing countries from the 'low-level equilibrium trap' and smashing the 'vicious circle of poverty' is congruent both with economic theory and historical experience. To be sure, different paths taken by different countries in the past have led to different outcomes in poverty reduction and employment generation. But robust evidence shows that the expansion of non-agricultural activity significantly influences employment, industrial production and exports with these activities constituting about 50 per cent of both rural employment and household income. While this distribution varies across countries and regions, Reardon *et al.* (1998) have demonstrated that rural Africa has the most diversified set of non-agricultural activities followed by Latin America (Reardon and Berdegué, 1999), East Asia and finally, South Asia. This distribution, however, masks considerable intra-regional disparity in almost all regions. J.O. Lanjouw and P. Lanjouw (1997) have persuasively argued that the non-farm sector is often linked in complex ways to country-specific agricultural settings. True, a uniform policy prescription is difficult because of ubiquitous diversification. But key elements of the growth theoretic are undoubtedly common to diverse settings, as, for example, revealed by the remarkable success of China's Township and Village Enterprises (TVEs). Table 1 brings out the average percentage share of per capita income, by source, for the rural population of India, in terms of quintile. An incisive analysis of survey data by Lanjouw and Shariff (1999) shows that the non-farm sector constitutes an important source of income to rural households. Occupational patterns, however, differ in their importance to the rural poor. There has been a convergence in the thinking of developmental economists about the hampering of the pursuit of development of RNFS by distortions in the labour market (*e.g.*, minimum wage legislation, mandated benefits and labour legislation) and capital market (*e.g.*, interest rate ceilings). There could, however, be situations, where imperfections in capital markets lead to rural industrialisation in communities with slim real economic opportunities despite large savings (Banerjee, 1997).

Unemployment generates and perpetuates a vicious circle. Hence supporting the process of reformation and creation of a market economy requires a thrust on a combination of basic education, vocational training and promotion of enterprises. This is a tall order, which requires a sharper focus on credit, marketing, technological upgradation, cluster development, infrastructural and institutional support mechanism.

TABLE 1: Income Sources in Rural India, 1994

Income sources	Per capita consumption quintile (percentage)					
	Bottom	2nd	3rd	4th	Top	Total
Cultivation	38	38	45	5	64	55
Agriculture wage labour	27	21	14	7	2	8
Non-agriculture						
Casual wage labour	16	15	11	7	2	6
Self-employment	12	17	16	14	8	11
Regular employment	4	7	12	18	21	17
Non-agriculture (total)	33	38	39	39	31	35
Other	2	2	3	3	3	3

Source: Lanjouw and Shariff, 1999.

A comprehensive study conducted by Swiss Development Corporation (SDC) and NABARD (National Bank for Agriculture and Rural Development) across eight states revealed:

- About one-fourth of the rural population does not work in the agricultural sector but in the rural non-farm sector;
- The service sector (transportation, trading, etc.) has great potential for new jobs;
- Agriculture and the non-farm sector are economically interdependent.

HISTORICAL INDIAN SETTING

In India, the role of cottage and small industries has always been recognised as an integral part of the development process of the country. In pre-independent India, Mahatma Gandhi emphasised the role of cottage and small industries for holistic development of villages — the place where real India lived — as reflected in village level self-sufficiency in his famous "constructive programme" way back in 1922. Mahatma Gandhi cogently argued "our villages are on the verge of destruction owing to the disappearance of village industries. They can be revived only through a revival of village industries". Subsequently, in post-independent India, the Industrial Policy Resolutions of 1948 and 1956 stressed the role of the non-farm sector in generating additional employment with low capital investment.

Historically, RNFS has enhanced regional/local capacity building in diverse areas, *e.g.,* Tilonia and Urmul in Rajasthan, Kala Raksha, Sandur, Berozgar Mahila Samiti, Aditi and Anwesha in Kutch, Karnataka and Bihar. The SEWAs all over the country represent a confluence of three movements: the labour movement, the cooperative movement and the women's movement. Further, long-term trends in infrastructure improvement, town growth and increasing population density lead to development of RNFS (Anderson and Leiserson, 1980). There is, however, a felt need to strengthen capacity building on a much larger canvas by enhancing the ability of RNFS to market their product outside the region. This would widen the economic base of the region, sustain the innovative products and processes of RNFS and strategies to significantly step up both production and productivity to achieve sustainable growth at the regional as well as the national level.

The development of entrepreneurship requires not just direct inputs but more importantly a broader framework of stable economic conditions, relatively easy access to capital and an efficient physical infrastructure. Bracing for tomorrow requires a paradigm shift from the ethos of dependency and vulnerability to self-reliance and competitive capability. The spectrum of these promotional measures influences the determinants of growth by removing bottlenecks to business development for RNFS. In its drive towards the state of maturity, the economy graduates from primitive structure dominated by agricultural sector to the stage of takeoff dominated by industrial sector and finally to the state of maturity, where services sector occupy the pride of the place. Worldwide experiences indicate that the relationship between RNFS/SSIs and large scale industries (LSIs) takes three forms: (a) the state of independence, where traditional SSIs covering village and cottage industries operate in an 'enclave' without competing with LSIs, (b) the state of competition where SSIs produce final consumer goods with low technology in competition with LSIs and (c) the state of complementarity where SSIs provide inputs to LSIs. In the Indian context, the traditional segments, such as, handloom, khadi and other village industries operate independently catering to the local market. Some RNFS/SSIs compete, however, directly with LSIs, especially in the low-value consumer goods sector. In several cases in the intermediate goods sector, RNFS/SSIs and LSIs are closely linked through forward and backward linkages. The time is now apposite to meaningfully strengthen and reorient the relationship between RNFS/SSIs and LSIs to make them partners in progress by adopting and adapting to technological upgradation on a large scale and creating a nurturing economic environment.

WINDS OF CHANGE

The process of structural adjustment programme (SAP), commonly referred to as economic reforms, initiated in July 1991 unleashed far-reaching policy changes in the pursuit of structural transformation of the economy. The era of globalisation and post-modernity refers to a multidimensional set of social processes that create, multiply, stretch and intensify worldwide social interdependencies and exchanges together with fostering in people a growing awareness of deepening connections between the local and the distant. The intensified challenges triggered by the increased complexity, uncertainty and turbulence of the business environment make it necessary to clearly distinguish between short-term palliatives and long-term practical, viable and feasible solutions. Accordingly, the financial reforms package needs to be fine-tuned to carry second-generation reforms to their logical conclusion by synchronising the intersecting themes of allocative efficiency and equity within the overarching context of India's efforts. This thesis could be substantiated by the exhortation of Amartya Sen, "we have to enhance human capability to lead more worthwhile lives." This enhancement of human capability is only possible if the RNFS is not seen as a quintessentially private enterprise. RNFS continues to be a matter for direct government involvement for socio-economic reasons. Hence, it needs to be encouraged to play its due role at this defining moment of history. Simultaneously, we must not be oblivious to the need of promoting RNFS because of its implications for heritage, culture, social structure, design vocabulary and design change. Such an ambitious growth agenda in a fast globalising environment requires an accelerated reform process to build a competitive, vibrant and integrated industrial structure. This necessitates adoption of a mechanism of incentives as integral part of a credible framework of consolidation of core competencies and exploration of new vistas of RNFS.

Reduction of regional and sectoral imbalances by exploiting the available potential with appropriate development and credit packages to check populism and the competitive policies of subsidies, strengthening the system of planning, policy and operations to promote sustainable growth in cottage and small scale industries, evolving developmental packages including credit support for diverse regions, mechanism for development of common pool resources with appropriate technological, economic, legal and institutional measures, preferential treatment to the credit needs of the project related weaker sections of the community needs to be stressed. Measures, such as, mechanism for providing consultancy and advisory services through advisory service centres, information shops and national centre for communication in collaboration with all concerned institutions, increased investment in research and development by public and private bodies, creation of eco-genial environment for higher efficiency, autonomy and self-sustenance would also help in streamlining the credit delivery mechanism. Limited options necessitate a thorough streamlining based on a careful and realistic assessment of the ground realities. As we can no longer be impervious to the needs of RNFS, growth-induced planned developmental efforts must be informed by an awareness of contemporary trends in inequality. The President of India, in his Republic Day address to the nation some time back trenchantly observed: "Our three-way fast lane of liberalisation, privatisation and globalisation must provide safe pedestrian crossing for the unempowered India also, so that it too can move towards 'Equality of Status and Opportunity'."

The dynamics of the underlying forces at work require a complete overhaul of the process of development of RNFS in the early part of the third millennium. As a part of the stabilisation-cum-structural adjustment programme, there is a pressing need for the enhancing the preparedness of RNFS in resolving basic distortions in the economy. Though market mechanisms are essential to engender efficiency and add value to the consumer, they need to be supplemented with a much broader growth strategy to create and retain value to uplift the living standards of Indian society. The Approach Paper of the Draft Ninth Five-Year Plan suggested devising of sectoral strategies for speedy enlargement of the village and small-scale sector (VSI) by emphasis on wide-ranging measures such as investment and technology upgradation, infrastructure support, marketing credit facilities, testing, quality certification and training facilities. Towards this end, there is a need (a) to strengthen flow of credit to the SSIs by introduction of factoring services to SSI in addition to the present system of discounting of bills, (b) organisational and financial streamlining of the KVIC to generate more job opportunities in the KVI sector, (c) technology development and upgradation in the VSI sector, particularly in the case of small scale industries, handloom, powerlooms, coir, handicrafts, wool, etc. and (d) evolution of new institutional mechanisms for improving the flow of credit to informal and rural non-farm sector. These measures are expected to result in enhanced contribution of the village and small-scale sector as also to contribute significantly in achieving the national goal of growth with distributive justice. Though credit is an essential input to foster the growth of RNFS, in the ultimate analysis, RNFS has to improve its productivity and efficiency by adopting modern technology to produce competitive goods and services.

The literature on extensively researched transformation process of the economy shows that RNFS constitutes an effective instrument of socio-economic development by addressing problems, such as, rural unemployment, urban migration, under-utilisation of know-how and rural resources. Apart from these goals, the RNFS also subserve the larger socio-economic objectives and the avowed national desideratum, such as, decentralisation and dispersal of manufacturing activities from metropolitan to non-metropolitan and rural areas, the reduction of regional economic imbalances and diffusion of entrepreneurial and managerial abilities and skills across industries for the optimum utilisation of the resource endowment of the region, restoration and promotion of traditional skills and craftsmanship and insulating the local culture from being swamped by outside influences. However, its ability to benefit from these opportunities depends on enterprise promotion, enterprise strengthening and enterprise management. Programmes for enterprise promotion include Rural Industries Programme, Micro Credit Programme, Entrepreneurship Development Programme and Project Idea Dissemination through television and publication of project profiles. Enterprise Strengthening requires specific programmes aimed at technology upgradation in identified industry clusters, technology transfer, quality enhancement and management development.

The long-term growth prospects of RNFS cannot be looked at in isolation with the growth prospects of the Indian economy. As RNFS is a microcosm of the economy, the withering of traditional arts and crafts as reflected in the precarious state of laheriya tie-dyeing of Jaipur, the folk-sarangi of the Punjab, Paithani weaving of Aurangabad, kasuti embroidery in Karnataka, Chamba rumal embroidery in Himachal Pradesh, Farrukhabad silk printing in Uttar Pradesh, Toda embroidery in the Nilgiris, metal blockmaking in Varanasi, etc. causes concern. Clearly, we have to go beyond tentative, half-hearted measures of the past for meaningful development of RNFS over the long haul.

The Approach Paper to the Tenth Plan emphasised the need for the agriculture sector to grow by 4 per cent for stepping up the overall gross domestic product (GDP) growth rate to 8 per cent per annum. The Planning Commission's Task Force on Employment Opportunities stressed that productivity growth of 4 per cent per year in agriculture would improve the quality of employment in the sector through faster growth in real wages of labour and in incomes per head of the self-employed. Despite agriculture contributing about 60 per cent of total employment, low farm sector employment elasticity (projected to grow from 0 per cent in 1993-2000 to 0.10 per cent in 2002-07) restricts growth in agricultural employment to only 0.4 to 0.45 per cent per year. With increasing accent on mechanisation for higher productivity and production gradually decreasing the labour force, the Task Force stressed the need for a long-term strategy for absorbing the rural labour force in the non-agricultural sector, *e.g.,* rural infrastructure like roads, market places and irrigation and water management. Further, it causes concern and consternation that public investment in agriculture declined in real terms not only in the 1980s but also in the 1990s. A sustainable growth of the Indian economy, therefore, depends not just on agricultural rebound but also a step-up in public investment. While investment in agriculture as a percentage of GDP stagnated to around 1.5 per cent over the years, the proportion of current expenditure declined from 3.4 in 1993-94 to 1.4 in 1999-2000. The resource crunch of the state governments together with the potential of increasing private investment by enhanced public investment in agriculture makes it necessary for the Centre to play a catalytic role in stepping up public investment in agriculture and allied activities. The inter-relations between farm and non-farm sectors, investment by the corporate sector in developing marketing links, storage and transportation facilities and the food-processing sector can also accelerate escalation of RNFS.

DEFINITIONAL AND CONCEPTUAL ISSUES

Empirical study of RNFS has been beset with practical problems and issues. While the Planning Commission uses the term "village and small industries" for "non-farm sector", the National Bank for Agriculture and Rural Development (NABARD), a pioneer in the promotion of RNFS, defines non-farm sector by cataloguing a "a spectrum of small, cottage, tiny and village industries". Similarly, the World Bank (1978: 11) maintained "most of the rural non-farm jobs are in small-scale construction, service, commercial transport, processing and manufacturing industries".

A close and careful examination of the various definitions of the Department of Small Scale, Tiny and Rural Industries, Government of India, the Khadi and Village Industries Commission (KVIC), the Census Commissioner of India and the Central Statistical Organisation (CSO) reveals that consensus on RNFS may be difficult because of the several models of development, various approaches and large number of assertions and averments. The centrality of RNFS lies, however, in the following dimensions:

(i) sub-sectoral — coverage of various types of activities.

(ii) spatial — location in the rural-urban continuum.

(iii) scale — size of enterprises.

An analysis of the sub-sectoral dimensions requires delimitation of various economic activities under RNFS. In terms of the Census classification, all workers are customarily divided into nine categories:

1. Cultivators
2. Agricultural labourers
3. (Workers engaged in) Livestock, forestry, fishing, plantations, orchards and allied activities
4. Mining and quarrying
5. Manufacturing, processing, servicing and repair:
   (a) In household industry
   (b) Other than in household industry
6. Construction
7. Trade and Commerce
8. Transport, storage and communication
9. Other services

Since RNFS basically relates to off-farm activities, we may justifiably exclude agrarian activities (1 to 3) because of their peculiar characteristics. In view of the diverse views on the spatial dimension, 'rural area' was defined in terms of Section 2(q)(b) of the NABARD Act, 1981 to mean the area comprised in any village and included the area comprised in any town, the population of which did not exceed 10,000 or such other figure specified by the RBI, from time to time. The increase in number of small towns with a population ranging between 10,000-50,000 and other relevant factors led to a subsequent modification by the Reserve Bank of India (RBI) in the definition of 'rural area' was to mean any village (irrespective of population) or town with a population not exceeding 50,000. In line with this revised definition, the NABARD Act was also amended.

Since the definition and configuration of projects in the RNFS poses theoretical and practical difficulties, the Central

Statistical Organisation's (CSO's) classification of units to categorise RNFS in terms of scale is some times used:

- "own account enterprises" (OAEs), which exclude hired workers or enterprises, employing only the owner/ worker or his/her family workers.
- "non-directory establishments" (NDEs), which are enterprises with five or less workers, of whom at least one is a hired worker.
- "directory establishment" (Des), which are enterprises with at least six workers, including at least one hired on a fairly regular basis. Within Des and NDEs, these units which are engaged in manufacturing are called MDEs and NDMEs respectively, the M representing manufacturing.
- Factories or manufacturing enterprises, which employ at least 10 workers if they use power or at least 20 without power.

The Government of India and the Planning Commission classified the industrial sector into major and medium industries and village and small industries (VSI). The VSI sector comprises sub-sectors, such as, traditional industries (handlooms, handicrafts, sericulture, coir, khadi and village industries), agro industries, modern industries (ancillarisation, mother units, common service centres), services and goods transport, etc. Almost the entire traditional industry and even some portion of the modern SSI form part of the RNFS, which represents a mainstream commercial activity, apart from being a cultural and creative manifestation. The Government of India notification dated December 10, 1997 defined a SSI unit as an undertaking with investment in fixed assets in plant and machinery upto Rs. 3 crore. Within the SSI, units with investment in plant and machinery upto Rs. 25 lakh are termed as tiny industry. However, in amendment of this order, the Government of India, Ministry of Commerce and Industry, (Department of Industrial Policy and Promotion), slashed the ceiling on investment in plant and machinery from Rs. 300 lakh to Rs. 100 lakh with effect from December 24, 1999.

The basic characteristics of RNFS could also be explored

in terms of qualitative criteria (Table 2) since standard quantitative yardstick have not yet been decisively established.

TABLE 2: A Systematic of Qualitative Criteria of RNFS

Sl. No.	Criterion	Characteristics
1.	Mode of Production	Low degree of division of labour, craft-type production.
2.	Market Position	Low degree of division of labour, craft-type production.
3.	Management Style	No professional management, no division between productive and management functions.
4.	Workers	High share of family members, low education requirements.
5.	Product Type	Low technology intensity, low production runs.
6.	Organisational Structure	Relations to employees, customers and suppliers.
7.	Legal Position	No formal registration.
8.	Output Markets	Locally limited.
9.	Input Markets	Utilisation of locally available resources.

H. Fahnel, J. Hartamann, W. Konig, R. Meier (1993):
"Aur der Suche nach neuen Konzepten der Kleinunternehmensentwicklung in Entwicklungslandern" in Gottingen Oktober 1992, Gottingen 1993.

The term RNFS is used in different senses — sub-sectoral, spatial and scale. This definitional issue of RNFS along three basic dimensions or axes (sub-sectoral, spatial and scale) is summarised in the diagram on next page.

RNFS is, however, increasingly used in the sense of a process through which all activities — off-farm and non-farm, outside agriculture and allied sectors, in secondary and tertiary services are carried out in or primarily benefiting rural areas. Various schools of thought have used several terminologies, such as model, process, theories, method, programme, and strategy in the field of RNFS. This is hardly surprising because in the economic history of India, rural development has not only been used as an instrument of economic emancipation but also as an instrument of social change of far-reaching ramifications. In view of the bewildering diversity of uses of the term RNFS, it becomes essential to clearly specify the

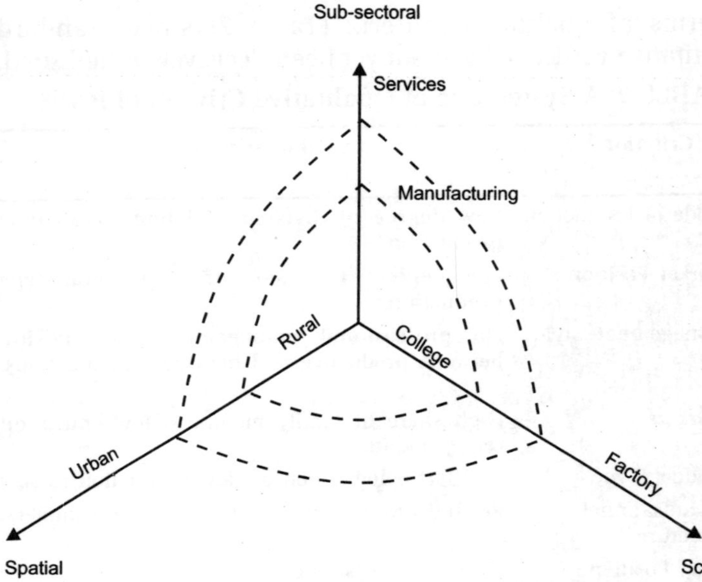

sense in which RNFS is used here. The paper uses RNFS in a broad sense including enterprises and artisans involved in a wide range of goods and services, which could generate employment for the rural work force without displacing them from their habitat. Conventionally RNFS could be defined as involving all off-farm and non-farm (outside agriculture and allied activities) enterprises and artisanal activities, which could be classified as household, decentralized, tiny and small scale enterprises involved in production/manufacturing, processing, preserving, storing and marketing of goods repairs, construction, trade transport, etc. and/or engaged in services and agro processing in villages and rural towns upto 50,000 population undertaken by enterprises varying in size from household (own account enterprises) to factories (*i.e.,* manufacturing enterprises employing at least 10 workers if power is used and at least 20 if no power is used). The slogan "leave the land but not the countryside; enter the factory but not the city" may have been coined in the context of China but it is no less relevant in contemporary India.

RNFS undoubtedly covers a wide spectrum of economic activities undertaken in the decentralised sector by artisans, craftsmen, non-agricultural labour in part-time activity. But it is customarily clubbed together without considering distinct individual identities. We can reasonably isolate three segments: (a) traditional industries producing handicrafts or rural household needs by conventional techniques, (b) industries producing modern high demand goods, such as, leather goods, brushes, etc. by largely traditional techniques, and (c) industries producing modern products in engineering, chemicals, toiletries, electronics, etc. These industries use modern techniques and also sometimes act as subcontractors or ancillaries to large scale industrial units. Chadha (1986) forcefully stressed accessibility of RNFS as follows:

> From the viewpoint of employment and earnings of the rural household it hardly matters whether non-farm employment is available in the village itself or in a nearby village/town. In other words, all economic activities which display sufficient strong linkages with rural households irrespective of whether they are located in designated rural areas or not, should be a part and parcel of their employment-income matrix. After all, many of the rural households derive employment and income benefits from diverse varieties of non-farm activities, whether completely in the rural areas or partly in the rural areas or partly in the nearby urban areas or though any other arrangement. The sheer existence and the accessibility of the non-farm employment is the real question.

Thus an examination of the genesis and evolution of the concept of RNFS reveals that this broad conceptualisation is by no means new. The importance of RNFS is, however, being increasingly realised as an instrument of meeting enhanced and varied requirements of rural industrialisation. An analysis of the Indian RNFS, in the past fifty years, unmistakably brings out its significant increase in terms of most parameters. The enhanced contribution of the sector is reflected in its contribution to investment, output, employment and exports due largely to the Government's conscious policy of protection and incentives. However, it received inadequate attention and remained restricted to the achievement of quantitative targets in terms of physical units and financial outlay. In the post-reforms period marked by the opening up of the economy and increasing alliance between the large and small scale segments of the domestic market, there was a paradigm shift in the concept of small scale industries/RNFS. The issues of speed, customer preference, quality management, technology upgradation, cost reduction, professional learning, innovation promotion and a modicum of social awareness could salubriously influence the growth process.

The case for a deterministic RNFS thesis in driving organic growth through diversification of assets, activities and incomes rests, *inter alia*, on the fact that export-led growth for agriculture is inconsequential to the marginal farmers, who practice largely subsistence farming. The task of transitioning businesses from a relatively protected environment to the rigours of a globalised market is impossible without an enhancement of capabilities. This is why modernisation, scaling up and skills upgradation of these multitudes and reduce their dependence on agriculture and allied activities by augmentation of viable and self-sustaining enterprises in rural and semi-urban areas obviously becomes the key to any sustainable economic expansion and the widespread problems of rural unemployment, urban migration, under-utilisation of physical resources and skills of the rural areas. Poverty alleviation, in the ultimate analysis, necessitates discernible improvement in the skill level of the youth by identifying the felt needs and catering to them to enable them to join the economic mainstream and the percolation of the benefits of market-dependent growth to them. As Noam Chomsky puts it, "freedom without opportunity is a devil's gift and the refusal to provide such opportunities is criminal. The fate of the more vulnerable offers a sharper measure of the distance from here to something that might be called civilisation".

RNFS has itself become an issue of debate and discussion. The main strands of this debate bring into question the established paradigms of RNFS, direction of change for fostering dispersed industrial growth and the attempt to replicate western models of development without considering the socio-economic conditions peculiar to India. In India, RNFS definitionally and conceptually denotes social, economic and technological programmes aimed at rapid transformation of the local economy by planned efforts.

EMPLOYMENT ASPECT OF RNFS-EMERGING CONTOURS

While the significance of RNFS for employment generation has long been understood, the implications of RNFS for creation of gainful employment have increasingly come to the fore in the difficult post-liberalisation scenario. This is a basic area, where viability ought to be assessed not merely in terms of monetary benefit but also in terms of its impact on the overall economy. In the overarching framework of economic liberalisation, let us not be oblivious of the fact that the principal goal of development is to create sustainable improvements not only in terms of per capita income, but also in the overall quality of life. The achievement of this goal requires a comprehensive approach to development. A focus on RNFS would help strike a judicious balance between the complex and challenging task of bringing about sustained growth and ensuring equity and orderly change. The Third All India Census of SSIs 2001-02 placed the number of SSI units at 105 lakh units (14 lakh registered + 91 lakh unregistered). The number of SSI units rose to 115 lakh as at end-March 2004 catalysing employment of 247 lakh persons. The works of Paul Streeten, Mahbub-ul-Haq and Dudley Seers in the seventies to the later works of Amartya Sen and Jean Dreze provide a strong theoretical basis of improving the quality of life and generating employment than to GDP growth *per se.*

Despite sharp reduction in the poverty ratio from 55 per cent in 1973-74 to 26 per cent in 1999-2000, rural India is home to 72 per cent of the Indian population and 75 per cent of its poor. No wonder then that poverty continues to be an abiding concern because of the staggering numbers involved. The occupational pattern of employment reveals a clear dichotomy in the sense that despite the share of agriculture being less than 30 per cent in GDP, it accounts for more than 60 per cent of the workers. As RNFS can help to rewrite the algorithm of growth to save the teeming millions from the scourge of poverty, it is necessary to examine the synergistic and interdependent relationship between RNFS and development. The requisite high rates of inclusive economic growth can only be sustained by putting in place an effective growth strategy for rural India. Given that creation of an additional job in RNFS costs only 10-20 per cent of the cost in a large industry and exacerbation of the already acute demographic pressures by rural-urban migration, promotion of RNFS is central to target transfers disproportionately populated by the poor and redress impediments to the smooth functioning of factor markets in labour, land and capital. The theoretical underpinning of the literature on economic development reinforces this thesis. The Lewis-Fei-Ranis economic growth model shows that urban wages need to be at least 30 per cent higher than the average rural income to induce workers to migrate from their home areas. At this urban wage level, the supply of rural labour is considered to be perfectly elastic. The Todaro migration model, however, demonstrates that migration proceeds in response to urban-rural differences in expected rather than actual earnings.

An analysis of data on National Sample Survey quinquennial surveys on employment and unemployment demonstrates that the spurt in rural non-farm employment (RNFE) was substantially responsible for the perceptible reduction in poverty in the 1980s. The percentage of RNFE in total rural employment steadily increased from 16.6 per cent in 1977-78 to 18.4 per cent in 1983, to 21.6 per cent in 1993-94 and to 23.8 per cent in 1999-2000. The latent RNFE potential is manifested in its 0.35 per cent yearly increase in total employment during the reform period ('93-94 to '99-00) — an increase in conformity with the trend analysis in the earlier periods. In absolute terms, the number of workers in RNFE shot up from 36.1 millions in 1977-78 to 44.9 millions in 1983 (CAGR of 4.06) and further to 62.98 millions in 1993-94 (CAGR of 3.28 during 1977-78 to 1993-94) and finally to 71.52 millions in 1999-2000 (CAGR of 2.14). It needs no clairvoyance to perceive that we must seriously debate available options and examine implications of not pursuing them because of the peculiar characteristics of RNFS and the concomitant risks. The lower employment growth in RNFE during the reform period ('93-94 to '99-00) *vis-a-vis* the pre-reform period needs to be tempered by the low overall employment growth (around 1 per cent per annum) during the reform period. 90 per cent of the incremental employment during the reform period emanated from RNFE as compared to 39 per cent in the earlier periods. The growth in RNFE, however, differed significantly with the growth in RNFE in males being much more pronounced.

Evidently then the salient features of the Indian economy unmistakably bring out the continued relevance of RNFS in the transformed economic reforms setting, where unemployment is at its highest now in four decades. The criticality of RNFS in addressing the deep-rooted malaise is reflected in the fact that incremental employment created during the period (1993-94 to 1999-00) was 8.54 millions. Of this increment, 3.1 million workers (36 per cent) were from the construction sector. 27 per cent was due to manufacturing and repair services (the share of repair services being 5.4 per cent) and 25.5 per cent was due to transport, storage and communication. The contribution of retail trade was 13 per cent while that of hotels and restaurants was only 4 per cent. Community and personal services witnessed a decline in employment but the employment of social services (education and health) rose. Around 63 per cent of the additional employment stemmed from construction and transport, storage and communications. The rapid growth in RNFE has been driven both by 'push' and 'pull' factors.

There is a fair measure of consensus among economists, planners and policy makers that employment expressed in terms of a single dimensional measure like person hours, days, month or year is grossly inadequate. Hence, it needs to be supplemented by corresponding data/information on qualitative characteristics like earnings, productivity, regularity, stability, physical conditions of work, etc. (Papola, *et al.*, 1999). Enhancement of the quality of employment and incomes in RNFS necessitates enabling Government policies, thrust on increased employment for unskilled workers and augmenting the incomes of the women by creating opportunities in the higher productivity sectors. Empirical evidence strongly suggests that identification of pro-poor growth engines at sub-sectoral level rather than at the level of broad sectors is of greater contemporary relevance.

Change, reform and radicalism are not abstruse doctrinaire reference points but an immediate necessity. The unique characteristics of Indian agriculture, however, render the task of fashioning growth strategies for rural India complex because of the variegated nature of work situation, modes of employment and attendant problems and issues. There is a preponderance of rainfed farming in the country and the proportion of tiny and fragmented farms [operational land holdings being in the range of 0-1 hectare (57 per cent) and 1-2 hectare (18 per cent) with limited labour absorption capacity] is simply overwhelming. The attempt to achieve economies of scale through corporatisation of farms and contract farming has not been successful because of fears of large-scale displacement of labour and apprehensions of exploitation by powerful corporate entities. Improvement in the skill levels of these multitudes and reduction in their dependence on agriculture and allied activities by ongoing efforts to facilitate greater access to credit, business and management training, improved technologies and production packages and competitive marketing strategies can gainfully employ the residual unabsorbed labour force. Thus increase in viable and self-sustaining rural and semi-urban enterprises can significantly alleviate the widespread problems of rural unemployment, urban migration, under-utilisation of physical resources and skills of the rural areas. There cannot, however, be sustainable employment generation without a comprehensive strategy, collective effort, shared commitment and vision in promotion and development of RNFS. Some of the key elements of this strategy to foster multi-dimensional and multi-layered growth of RNFS include differentiated growth and stabilisation, greater private investment, aggressive marketing, robust infrastructure and adequate credit.

COMPLEXITIES OF RNFS

The bewildering complexities of RNFS emanate, *inter alia*, from the large number of decentralised tiny units, enormous range of products — both traditional and non-traditional, vast disparity in technology employed as well as in the scale of production, absence of standard products and diverse local, regional, national, international markets. Serious infrastructural constraints, financing, marketing and managerial deficiencies, absence of systematic extension efforts in use of new tools, techniques of production, etc. and the tendency among entrepreneurs to remain small also circumscribe development of RNFS. These complexities of RNFS make it difficult to identify, map, profile the existing RNFS along with the distribution and evaluate the effectiveness of past policies and programmes, examine segments/sub-segments with a faster growth potential in terms of market demand, resource base, sustainable employment, income generation, improved technology, suggest support-mechanisms for creation of marketing synergies, technology upgradation, credit delivery, ancillarisation, subcontracting and promotional support through NGOs/VAs in the light of the central tenets of RNFS and investigate policy and regulatory frameworks in relation to RNFS. There is also a need to assess the potential for RNFS (in terms of number of enterprises, employment and credit use) in sync with existing infrastructure, technology, marketing, entrepreneurship and promotional and extension services in view of the emergence of new paradigms and techniques for effective management of change and develop a concrete action plan for sustained development of RNFS with physical and financial outlay and non-credit plan for non-credit inputs, including the role of various agencies involved in promotion and development and coordination of various activities and institutions involved in generation of sustainable development of RNFS.

ISSUES FOR DEVELOPMENT

A scan of the global literature on RNFS as well as field level experiences strongly suggests that there are certain key issues contributing to the success of RNFS. Accordingly, in drawing up RNFS development plans, we have necessarily to identify these key issues for their successful implementation. These include aspects, such as, identification and diversification, holistic versus piecemeal, bottom up versus top down, demand driven versus supply driven, group approach versus individual approach, subsidised input cost versus full recovery, vertical and horizontal linkages between RNFS and large industries, effective management, participatory planning and institutional restructuring. Against this backdrop, the issues of productivity, value addition, marketing, credit, infrastructure, resource and technology dissemination, resource management, etc. need to be examined in an ambience of liberalization, structural reform and globalisation for the RNFS to successfully meet the relentless onslaughts of the market forces. The concept of 'flexible specialisation' has been widely debated in the literature on development economics but its adaptability to the ground level realities is yet to be conclusively established. In analyzing the impact of RNFS on development performance, it is important to ask three questions: Is delivery of financial and promotional support to RNFS adequate and appropriate? What needs to be done for creation of an enabling environment for enhanced private investment for RNFS? Whether these enterprises can perform their conventional roles of employment and decentralised development under a free market mechanism or a new set of policies tailored to their specific needs of RNFS is called for to foster a virtuous cycle of regenerative, broad-based growth? These questions are not merely academic but are fundamental to the emerging process and pattern of economic development in India.

CREDIT DISPENSATION TO SSIs

Three types of institutions purvey credit to RNFS both for fixed assets creation and working capital. The formal banking system provides a range of modalities and terms for loans aimed at enhancing performance of RNFS. The sub-sector specific promotional institutions provide a range of financial and non-financial services. Finally, the informal credit channels in the private sector charge exorbitant rates of interest but provide a more efficient service. All these virtually parallel systems in the public, private and cooperative sectors of the Indian economy met the progressively larger credit needs of RNFS in expanding output, employment and exports (Table 3) and influenced both the development of forces of production and the relations of production in a chain of 'cumulative causation'. But the export value realization from these products has been low in value terms, marked product concentration inasmuch as 70-80 per cent of SSI exports were accounted for by ready-made garments, leather products, basic chemicals, marine and processed foods and some engineering goods. Further the outreach of the credit institutions remained restricted and a stunted financial sector was decidedly anti-poor.

TABLE 3: Performance of Village and Small Industries Sector

	Production (Rs. Crore)		Employment (Lakh Nos.)		Exports (Rs. Crore)	
	1990-91	2002-03	1990-91	2002-03	1990-91	2002-03
Modern SSIs						
SSIs	1,55,340	7,60,844	125	200	9,664	81,930
Powerlooms	14,306	27,838	52	43	662	6,883
Sub-Total	1,69,646	7,88,682	177	243	10,326	88,813
Traditional Industries						
Khadi & Village Industries	2,280	8,250	48	65	6	26
Handlooms	3,974	16,900	92	125	407	2,616
Sericulture	866	1,477	52	57	441	2,200
Handicrafts	11,325	22,765	44	60	8,100	10,934
Coir	279	1,458	5	5	48	375
Sub-Total	18,724	50,850	241	312	9,002	16,151
TOTAL	1,88,370	8,39,532	418	555	19,328	1,04,964

Source: SIDBI's Annual Report, various years.

Micro Finance Institutions (MFIs) have helped to streamline the existing credit delivery mechanism by increasing the outreach of credit and enhancing the viability of institutions purveying rural credit. While the absolute number of households or enterprises (or relative market penetration) in the target population reached by the population measures the outreach, the number of underserved (women, minorities, and rural poor) served by it, who were traditionally by-passed by formal credit institutions measures the depth. Micro credit and poverty alleviation programmes are inextricably linked because of the potentiality of micro credit programmes to link the formal banking structures to the rural poor by stimulation and mobilisation of savings and promotion of entrepreneurial endeavour. Recent developments have underscored the urgency to sensitise the rural financial institutions (RFIs) to work as effective instruments of rejuvenating the credit delivery system. But RFIs are confronted with the problems of sustainability primarily due to the absence of appropriate governance and ownership structure, legal form, regulatory framework and more importantly, on account of a lack of dependable source of medium to long term capital.

Development is a complex, interlocking process of a "chain of disequilibria", which must keep alive rather than eliminate the disequilibria. This requires credit expansion on a large scale together with constructive policy changes to support reforms that will enhance development activities. The significance of credit and technology to produce globally competitive goods and services increased in the post-reforms period. But the dramatically transformed scenario necessitates effective management of change so that RNFS do not get swamped in the new order. In reshaping their strategies for the future RNFS must draw on the lessons of recent experience for secular dynamic change and structural transformation. This requires transcending of the physical and financial achievement in quantitative terms and a thrust on various inter-related issues, *e.g.,* flexible specialization, speed, production networking, sub-contracting and ancillarisation, quality certification, technology and skill upgradation, innovation and incubation, marketing development and infrastructural support.

ROLE OF FIs AND BANKS IN FINANCING

Entrepreneurs need shortterm, medium term and long term finance. The conventional mechanism for financing of SSIs in India stressed provision of term capital and working capital. Public and private sector banks, Small Industries Development Bank of India (SIDBI), National Bank for Agriculture and Rural Development (NABARD), Regional Rural Banks (RRBs), Urban Co-operative Banks (UCBs) and foreign banks meet the financial and credit needs of the sector. Public Sector Banks (PSBs) were conceived and functioned as instruments of social change and emancipation and also played a pivotal role in developing SSIs. Banks have been involved in directed lending for poverty alleviation/self-employment programmes to enhance the standards of living. The RBI's consistent direction to PSBs to allocate 40 per cent of their lending towards the priority sector, *i.e.,* agriculture, small scale industries, tiny sector, village and cottage industries, small traders, professionals and self-employed, etc. is sometimes held responsible for a higher level of NPAs in these sectors.

In view of the genuine difficulty of many SSIs, particularly the first generation entrepreneurs, in accessing bank credit because of their inability to provide adequate collateral security, the Government of India (GoI) launched a Credit Guarantee Fund Scheme.

The Credit Guarantee Fund Trust for Small Industries (CGTSI), set up by the GoI and SIDBI, is the nodal agency for the scheme. The CGTSI helps make collateral-free credit, both term loans as well as working capital, available to SSIs, particularly tiny units, by guaranteeing 75 per cent of the credit risk of eligible lenders, *viz.,* banks and institutions subject to a loan cap of Rs. 25 lakh and guarantee cap of Rs. 18.75 lakh per borrower.

State Financial Corporations (SFCs) were mandated to serve as regional funding agencies for promoting regional growth through SMEs development by grant of term loans for purchase of land/machinery and equipment/construction of factory premises for setting up new industries or modernising existing ones and participating in their equity base (Table 4). But a complex interplay of structural, managerial and financial problems ails the SFCs. The progressive deterioration in the financial position of SFCs not only wiped out their net worth

TABLE 4: Assistance Sanctioned by SFCs to Small Scale Sector

(Rs. Crore)

Year	No. of Units	Total Sanctions	Sanctions to SSIs	SSI sanctions as % of Total Sanctions
1991	45,092	18650	14920	80
1992	42,554	21890	18720	85.5
1993	36,713	20170	16860	83.6
1994	28,279	19080	15610	81.8
1995	28,331	27000	19200	71.1
1996	30,224	41880	25130	60
1997	26,473	35430	21150	59.7
1998	NA	26270	17680	67.3
1999	NA	18650	13650	72.2
2000	NA	22030	16170	73.4

Source: IDBI Report on Development Banking in India (various issues).

but also led to negative net worth. Accordingly, the GoI amended the SFCs Act and formed the G.P. Gupta Committee for examining the functioning of SFCs and suggesting measures for restructuring and revitalisation. These attempts, however, were not enough to rehabilitate SFCs as the viability of SFCs is inexorably linked to business-related factors, *e.g.*, high transaction cost, high-risk costs, low margins, high NPAs and low capitalisation. Khadi and Village Industries Commission (KVIC) and Khadi and Village Industries Boards (KVIBs) assist in financing khadi and village industry sector. National Small Industries Corporation (NSIC) and State Small Industries Corporations (SSICs) strove to develop SSIs by supplying machinery on a hire-purchase basis to small scale and ancillary industries, inclusive of the value of machinery and equipment already installed (Table 5).

TABLE 5: Sanctions & Disbursements of Term Loan by SIDCs/SIICs

(Rs. Crore)

Year	Sanctions				Disbursements			
	SSI	Non-SSI	Others	Total	SSI	Non-SSI	Others	Total
1995-96	3070	11510	8550	23130	1120	7390	7330	15840
1996-97	3790	9130	8590	21510	1600	8960	7700	18260
1997-98	3880	8990	9670	22540	2220	6620	9080	17920
1998-99	NA	NA	NA	22810	NA	NA	NA	21760
1999-00	NA	NA	NA	16480	NA	NA	NA	17410

Source: Reports of SIDCs/SIICs & IDBI Report on Development Banking in India (various issues).

FLOW OF CREDIT TO SSIS

The overall framework of the credit dispensation was inadequate in meeting the need for sufficient and timely institutional credit to the SSIs. An expert committee (Chairman: Dr. Abid Hussain) and an informal group of the Planning Commission (Chairman: Dr. G. Thimmaiah) examined the role of bank credit in development of SSIs. Subsequently, the S.L. Kapur Committee Report emphasised that only 15-20 per cent of the credit needs of the sector were being met. Accordingly, it suggested several initiatives to increase credit to the SSIs. Considered in a proper historical and comparative perspective, PSBs, Regional Rural Banks (RRBs) and SFCs increased the flow of credit to SSIs through bankable schemes. 27 PSBs through their countrywide network of over 45,000 branches, including 395 specialised SSI branches, meet the working capital requirement of SSIs. The statistics are revealing: the outstanding amount of credit to the SSI sector by PSBs rose from Rs. 42,591 crore in 1999 to Rs. 48,445 crore in 2001 and further to Rs. 49,743 crore in March 2002. But the percentage share of SSIs in net bank credit (NBC) progressively declined from 16.1 per cent in 1998 to 14.4 per cent in 2001 and further to 12.5 per cent in 2002 (Table 6). Such consternation emanates at least partly from the difficulty of SSIs in surviving the screening of the credit mechanism set up by commercial banks, which pursue "reasonable risks and prudent stable returns". This causes a disconnect between

TABLE 6: Flow of Credit to SSI Sector by Public, Private Sector & Foreign Banks

(Balance outstanding as at end-March) (Rs. crore)

Banks	1969 Amount	1999 Amount	2000 Amount	2001 Amount	2002 Amount
PSBs	257	42,591	46,045	48,445	49,743
	(8.5)	(16.1)	(14.6)	(14.2)	(12.5)
Indian Private Banks	NA	6,451	8,000	8,158	8,613
		(18.9)	(16.5)	(14.4)	(13.7)
Foreign Banks	NA	2,460	2,990	3,716	4,561
		(11.0)	(10.6)	(11.0)	(11.6)
Total	—	51,502	57,035	60,319	62,917

Figures in parentheses represent percentage share of Net Bank Credit (NBC).
Source: RBI Report on Trend & Progress of Banking in India (various issues).

SSIs' need for funds and their raising of finance since the access of small business/enterprise to external financing is beset with several operational problems. SSIs continue to be an integral part of the blueprint of development. Hence management of change requires not rhetoric but immediate and effective action reflected in various parameters, including a reduction in the debt equity ratio, *i.e.,* debt/shareholders' fund ratio. This point of view has also been strongly urged by the recent Parliamentary Standing Committee on Industry (129th

Report on Credit Flow to the SSI Sector). The Committee suggested relaxed bank norms for declaring SSI units as NPAs by considering factors, which hinder growth of the SSIs. These factors include delayed payments, blockage of credit flow and the enactment of the Securitisation Act. Banking and financial institutions can no longer afford to exist in cocoon or adopt an ostrich like attitude. These institutions need to adopt new practices by training staff members and eliminating unnecessary rules and regulations to adopt a customer-centric approach.

Empirical surveys by Confederation of Indian Industry (CII) have revealed that the country's SSI/RNFS is steadily losing out to China not on quality but price. Accordingly, timely availability of affordable finance could address this issue to a great extent. Evidently, there are persistent problems involved in credit to RNFS — the problems of physical and financial parameters, inadequate and delayed credit, linkage of SHGs and NGOs with banks, refinance for cash credit limits, etc. Consequently, apex institutions like NABARD and SIDBI successfully introduced several measures to enlarge and diversify credit and developmental activities in rural areas. The basic objectives of these programmes is to generate or enhance opportunities for livelihood, both in terms of income and employment in rural areas in a sustainable, demonstrative and cost-effective manner. But with the spreads of these banks coming under increasing pressure, the margins squeezed all the time and refinance drying up fast, these institutions need to alter their policies to meet the challenge of time. Stepping up the flow of credit to the sector to meet the projected plan requirement requires concerted and coordinated attempts by all Banks and FIs to achieve a more sustainable growth trajectory of RNFS.

CLUSTER APPROACH TO DEVELOPMENT OF RNFS

The cluster approach to enterprise promotion draws sustenance from backward and forward economic linkages and provides an active base for business and social interaction. Backward linkages connect a sector to those sectors from which a micro and small enterprises (MSE) purchases inputs and forward linkages indicate the interconnection of a sector to those sectors to which it sells output. The economies of agglomeration have decidedly emerged as effective instruments of realising the potential of "collective efficiency" through provision of raw materials, equipment, machinery, spares, repair and other services that would otherwise have not been possible. This approach with emphasis on its significance to the economy and the region's environment, replicability, viability, promotability, potential for complementarity and subsidiarity provides productivity gains in a mutually beneficial network. This is reflected in business operations on a continued basis and creation of sustainable mechanism of sub-contracting and linkages between firms. 350 modern SSI clusters exist in India in addition to the 2,000 artisan-based rural clusters (Gulati, 1997). The United Nations Industrial Development Organisation's (UNIDO's) study on the restructuring and the modernisation of small industry clusters in India was based on 138 clusters (125 natural, 13 induced) in 16 states covering 18 types of industries. It is necessary to bridge critical infrastructure gaps through strengthening National Cluster Development Programme, including identification of critical infrastructure gaps on cluster basis and functional Industrial parks. Successful clusters are characterised by a critical mass of similar or related economic enterprises, competing with each other, to spur innovation, availability of specialised services and infrastructure within the cluster that facilitates the production systems in an efficient manner, accessible and rapid exchange of information and knowledge and high rate of new business formation. This approach, therefore, must be accorded high priority in identified industrial sub-sectors and geographical clusters to facilitate vertical expansion of units.

CRITICAL SUCCESS FACTORS

Speedy implementation of structured multi-dimensional programme requires thrust on marketing, credit, technology and infrastructure. Studies conducted by the Centre for Studies in Decentralised Industries, Mumbai and the Technical Consultancy Organizations brought into sharp focus some of the basic problems RNFS is saddled with — the problems of inadequate availability of raw material at reasonable price, marketing deficiencies, etc. There has been an increase in marketing activity because of the inexorable process of economic reforms. Coordination between banks and extension agencies, industry associations, etc., needs to be based on synergies and locational and business specific complimentarities of the concerned institutions. In the wake of intensified competition and increased business complexities, such attempts are necessary to secure competitiveness of RNFS. After all, who does not look ahead will always remain behind. Effective marketing for dealing effectively with the increasingly volatile business environment could be supplemented by environmental analysis to overcome inadequacies of marketing outlets and managerial deficiencies. Such attempts would help not only to retain but also to enhance the customer base.

Technological obsolescence coupled with the need to improve product quality is a prerequisite for development of RNFS. Measures aimed at technology upgradation and skill development need to be examined against the concept of intermediate technology considered productive in a rural setting by Schumaker. In India, this concept was modified to imply appropriate technology so as to be in conformity with the resource endowments and the productive potential of the region. This attempt to get popularity failed because of inadequate development of rural enterprise and the indifferent attitude of technology promoting institutions. The Report of Expert Committee on small enterprises (1997) chaired by Dr. Abid Hussain rightly said that 'traditional industries with low levels of technology reached their peak and unless enterprises ventured to new generation of products the dynamism of growth slows down'. In order to embrace and benefit from the convergence of telecommunications, multimedia and broadcasting technology, giving rise to the concept of Information and Communications Technologies (ICTs), basic questions relating to the role of information system (IS), Information Technology (IT) and information management (IM) in streamlining the production process to create and improve products need to be resolved.

Poor basic infrastructure — electricity, power, transport, communication and availability of ancillary and allied services, *viz.*, supply of raw materials and other inputs, semi-skilled labourers, power, transport and communications, etc. seriously constrains the intensification of production and marketing systems. There is a need for the increased role for private sector financing in the present milieu because of the shifting paradigms in infrastructure financing. The role of bottlenecks in respect of four identified factors could also be analysed to explore approaches for solutions. We must, therefore, explore the support mechanism aimed at creating conducive policy environment for sustained growth of RNFS by modifying generic strategies.

The GoI formulated a common production strategy for balanced development of large scale, small scale and village industries. Rural Industrial Projects, Rural Marketing Centres and District Industries Centre were also set up at the district level as a single window for providing a big push to rural industrialization. With a view to making RNFS a healthy adjunct of competitive and growing Indian industry, certain changes in the operational strategy for strengthening the credit delivery system, including the development of industrial estates/areas, revitalising the District Industries Centre (DIC), efficient conduct of EDPs, emphasis on homogenous cluster of RNFS and supplementing the strategy of flexible specialisation by nurturing of an entrepreneurial culture are necessary.

RURAL INDUSTRIALISATION

The basic strategy of rural industrialisation in India comprises resuscitation of traditional village industries by facilitating technological upgradation, diffusion and dispersal of modern manufacturing activity in the rural areas with perceptible forward and backward linkages, ethnic distinctiveness and high labour inputs on the production line in conformity with the resource endowment of the region and the needs and requirements of the persons. The rural industries supplement income as well as provide part/full time employment activity for the rural artisans, landless labourers, women and educated unemployed. Compelling and incontrovertible cross-country evidence show that a thorough understanding of the modern and indigenous perceptions in small enterprise work place can be incorporated in a new development model with specific roles for credit, profit, output and quality control. As the S.L. Kapur Committee Report on

Credit to SSIs definitely and unerringly pointed out, SSIs need "to develop a global vision, respond to more demanding standards of the customers, identify the patterns of shifting values and craft the key strategies that will leap frog them ahead of competition". This is a tall order, which necessitates synchronised and concerted efforts of all players in this game, *viz.*, the artisans themselves, the government, the business sector, mediating organizations like non-governmental organizations (NGOs), voluntary agencies (VAs), etc. and the market. There has also been a steady increase in the flow of bank credit to micro enterprises in rural areas set up by the vulnerable sections of society, including women (Sharma, 2001). All these aspects coalesce into the central theme of bringing about a reappraisal of the ways in which institutions and networks of support for RNFS are managed to bring about a silent revolution in rural areas. India must grapple with this concern if the positive cascading effects of the much needed 'take-off into a stage of self-sustained growth' in the post reforms era have to be enduring.

The Rural Industry Programme (RIP) of SIDBI attempted to foster faster development of RNFS through better commercial exploitation of local resources by providing finance by primary lending institutions like banks/SFCs and selected NGOs. SIDBI also attempts to provide other critical inputs like information motivation, training and credit, backed by appropriate technology and market linkages for healthy growth of enterprises. Under RIP, identified implementing agencies provide a cohesive and integrated package of basic inputs and services to potential entrepreneurs to set up their own enterprises. The package of services, *inter alia*, included identifying and motivating rural entrepreneurs, project identification, training, appropriate technology, finance tie-up and market linkages. RIP not only exposed the local entrepreneurs to improved production techniques but also paved the way for chalking out the growth plans for these units. Apart from the technology related aspects, the group of entrepreneurs/artisans were also counselled by bank representatives on financial aspects. The salient features of RIP were as under:

Payment to the implementing agencies for their

professional inputs provided mainly by results in terms of enterprises grounded.

- Focus on entrepreneurial competence of rural poor rather than on their social status.
- Facilitating suitable inputs in the areas of entrepreneurship and skill development, finance, appropriate technology, marketing and suitable post-sanction follow-up.
- Networking with concerned institutions like NGOs, banks, technology institutions, corporate bodies and Government agencies.
- Enterprises grounded on technological and economic consideration.
- Concurrent monitoring of the programme by professional agency.
- Special skill upgradation workshops and training programmes for the field level officials of the implementing agencies.

SIDBI's experience strongly suggests that RIP, as compared to subsidy oriented schemes, is a cost-effective and sustainable alternative for promoting rural enterprises in the tiny sector. It vindicates that suitable industry-specific interventions under RIP backed by positioning of professional teams at field level to provide consultancy and escort services to rural entrepreneurs can holistically develop backward regions. The coverage of RIP thus needs to be expanded and strengthened in terms of marketing and technology linkages for increased overall effectiveness. Given the diversity of natural resources in villages and the traditional skills of the artisans, RIP type initiatives based on rural cluster methodology are aimed at accelerating the pace of rural industrialisation and their multiplier effect has the potential for large scale replication. Independent objective assessment by National Institute of Rural Development (NIRD), Hyderabad strongly suggests that it could mark a welcome change from subsidy-oriented schemes to sustainable alternatives for promoting rural enterprises in the tiny sector. In the present context of sweeping economic reforms, suitable industry-specific initiatives together with positioning of professional teams at field level to provide consultancy and escort services to rural entrepreneurs can help in integrated, holistic development of backward regions. Given wide diversities in the resource endowments and skills, there cannot be a standard approach to the evaluation of small enterprises development (SED) (Harper, *et al.*, 1998). But such cluster-based initiatives have the potential of significantly altering rural industrialisation. Strengthening of rural artisan complexes, modernisation and capacity building in Villages industries and a special thrust on small agro-industries would also be helpful in boosting RNFS.

NINTH PLAN STRATEGY

RNFS has made a perceptible impact the world over in ameliorating the living conditions of the common man. This is why in India, concerted attempts have been made to spearhead rural development by widening and deepening RNFS across areas. The worry lines are, however, clearly etched as successive Five-Year Plans made inadequate provision for financing of RNFS programmes. The Eighth (1992-97) and the Ninth (1997-2002) Five-Year Plans stressed the importance of RNFS in economic planning because of the pivotal role it plays in poverty alleviation programmes, environment protection and increasing productivity in all sectors of the economy. The Plan document envisaged incremental employment generation of 26 million by 2000 from NFS alone with high latent potential in trade, transport, manufacturing services, etc. Towards this end, the Ninth Five Year Plan spelt-out the following measures: (i) provision of incentives and support to small scale and village industries to facilitate their growth and employment and the non-displacement of such industries by foreign investment, (ii) stepping up the flow of credit to SSIs and encouragement to factoring services apart from discounting of bills, (iii) evolution of new institutional mechanism to augment credit to informal and RNFS, (iv) increase in the investment limit for SSIs to account for inflation and to achieve minimum economies of scale and technological upgradation to face emerging challenges, (v) review of list of items reserved for SSIs with a view to achieving economies of scale, technological upgradation, export capabilities, etc., (vi) enlarged coverage of schemes, such as, the PMRY to create self-employment opportunities for educated unemployed, (vii) organisational and financial strengthening of the KVIC to create more employment opportunities, and (viii) technological development and upgradation in the VSI sector, particularly SSIs, handlooms, powerlooms, coir, handicrafts, wool, etc. These principles aimed at resuscitating the sector are eminently sound and sensible and could arguably form the basis of placing the growth of the RNFS as a whole on a higher and more sustained growth path. Consequently, it is contended that nothing less than a fresh approach, which implies a paradigm shift, would serve to redefine the parameters governing the RNFS in a meaningful manner. Questions such as how do various sub-sectors of the RNFS work together in development; whether there are alternative schemata being activated in simultaneously sequential or parallel development and the relationship between individual and societal expectations, frameworks and goals need to be explored and examined. Promotion of the RNFS with customer-centric strategies, which provides a range of options for restructuring the Indian economy, could thus work as a trigger mechanism in fostering faster development. For, it is absolutely unrealistic to preach equity at the global level but perpetuate inequities within the country. Charity must indeed begin at home and the resources allocated for wholesome development must be used for well-defined purposes, otherwise it would have a deleterious effect on wholesome development. These expedient measures would also significantly help to realise the unswerving objective of growth with distributive equity. This is why in the constantly evolving situation, we need to nuance our approach by giving a renewed thrust to the RNFS to meet the challenges of the present and the expectations of the future. Accordingly, the Draft Approach Paper to the Tenth Plan stressed the imperative necessity of broad-based decentralised growth: "It is important to emphasise that the equity-related objectives of the Plan, which are extremely important, are linked to the growth objectives, and the attainment of one may not be possible without the attainment of the other. For example, high rates of growth are essential if we want to provide a sufficient expansion of sustainable high quality employment opportunities to the expanding labour force and ensure a sufficient increase in income of the poor and the disadvantaged." Hence, the deployment of RNFS as an instrument of transformation becomes an important variable in the strategy of sustained development. RNFS and the associated methodology must be brought into the main theme of economic planning in the emerging contemporary global milieu by meshing together of all the different perspectives of RNFS for optimum results. Some of the basic elements of the technology-driven, customer-focused and market-driven strategy to streamline monitoring framework, data collection methods, environmental indicators, data management, assessment and reporting approaches for RNFS relate to —

- Formulation of a structured survey to ascertain and develop a comprehensive mapping and business database;
- Development of a methodology for determining cost of poor quality and non-value-adding activities in financial terms;
- Emphasis on research and development (R&D);
- Refashion test laboratories and government establishments to enable them to launch commercially viable products;
- Proactive role of banks and financial institutions to further RNFS in a big way;
- Establish vision, direction and shared values. Set challenging goals and implement strategies to achieve them. Train, facilitate, and empower people.

CONCLUDING OBSERVATIONS

With emphasis on physical and geographical features, availability of resources — natural, human and infrastructure — an attempt has to be made to identify and analyse the potential for development, use forward and backward linkages and formulate a proactive role for banks in streamlining the credit mechanism for accelerating the pace of rural industrialisation. More specifically, an expansion of existing activities and exploration of areas to achieve sustainable employment, income generation and growth is urgently needed. In view of the influence of RNFS on future pattern and process of growth, the competitive advantage of RNFS with large and immediate effects both on the sector and the economy as a whole requires to be strengthened. Some of the basic elements of this thematic pattern of retooling the development strategy include greater independence, flexible specialization, working capital management, inventory control, modernisation and technological upgradation, creation of marketing synergies, customer-focused intervention, networking, etc. The significance of ancillarisation, subcontracting, processing and job work has increased manifold in the last few decades because of the advantages gained by large-scale industries by farming out certain parts, components and sub-assemblies. We must work for this new paradigm, which is founded on the principles of strengthening of semi-market transactions occurring in inter-firm network, development of RNFS as ancillaries, subcontractors, as partners in development and in certain industries as niche technology builders and suppliers to surmount obstacles and achieve the cutting edge of development.

The overwhelming task of reducing poverty and the resultant social inequity persisting for far too long requires greater emphasis on egalitarian dimension of the growth process. A direct assault on the intractable problems of poverty, unemployment and the skewed pattern of distribution of income and wealth is inconceivable without a renewed thrust on RNFS. It is necessary to reevaluate the development paradigm that facilitated the fast track growth of some states, and modify it in the light of the resource endowment and the peculiarities of the state to eradicate the poverty that stymies growth. To be sure, stimulating productivity is not easy because of the devastating effects of the combination of competitive volatility, market complexities and worker anxiety. But there is little doubt that the services sector can provide a momentum to the growth process. Synergies between technologies and improved human capital and fine-tuning of the mix of policies can result in a new state of economic success. Energising of rural development in future requires diversification and the growth of the services sector to create new and manifold employment opportunities. These broad principles and actions may be difficult to be implemented immediately. But a pro-active role by Banks, FIs, VAs/NGOs and, of course, the Government is imperative. Consequently, a sharper focus on strengthening of the pre-requisites for development of RNFS, such as, credit, marketing, technological modernisation and infrastructure are important desideratum of the strategy to resuscitate the RNFS in the new millennium. As Swami Vivekananda exhorted in his stirring address over a century ago: "arise, awake, sleep no more". There is thus a manifest need to work toward a vision that is more prosperous, better governed, more cooperative, and less poor, based on development that cares in particular for the most vulnerable sections of society — sections deprived of basic opportunities in the 'trickle-down' process of economic growth. This would also mark an important step forward in the move towards suraj (good rule) from swaraj (self-rule) in the Gandhian terminology and help in the realization of development with the changing face of India — a face designed to reflect vibrancy, resilience and efficiency despite structural bottlenecks and vicissitudes.

REFERENCES

Anderson, D., and M.W. Leiserson (1980): "Rural non-farm employment in developing countries", *Economic Development and Cultural Change,* Vol. 28, No. 2.

Banerjee, A.V. (1997): *Notes toward a theory of industrialisation in the developing world.* Mimeo Cambridge: Massachusetts Institute of Technology.

Chadha, G.K. (1986): "Non-farm Employment for Rural Households in India", *Indian Journal of Labour Economics,* No. 3.

Fahnel, H., J. Hartamann, W. Konig, R. Meier (1993): *Aur der Suche nach neuen Konzepten der Kleinunternehmensentwicklung in Entwicklungslandern* in Gottingen Oktober 1992, Gottingen 1993.

Harper, Malcolm and Gerry Finnegan (1998): *Value for Money: Impact of Small Enterprises Development,* Oxford and IBM Publishing Company Pvt. Ltd., New Delhi.

Lanjouw, J.O. and Lanjouw, P. (1997): *The rural non-farm sector: an update,* Mimeo. Development Economic Research Group, Washington, D.C: World Bank.

Lanjouw, P. and Shariff, A. (1999): *Rural poverty and non-farm employment in India: evidence from survey data,* Mimeo. Department of Development Economics. Amsterdam: Free University of Amsterdam.

Gulati, Mukesh (1997): "Restructuring and Modernisation of Small Medium Enterprise Clusters in India", *UNIDO Report,* UNIDO.

Hartamann, J. *et al.*, (1990): "Informal Small Business in Rural Areas of Developing Countries", *International Small Business Series,* No. 5, Gottingen 1990.

Industrial Development Bank of India: *IDBI Report on Development Banking in India* (various issues).

Papola, T.S. and Alakh N. Sharma (eds.) (1999): *Gender and Employment in India,* Indian Society of Labour Economics, Institute of Economic Growth and Vikas Publishing House Pvt. Ltd., New Delhi.

Reardon, T. *et al.* (1998): "Diversification of household incomes into non-farm sources: patterns, determinants and effects." Paper presented at *Strategies for Stimulating Growth of the Rural Non-Farm Economy in Developing Countries,* International Food Policy Research Institute Conference, May, Airlie House, Warrenton, Virginia.

Reardon, T. and J. Berdegué (1999): "Rural Non-farm Employment and Incomes in Latin America". Paper presented at Seminar *Desarrollo del Empleo Rural No Agrícola* sponsored by the Inter-American Development Bank, the UN Economic Commission on Latin America, FAO, and the International Farming Systems Research Methodology Network (RIMISP), Santiago, Chile, 6-8 September.

Reserve Bank of India: *Report on Trend & Progress of Banking in India* (various issues).

Sharma, Manoranjan (2001): "Rural Financial Institutions In Early Third Millennium: Present Position, Expedient Issues and Emerging Challenges", *Emerging Institutions for Decentralised Rural Development,* NIRD, Hyderabad.

SIDCs/SIICs: *Report* (various issues).

Small Industries Development Bank of India, *Annual Report,* various years.

Sundaram, K. (2001): "Employment and Poverty in 1990s", *Economic and Political Weekly,* August 11-17.

World Bank (1978): "Rural Enterprises and Non-farm Employment", *A World Bank Paper,* Washington, D.C.

—— (1978): "Employment and development of small enterprises", *Sectoral Policy Paper,* World Bank, Washington, D.C.

7

Exchange Rate, Food Price Stabilization and Inflation

ASHIMA GOYAL

ABSTRACT

Food price stabilization is essential in developing countries to provide food security and incentives for farmers. But some of the means used are inefficient and others lend themselves to capture by interest groups. Two changes suggest a possible new solution. First, trade at the margin in agriculture should rise with new agreements under WTO. Second, the currency crises of the nineties have shown the superiority of a managed float for developing country exchange rates. If the exchange rate has to be managed, one way to do so is to vary the nominal exchange rate to partially neutralize variations in world food prices. This combined with more liberal agricultural trade, can help to stabilize agricultural prices, lower the dependence on the other more distortionary policies, and provide a possible resolution for political deadlocks that make it difficult to remove subsidies. The benefits for macroeconomic policy come from inflation stabilization, more degrees of freedom, and exchange rate behaviour that reduces currency risk. An analysis of Indian experience in the nineties suggests that the rule would have been beneficial.

JEL Classification nos. Q18, F31, O11

KEY WORDS: Food Price, Trade, Managed Float, Policy Rule.

1. Introduction

Onions are widely consumed by the poor; so when their prices shot up in 1998, the anger of the electorate almost brought down the Indian government. A cartoon pictured Amartya Sen, who had recently been awarded the Noble Prize in economics, talking on the phone: 'Yes Minister, thank you Minister, no, I do not have a theory to bring down the price of onions.' But economists have devoted a lot of thought to, and policy makers have often attempted to intervene in the pricing of food. Newbery and Stiglitz's (1981) exhaustive work indicates that the microeconomic benefits of price stabilization (based on current theorizing) are minor. This, however, leaves open the question of why consumers and therefore politicians dislike food-price instability. A potentially important, relatively unexplored answer is impact on inflation and wages.[1]

Countries in South-East Asia have long stabilized food price in order to minimize shocks to the poor. But the methods used bred inefficiencies and created interest groups. Even so, East Asian countries had rapid growth, food budget shares have fallen and they have shifted from protecting the consumer to subsidizing the farmer. With green revolution technology productivity has risen, and most countries are now self-sufficient in food grains. It is now possible for them to allow more trade in agricultural products, without severely compromising food security. Moreover, as the post-Uruguay round WTO agreements come into effect agricultural trade will open up more. In countries where poverty remains high but interest groups have made old methods of price stabilization costly, compensating variation in nominal exchange rates is a way to by-pass these vested interests and deliver part of the required protection more efficiently. That is, the nominal exchange rate can be varied to partially neutralize the effects of variations in world food prices on domestic food prices, in the context of freer trade, where both prices now move more closely together.

In addition, with the changes in global capital flows, a consensus is forming that one of the best exchange rate regimes is a managed float.[2] This requires that central banks induce some variation in the nominal exchange rate, yet allow the system to move towards equilibrium exchange rates. Partially linking the variation in the nominal exchange rate to world food prices can give some variation in nominal exchange rates. Moreover, this aids in stabilizing food prices. Since wages rise with food prices in developing countries, stabilizing food prices lowers inflation. If the nominal exchange rate is fixed, inflation leads to an appreciation of the real exchange rate. By aborting this process, the suggested exchange rate policy prevents misalignments in the real exchange rate. Moreover, the flexibility in nominal exchange rates gives some monetary flexibility to adjust interest rates to the domestic cycle, and thus improve fundamentals and move towards a regime of stable real equilibrium exchange rates. Therefore the policy contributes to stabilizing food prices, and lowering the probability of currency crises. It is only an additional means of food price stabilization, not the only one. But there is a synergy that could be exploited.

Svensson (2000) emphasizes that the exchange rate plays a very important role in inflation targeting for an open economy. He demonstrates that a change in the exchange rate has the lowest lag among all policies in reaching a consumer price index target. In this paper we focus on food price stabilization, since food has the highest weight in the Indian consumer price index, the arguments would carry through using any other dominant commodity or commodity group. For example, oil should be included in the basket for a country that is dependent on oil imports.

The structure of the paper is as follows: Section 2 makes a critical survey of the working of current methods of price stabilization. Section 3 shows how the exchange rate based policy rule would work. Section 4 has a historical and counter factual analysis of its application to Indian in the nineties.

2. Methods of Price Stabilization

Williamson (1991) in collating the lessons of history on the interactions of growth with poverty and inequality, remarks that it is shocks to food prices that have had the largest impact on poverty. Technological progress in America during the industrial revolution favoured essential consumer goods; therefore poverty remained lower than in Europe at a comparative period. Conscious policies to stabilize the price of basic food were widely adopted in Asia in the sixties. These arose in the context of widespread poverty, absence of full income indexation, and the disastrous political consequences of food shortages. The objectives were wider than just price stabilization. There was a desire to achieve self-sufficiency in the production of basic food and to break the nexus between food prices-wages-inflation, of which there was an implicit understanding. Policies followed were different for food importing and exporting countries. But no poor populous country could afford to let imports form a large percentage of domestic consumption needs. Political problems had occurred in connection with food imports and food supply was a sensitive issue.

In implementing the policies, a floor price was required to maintain incentives for producers and a ceiling price to protect consumers. The floor price was considered necessary to induce the adoption and wide diffusion of new agricultural technology including high yielding and pest- and disease-resistant crop varieties. In pure price stabilization a sustainable target price must be the mean between the high and low prices, and is not necessarily linked to any such floor or ceiling. Low and stable price of the basic food grain was thought desirable to keep down inflation, reduce upward pressure on wages, and improve the profitability of the industrial sector.

In Thailand a cheap rice strategy was regarded as a substitute for salary increases. South Korea, Taiwan, and Japan all kept food prices low and stable in the period when food budget shares were high.[3] In Pakistan, for example, the increase in flour prices was tied to the increase in wages for industrial workers rather than to the costs of marketing and distribution.[4]

An alternative to price stabilization, that can protect producers at least, is the development of crop insurance and futures markets in agricultural commodities. But crop insurance has never been very successful. One reason is the frequency of adverse selection and moral hazard in agricultural markets; second, crop failures are sometimes global problems so that the losses to be compensated become too large. Futures markets are touted as a modern panacea. But selling forward only reduces uncertainty regarding revenues; it does not reduce price variability, since forward and futures prices move in line with cash prices. Moreover futures markets do not eliminate production risks; they have a short time horizon; transaction costs are too high; small farmers suffer from a lack of information relative to large traders and may be afraid of market manipulation. At best futures will work for a few cash crops with high price volatility. Therefore additional stabilization measures will continue to be required.

The types of interventions commonly followed were procurement, buffer stocks and distribution by the government, imports, taxes and subsidies. If prices are not to respond fully to production variations, they have to be offset by variations in trade or stocks rather than in consumption. A price band has to be fixed around an average price, taking into account the supply response to the new price regime. The major thrust of domestic stock operations has been toward seasonal price stabilization, whereas imports have been the major instrument for inter-year price stabilization. Carrying buffer stocks for long periods is costly.

Although these public price stabilization schemes based on buffer stocks or trade measures were not efficient, they did lower variability of domestic prices compared to international prices.

The primary beneficiaries of the system were not the consumers or the farmer, but the flour millers, the ration shopowners, and the officials of the government distribution agencies. The subsidies involved were quite high. The Ministry of Food had an interest in larger procurement at a low price, to benefit customers of the food distribution system. The Ministry of Agriculture wanted a high price to please farmers and stimulate production. In Thailand, rice exporters were subsidizing consumers. Domestic rice prices were kept below the international price, and a subsidy of ten per cent below the open market price was provided to consumers. Since the aim was to protect both the consumer and the farmer paradoxes arose, such as taxing farm exports yet providing price support to farmers through the procurement programme.

Export taxes and import subsidies can protect domestic agents from fluctuations in international prices. For example if export taxes rise with international prices, price realizations by domestic farmers would be unchanged. The trouble with this is that a frequent change is required in tax rates, but bureaucracies are not nimble footed. In democracies changes in tax rates have to be approved by parliament. Often one group gains at the expense of another, groups that are hurt can cause further delays. The exchange rate is much more solely within the control of the Central Bank, response times can be fast, and moderate but frequent two-way variation will ensure that gains and losses are evenly distributed and can be covered in forward markets.

Private traders, in both foreign trade and domestic markets, respond to market signals faster, and should be encouraged. They like a wide margin is required between floor and ceiling price, but a more efficient way of stimulating private trade is investment in transport and communication infrastructure and the development of institutions to finance trade. Public stocks have to be adequate to defend floor and ceiling prices. If speculation is absent, public stocks can be smaller. Traders will expect future prices to move in line with the government's projections only if the government has a credible purchase and sales policy.

With improved self-sufficiency as well as growth in per capita incomes, food price fluctuations become less important. In some Asian countries, imports of the basic cereal consumed, as a percentage of net supply, have fallen from double digits in the sixties to single digits in the eighties. But the impact of a price rise on the poorest consumers, and collapse in producers' prices due to an unusually large harvest is still a concern. As markets get better integrated, and transaction costs in trade fall, trade policies become cheaper compared to buffer stocks. Costs of trade contacts and negotiations will fall as use of the Internet becomes widespread. But an improvement in the physical infrastructure, such as port facilities and the links between ports and internal markets is also required.

Macroeconomic implications of food prices need to be worked out more fully and linked to the major re-thinking going on with respect to exchange rate regimes. Most countries had fixed nominal exchange rates through much of the period. The East Asian crisis has underlined the problems associated with fixed exchange rates, but the European crisis before that implicated floating exchange rates. Some kind of exchange rate management is required that allows exchange rates to approach equilibrium exchange rates without large fluctuations. Islam and Thomas (1996) found that although nominal exchange rates were fixed for the countries they studied, still changes in nominal protection rate occurred more due to changes in the real exchange rate, than due to policies to stabilize domestic prices. Simulations showed that under equilibrium exchange rates price variability is lower and benefits from free trade rise, compared to a price band scheme. The implication is that the exchange rate has a major impact on price stabilization; this impact can be leveraged in a systematic way.

There is also very little work on the impact of the exchange rate regime followed on poverty. Since wage adjustment is lagged, particularly for the poor, they suffer if there is a rise in prices of the goods that dominate their consumption basket. As a currency crisis escalates into a recession the major impact is on the poor who loose livelihoods and are often without any buffer. Therefore if an exchange rate policy could help stabilize the price of their food basket and lower the probability of currency crises, it would benefit them.

In a populous developing country, food prices affect poverty in the short-run and inflation in the medium-run, as wages rise with food prices. In an open economy, there is a target level of the real exchange rate that delivers socially acceptable wage rates. If the actual exchange rate is more depreciated than this target, inflation and real appreciation results, as nominal wages rise in an attempt to reach the target wage and prices follow. If the nominal exchange rate is set to equal a sustainable level of domestic food prices to world prices of a basic food grain, and then varied to partially neutralize random world price movements, domestic food prices would be stabilized. Since inflation would be moderated, domestic macroeconomic policy would be freed to improve fundamentals, such as investment and productivity, thus allowing the real exchange rate to move in sustainable directions. The nominal exchange rate would be subject to small random fluctuations compatible with deepening and strengthening foreign exchange markets. These fluctuations would be below those in international food prices, since other measures of food price stabilization can continue to be used. Most developing countries tax agriculture, and shift to subsidizing it only when per capita income levels rise. Therefore tariffs are normally below those permissible under the Uruguay round agreements, and variation in these tariffs is available as another measure of stabilization.

No developing country government will allow very high import dependency in grains, since this may compromise food security. But at current productivity levels, freer trade in food grains is compatible, for many low-income countries, with politically acceptable imports at less than 10 per cent of domestic requirements.

3. An Exchange Rate Based Policy Rule

A rule for determining the nominal exchange rate can be devised, that will moderate inflationary pressures, and stabilize food prices.

Policy Rule: The float of the exchange rate should be managed such that the depreciation of the exchange rate, ε, moves in the opposite direction to πF^{a^*} where πF^{a^*} is the average inflation in world food prices.

The rule would partially offset movements in foreign food prices by opposite changes in the nominal exchange rate. It is written in terms of the depreciation of the exchange rate, ε, and rates of inflation so that it is equivalent to relative purchasing power parity in food products.

If written in levels the rule is equivalent to absolute purchasing power parity. That is, $EP^*_F = P_F$, where E is the nominal exchange rate, and P stands for the nominal price level. $(EP^*_F)/P_F$ is the real food exchange rate. Given exogenous world food prices, $EP^*_F = \bar{P}_F$ determines the feasible level of the nominal exchange rate since it sets domestic food prices at the level $\bar{P}_F$, defined as delivering the socially acceptable wage level. If the relationship in levels determines the level of the nominal exchange rate, it can then be varied according to the relative purchasing power parity rule. If when world food prices rise, the nominal exchange rate appreciates, domestic food prices P_F equated to border prices, will not change. If exports or imports can balance supply to domestic demand at these prices P_F, would be stabilized. Since food price shocks would no longer trigger the wage-price mechanism, inflation would be moderated. Then there would be no rise in poverty in the short-run and in nominal wages, food prices and inflation in the longer run.

Three considerations arise. First, will exports be competitive at the level of E determined? The answer is that since world food prices reflect a higher level of labour productivity in developed countries, the E that gives absolute purchasing power parity with world food prices will have to be depreciated enough to be competitive for the developing country.[5]

Second, if, however, labour productivity is very low so that competitive exports require $E > \bar{E}$, policy would have to concentrate on measures to improve productivity. There will be some inflation, since with a more depreciated nominal exchange rate real wages will be below the target and nominal wages will tend to rise, pushing up prices. But since tariff levels are often low, adjusting tariffs within the WTO feasible range would offer degrees of freedom in stabilizing food prices.

Third, E can be kept at $E > \bar{E}$, above the level that gives the target wages, even if productivity is high enough to have $E > \bar{E}$, in order to stimulate exports. In any case, at this stage, since per capita income levels would be high, food price stabilization would cease to be a major issue; E can be allowed to appreciate and food prices rise.

Fourth, as, productivity rises with development, the bands of variation can be adjusted to allow the real exchange rate to appreciate. A simple way to do this is if E is appreciated fully when world food prices fall, but depreciated less than fully when they rise. The process of adjustment will be smooth, and without excessive exchange rate volatility.

The rule will especially benefit developing countries in which average food budget shares are high, so that food price stabilization has a major impact on inflation. Since trade costs and tariffs provide a margin the rate version of the rule is sufficient; the domestic price level chosen can include some margin over world prices.

Most Asian countries have improved agricultural productivity, over the past few decades, with green revolution technology, so as to reach self-sufficiency in food. But countries in South Asia that have not raised their per capita incomes substantially still have high food budget shares for the majority of the population. The food real exchange rate will reflect the lower productivity of the developing country and allow it to export or import food depending on fluctuations in world food output and price. When food budget shares become low, countries shift from taxing to subsidizing agriculture in order to protect farm incomes. The latter start to shrink[6] as consumer demand diversifies away from food. At this stage farm subsidies are not a major burden on the exchequer as the farm dependent population is small.

Post-Uruguay round changes will benefit developing countries as WTO guidelines, which require all subsidies above 10 per cent to be removed[7] are followed. Export markets will open for their agricultural products. Since their subsidies are normally below permissible norms they will have some scope for protecting agriculture if it becomes necessary. Perhaps that is why the major resistance to implementing the changes is coming from the developed countries, as the Doha round in 2003 demonstrated. The link to border prices of food will help policymakers to resist farm lobbies, which press for higher support prices. What farmers really need are stable prices, not rising ones. Stable procurement prices for grain will give farmers security and export markets for high value added products will give them high risk high return opportunities.

Mild volatility imparted to the nominal exchange rate will justify the effort or the expense of using hedging devices. Since participants in the exchange rate market would be insured against small losses, these would not trigger a panic. International commodity prices would be only one of the factors influencing exchange rate policy therefore market players would not be able to manipulate monetary authorities. If the exchange rate policy is credible enough to anchor expectations, trading will help to achieve the desired variation. After the East Asian crisis the consensus has veered around to some kind of managed float being the best exchange rate policy. If the managed float is to be followed in any case a float linked to international food prices would help to achieve other policy objectives. Macro policy would be freer to stimulate the investment and productivity increases that would allow an eventual appreciation real exchange rate without harming exports.

4. Food Price Stabilization for India

Although a trade and domestic consumption weighted basket of imported prices can be used in more sophisticated applications of the rule, we develop an example of its functioning based on wheat prices. Wheat and rice are the major grains consumed in developing countries; food security issues are tied up with their production, availability, prices and trade. The world rice export market is narrow, but wheat is well developed.

The first 3 columns in Table 1 present the Indian nominal exchange rate in rupees per dollar; price of US wheat in dollars per quintal; and the average Indian free market price of wheat in rupees per quintal. Since there were restrictions on the free movement of wheat across Indian States, wholesale wheat prices show considerable variation across States and over the years. The prices in the table are calculated by taking Rs. 465 as the average for 1997-98 (since the variation in that year was over Rs. 445 to 485). The Government wheat price index, based on an average across weeks, is applied to that level. Official support prices in the active Government procurement and distribution programme are given in the fourth column. The fifth column calculates the wheat exchange rate for India as a ratio of Indian to US wheat prices. The trade and transaction cost factor (also reflecting tariff barriers) t multiplying the price ratio is kept at 0.22. The wheat exchange rate shows that the nominal devaluation of 1992-93 was too steep. If the second stage devaluation had been to our calculated value of 26.59 Rs./$ it would have avoided part of

TABLE 1: The Wheat Exchange Rate for India

Years	E (Rs./$)	P^*_W	P_W	P_s	$\frac{1+tP_w}{P^*_w}$ (Rs./$)	$\frac{1+tP_w\,(1993-94)}{P^*_w}$ (Rs./$)	π(%)
(1)	(2)	(1)	(4)	(5)	(6)	(7)	(8)
1990-91	17.54	11.8	270.8	215	27.99		10.25
1991-92	25.83	15.0	303.7	225	24.7		13.74
1992-93	31.25	14.3	311.7	275	26.59		10.05
1993-94	31.5	14.3	369.8	330	31.55	31.6	8.35
1994-95	31.5	15.7	371	350	28.83	28.75	10.85
1995-96	34.63	21.6	378.4	360	21.37	20.9	7.68
1996-97	35.05	18.1	460.8	380	31.06	24.94	6.36
1997-98	38.03	14.4	465	475	39.4	31.35	4.8
1998-99	41.45	13.1	518.1	510	48.25	34.46	6.9
1999-00	43.42	12.8@	604.4*	550	57.61	35.27	3.0

Note: P^*_W price in $ per quintal of U.S. no.2, Hard Red Winter Wheat (ordinary) f.o.b. Gulf.
@ for July 1999. P_W: free market price of wheat.
*for December 1999. P_s, minimum support price of wheat in rupees per quintal, *t*, imputed transaction cost factor, π measured as the rate of change in the wholesale price index, average of weeks.

Sources: FAO, Geneva (www.fao.org), Economic Survey, various issues, Report of the Commission for Agricultural Costs and Prices (1998).

the subsequent rise in support and free market prices or wheat and the aggregate inflation that brought about a real appreciation of the exchange rate. There were restrictions on trade so that price arbitrage was far from perfect, but part of the justification for the steep rise in domestic support prices was to close the gap between domestic and border prices after the devaluation.

By July 1994 domestic wheat prices had risen by enough to equate the two exchange rates. After that as international prices rose, the nominal exchange rate could have been appreciated, without causing a rise in domestic prices. But policymakers wanted to depreciate the exchange rate somewhat to correct for the real appreciation from past inflation. Domestic wheat prices continued to rise, far beyond what was justified by the depreciation. They rose even though international wheat prices started to fall steeply in 1997-98. The rise was bolstered by steep annual hikes in support prices from 1997. The commodity exchange rate was close to the actual nominal exchange rate again in 1997-98, and then overshot as domestic wheat prices exceeded border prices. Inflation had been falling (column 8) as reforms, restructuring and competition lowered industrial prices. But agricultural prices rose by an unprecedented 25 per cent in the nineties and were responsible for the high inflation of the mid-nineties. Since wages, especially of the poor, rise only with a lag, inflation hurts the poor the most. Food security is defined not only by available quantity, but also affordable price. Early studies showed that rural poverty had hardly been dented by the reform, but later studies showed that poverty fell decisively in the last two years of the nineties.[8] These were the years when inflation fell as border prices began moderating food price increases. Inflation is a very politically sensitive issue. The high inflation of the mid-nineties had brought down the Congress government that initiated the reforms.

Given that industrial prices were falling, stabilizing food prices would have meant a lower rate of inflation. Column 7 gives the level of the nominal exchange rate that, together with freer trade, would have maintained domestic wheat prices at Rs. 370, the level in 1993-94. The nominal exchange rate, international and domestic prices were stable at this level for two years each; suggesting that this was a feasible level for the exchange rate. An appreciation of the exchange rate would have been followed by a return to about Rs. 35 per dollar. If inflation had been lower the depreciation that actually occurred would not have been required. But even if the appreciation chosen had been lower than that shown in column 7, the exchange rate could have been at the year 2000 level, with domestic wheat prices at Rs. 470, much lower than actual levels, and lower inflation.

Further advantages would have been that the two way movement in nominal exchange rates would have encouraged hedging of foreign exchange transactions; bouts of high volatility in exchange rates in 1995 and 1999, that had adverse macroeconomic consequences may have been avoided. In the mid-nineties a steep rise in interest rates led to an industrial slowdown.

The sharp increases in support prices exceeded those recommended by the Commission on Agricultural Costs and Prices (CACP). The farm lobby was able to exert strong political pressures. Benchmarking domestic support prices to border prices would have been a way to side-step these pressures. The farm lobby had long been agitating against domestic grain prices that were lower than international, while exports were restricted. Therefore they could not easily have pressed for support prices that exceeded border prices, especially when industrial prices were falling in a more liberal import regime.

More detailed analysis used monthly data over 1994-97. The price series are stationary in first differences. The coefficient of regressions of domestic on US wheat prices (in first differences) is significantly different from unity, implying that trade arbitrage in wheat is not perfect. The result does not support even relative purchasing power parity in wheat. This is to be expected because trade in grains had many restrictions in this period. But there is a positive correlation coefficient between the two prices of 0.4011; they do move together. The coefficient of variation of US prices at 0.2312 exceeds that of domestic prices at 0.1883. The procurement and food price stabilization policies currently followed have been able to lower domestic food price volatility. In the period of analysis domestic volatility in prices was driven by external volatility plus the variations in the nominal exchange rate. Although Indian monsoons were normal in the period, agricultural output growth was below trend, with regular fluctuations.

The data and simple manipulation with it suggest the rule would have worked well in the nineties. To sum up the policy lessons:

First, if the objective is to stabilize domestic wheat prices the nominal exchange rate should rise (fall) when international wheat prices fall (rise). The nominal exchange rate would then have a coefficient of variation of 0.2 but the real exchange rate would be more stable.

Second, to minimize inflation the rupee can be depreciated less than fully if international grain prices fall, and appreciated less than fully if they rise.

Third, if stimulating exports is a major policy objective, depreciation should be full, but appreciation should be only a fraction of the fall in international prices.

Fourth, domestic output shocks can be offset by trade.

Fifth, trend rise in domestic productivity would require a trend appreciation, which could be achieved by appreciating more and depreciating less over international food price shocks.

The increase in poverty in India immediately after the devaluations of the early nineties was caused by the steep rise in food support prices to match the new border prices. Figures to support this come from the regular surveys of per capita consumption expenditure (PCCE) conducted by the National Sample Survey Organization of India. Since 1972-73 (when the surveys were started) PCCE has been increasing for the rural population in both the states where it is highest (Punjab) and lowest (Bihar). But between 1992 and 1994, years of high agricultural price inflation real PCCE fell by -0.37 and -1.87 per annum respectively in Punjab and Bihar. The inflation precipitated social discontent; the Government imposed monetary tightening to lower inflation before the elections but was voted out of power and the economy slipped into a recession.

In the mid-nineties wheat was at around border prices at the prevailing exchange rates, and oilseeds were protected, and India had a clear comparative advantage in rice, vegetables and fruits (Gulati and Sharma, 1997). If imports of wheat are privatized, but exports remain canalised, prices cannot fall below the border price since government would buy and cannot rise above it since private parties would import. Both the very poor and farmers would be protected from extreme price fluctuations. In wheat production, farmers would get the highest incentive commensurate with low inflation. With the latter, a real appreciation of the exchange rate would not occur. If trade is facilitated in horticulture etc., farmers will have other profitable opportunities. Consumers of such products are less vulnerable to price fluctuations. Farmers would be able to hedge their bets by producing a mixed portfolio: grain, which they could sell at a stable support price, and high risk-high return high-value added products.

The nominal exchange rate would vary with fluctuations in world agricultural prices, but the variation could be restricted to a policy determined band which could be narrower than the variation in world food prices. Hedging devices such as futures are easier to use in foreign exchange markets compared to agricultural markets. With the random fluctuation in the nominal exchange rate, the habit of using them would be encouraged. Use of such risk lowering devices combined with a monetary policy that targets real fundamentals by bringing real interest rates close to world rates would lower the probability of currency crises.

5. Conclusion

Ensuring food security is a vital issue, at low levels of per capita income, because food has the major share in the consumption basket. A large rise in its price has serious consequences in hunger and deprivation. Food security for the poor comes when food is available at prices they can afford. Improvements in agricultural productivity and therefore the supply position, is the necessary long-run solution. But the means used to smooth short-run fluctuations in food prices and make food available at affordable prices to the poor have been food stocks, subsidies and public distribution, taxes and tariffs. Some of these are inefficient and others have been, captured by interest groups. They have provided only partial food security and at high cost.

Meanwhile, the green revolution technology has allowed many developing countries to reach self-sufficiency in food; and, in the post-Uruguay round world they are more open to trade at the margin in agriculture. They no longer fear that it will seriously imperil their food security; for some of them it will open export opportunities. Moreover, the East Asian and other currency crises of the nineties suggest that small managed fluctuations in the exchange rate are desirable. If the exchange rate has to be managed, then the range of variation can be linked to world food prices. This combined with more liberal agricultural trade, can help to stabilize agricultural prices, lower the dependence on other more distortionary policies, and provide a possible resolution for political deadlocks that make it difficult to remove subsidies.

Food prices can be stabilized by a rule that varies the nominal exchange rate to neutralize variations in world food prices. The level of domestic food prices and nominal exchange rate would have to be such that real exchange rates are close to their sustainable levels. These levels would change with productivity growth.

Inflation in India in the nineties was largely fueled by food prices. If the rule had been applied it could have effectively stabilized these and greatly benefited the poor. It would also have curbed high volatility in the exchange rate. Therefore the option should be considered for the future.

ACKNOWLEDGMENT

I thank David Bigman for pointing out to me that the impact of the exchange rate regime on poverty was an important and under researched area; and Anurag Sharma and Soma Dey for research assistance.

NOTES

1. Politicians are especially concerned about this when food comprises a large part of the average budget. But the issue has not received much analytical attention.
2. See, for example, Asian Development Bank Institute (2000), Corden (2002).
3. See Goyal (2003) where these policies are analytically examined and it is argued that they contributed to rapid development.
4. See, Islam and Thomas, 1996.
5. Anderson (1994, p. 17) computes from the historical experience of high-income countries that, for a country that would be self-sufficient in food in a world of free trade, the switch over from taxing to assisting agriculture directly would occur when its per capita income reaches 2.6 times the global average income. If this can be taken to imply that international grain prices reflect a purchasing power of about 3 times the world average, the nominal exchange rate implied by the rule would be competitive. The Indian purchasing power, for example, is below world average, at dollars 360 per capita.
6. In Taiwan and Korea food budget shares fell below fifty per cent in the sixties. In Korea, expenditure on food as a percentage of total expenditure of urban households was 45 per cent in 1960. Income per farm household as a proportion of income per non-farm household fell in Korea from

99.7 in 1965 to 67.1 in 1970. In Taiwan it fell from 94.8 in 1966 to 79.1 in 1971 (see, Francks *et al.*, 1999).

7. Subsidy rates in 2000 were at around 11 per cent for America, 80 per cent for Europe, and 3 per cent for Australia, in food grains. What is worrying is the tendency to shift subsidies under permissible green box or environment related categories. Such tendencies need to be taken up and countered at the WTO level. East Asian countries have protected domestic farmers by preventing imports, rather than subsidizing exports. Since the major grain surplus countries are America, Australia, and perhaps Europe, WTO compliance is not likely to have much impact on grain prices. World prices have been trending downwards since the eighties and this is expected to continue.
8. Poverty ratios based on thin samples conducted by the National Sample Survey Organization (NSSO) showed little evidence of reduction in poverty up till the middle of 1998. The detailed 55th round quinquennial survey of 1999-2000 showed substantial reduction that survived adjustments for non-comparability with the earlier detailed round (see, Datt, 1999, Deaton, 2003). It is clear that poverty fell steeply after 1998.

REFERENCES

Anderson, K., 1994, 'Food Price Policy in East Asia', *Asian-Pacific Economic Literature,* 8(2), 15-30.

Asian Development Bank Institute, 2000, *Newsletter,* January, 2, 1, 1-3, Tokyo, http://www.adbi.org/news/news3.htm

Commission for Agricultural Costs and Prices, 1998, *Report of the Commission for Agricultural Costs and Prices,* Department of Agriculture and Cooperation, Ministry of Agriculture, Government of India, New Delhi.

Corden, W.M., 2002, *Too Sensational: On the Choice of Exchange Rate Regimes,* Cambridge MA: MIT Press.

Datt, G., 1999, 'Has Poverty in India Declined since the Economic Reforms?' *Economic and Political Weekly,* 34, December 11-17.

Deaton, A., 2003, 'Adjusted Indian Poverty Estimates for 1999-2000', *Economic and Political Weekly,* January 25, 38, 4, 322-26.

Francks, P., Boestel, J., and Kim, C.H., 1999, *Agriculture and Economic Development in East Asia,* Routledge, London.

Government of India, *Economic Survey,* Ministry of Finance, Economic Division.

Goyal, A., 2003, 'Agriculture and Industry: Enhancing Mutual Gains', *Decision,* July-December, Vol. 130, No. 2.

Gulati, A. and A. Sharma, 1997, 'Freeing Trade in Agriculture: Implications for Resource Use Efficiency and Cropping Pattern Changes', *Economic and Political Weekly,* 32, December 27, A-155 to A-164.

Islam N. and S. Thomas, 1996, *Foodgrain Price Stabilization in Developing Countries: Issues and Experiences in Asia*, International Food Policy Research Institute: Washington D.C.

Newbery, D.M., and J.E. Stiglitz, 1981, *The Theory of Commodity Price Stabilization: A Study in the Economics of Risk*, Oxford, U.K.: Oxford University Press.

Svensson, L.E.O., 2000, "Open-economy Inflation Targeting", *Journal of International Economics*, 50, 155-83.

Williamson, Jeffrey G., 1991, *Inequality, Poverty and History*, Basil Blackwell.

8

Shadow Economy: A Conceptual and Methodological Policy Frame

AMITABH KUMAR

PERSPECTIVE

The issue of the shadow economy has been an abiding concern for economists, planners, policy makers and the general public down through the years. In the context of the liberalization of markets, the privatization of ownership and the globalization of the economy, the issue has acquired a sharper focus across the development spectrum. In common parlance as well as the steadily burgeoning literature on economic development, the teem shadow economy implies a wide area of economic activity outside the pale of Government accounting. This is customarily referred to as shadow, informal, hidden, black, underground, clandestine, illegal and parallel economy.[1]

Bewildering complexities inherent in the very nature of the shadow economy makes it difficult to hazard a guess about the size of the shadow economy. Recent estimates of the shadow economy place it at $9 trillion worth of output. This estimate is based on seminal study by Schneider and Enste,[2] which aimed at measuring the size of the shadow economy in developed and emerging economies. This study disconcertingly found that underground activity accounted for 15% of the officially reported GDP, on average, in rich economies and around one third of the GDP in the emerging economies. The IMF estimated the official global GDP at $39 trillion in 1998. Accordingly, the size of the shadow economy worked out to around $9 trillion. Clearly it needs no clairvoyance to perceive that the issue of shadow economy is of considerable contemporary significance. This assumes further importance in the light of the close connection between shadow economy and acts of terrorism. Consequently, the issue needs to be looked at in a holistic manner for comprehensive assessment and perspective.

MEANING AND CONCEPT

This paper attempts to measure the size of the shadow economy using a theoretical sound model, a scientific method and few assumptions. It can justifiably be maintained "...the subject of shadow economy seems to arouse a mixture of outrage, guilt, curiosity and incredible admiration" (Cowell, 1985: 1). Despite shadow economy being a "fuzzy concept", it dismays some people but interests quite a lot of them. While different interpretations of its meaning have made it difficult to develop an uniform understanding, researchers have increasingly become conscious of the importance of the shadow economy for the official economy. The shadow economy has been defined in different ways because of the semantic difficulty in conveying various meanings and connotations implicit in the term. Consequently, attempts need to be made to formulate a working definition of the shadow economy in the light of continuity and change in the definition of the shadow economy over the long haul.

In view of the multi-dimensional and multi-layered nature of the shadow economy, the definition has evoked heated debates. Two main strands of this debate relate to the definitional approach (*i.e.*, simply unrecorded economic activity) and the behavioural approach. The proponents of both these approaches differ in their inclusion of components and thus the two sets of definitions cover somewhat different grounds of the shadow economy.

The definitional school of thought argues that it is difficult to provide a formal definition necessitating coverage "of those activities which...are not recorded in the national income accounts".[3] Many refer to the hidden economy as unrecorded national income calculated as the difference between the 'potential' national income for the given currency in circulation and the recorded national income.

In contrast to the definitional approach, the behavioural approach lays stress on the shadow economy in terms of particular behavioural characteristics of activities. It has been persuasively argued that the point of departure between official economic activity and informal activity is "whether activity adheres to the established, prevailing institutional rules of the economy,.... Adherence to the established rules constitutes participation in the formal economy...whereas non-compliance or circumvention of the established rules constitutes participation in the informal economy.[4]

Feige makes a distinction between unreported economic income and unreported fiscal income. While unreported economic income is "under estimation of total economic income", unreported fiscal income is "empirical understatement of total taxable income" (Feige, 1987: 90).

Fortunately, there seems to be consensus about its existence.[5]

The existence of a shadow economy implies that the output of this sector is not reported to the revenue authorities. If the unreported output is taken out of the country, scarce capital is made scarcer and the country's economic development suffers. This is true for developing as well as most developed countries. There may be a case, albeit a weak one, for such transfers of capital from capital-abundant countries. It is a weak case because such capital may be used to finance undesirable activities. If the unreported output is retained within the country, it may be accumulated in the form of gold, cash, real estate (which are mostly unproductive assets and investment in these raise their prices artificially), or may be used up in 'conspicuous consumption'. Taking a chunk out of the productive channels obviously slows economic development. 'Conspicuous consumption' has undesirable 'demonstration effect', motivating non-evaders to follow suit. One can argue that if unreported output is kept in productive channels there will be no ill effects. "One of the major benefits is often considered to be a fact that it is one of the most productive and enterprising sector of the economy, without which the population would be materially much worse off" (Frey, 1989: 11). This argument does not take into account the consequences of the shadow economy on government finances. Public spending has been on an increase in the recent past. In order to finance its ever increasing activities, modern governments rely on taxation. If taxes are not paid, the government will be forced to either increase tax rates, or rely on borrowings, both of which have harmful effects. There is evidence to suggest that the size of the shadow economy increases with a rise in tax rates.[6]

There could be favourable case in terms of reduced distortion of the taxes "...if taxes are distorting and evasion provides a way of overcoming such distortions then the social value of reduced evasion becomes ambiguous" (Cowell, 1985: 34).

It is generally agreed that tax evasion works against horizontal equity since evaders pay less than others having same income. People with high incomes can be expected to evade more since they have better opportunities to evade and face higher rates of taxes. If this is true, evasion works against vertical equity as well.

Measurement of the size of the shadow economy is the central theme of this paper. There are many methods and many estimates for any country. The existing methods suffer from weaknesses, making it imperative to evolve a new one. "On balance existing plans of estimation seem highly questionable, it would, therefore, appear foolish to place too much faith on estimation reported.... Further research along with these lines would appear futile" (Pyle, 1989: 175). Such strong statements cause serious doubts on the existing methods of estimation. A new method is suggested in this paper, mainly based on the work of Professor D.A. Collard of Bath University, U.K. (Collard, 1987). It is based on a functional relationship between tax revenue and administrative expenditure incurred to calculate it.

The shadow economy is a complex phenomena. The fact that it cannot be observed directly renders its direct measurement impossible. The existing estimates are based on different methods of capturing the traces it leaves. Various methodologies have been used for estimating the size of the shadow economy. Let us now attempt to briefly explain some of the major methodologies.

1. Monetary Approach

(i) **Currency ratio:** The key variable here is the ratio of currency in circulation to bank deposits. Gutmann in the United States pioneered this approach. He took 1937-41 as the base period during which he assumed the absence of shadow economy. He treated the desired ratio in the legitimate economy as constant and prescribed changes in the ratio to changes in the size of the shadow economy. The estimate by this method is very sensitive to the choice of the base year. Gutmann also assumed that velocity of circulation is the same in both the reported as well as unreported sectors of the economy; an assumption which is yet to be proved. Gutmann's another assumption that currency is the sole medium of transaction in the shadow economy does not seem to be necessarily true. O'Higgins found the currency ratio declining in UK during 1963-81 and rightly concluded that this method cannot be used to estimate the size of the shadow economy (O'Higgins, 1989: 189-90).

(ii) **Transaction ratio:** On the basis of the quantity theory of money MV = PT, Feige pioneered this method to estimate the size. This method looked at the relationship between the total value of transaction in the economy and the recorded GNP. Any increase in the ratio of these two is attributed to an increase in the size of a shadow economy. While estimating the size of the shadow economy in the USA, he took 1939 as the base year and assumed that there was no shadow economy in that year. His estimates are sensitive to these two assumptions. Feige also made assumptions regarding life of paper currency. "It is worrying...that his estimates are so sensitive to changes in some of his assumptions" (Pyle, 1989: 29). Feige too assumed that cost is the sole medium of transaction in the shadow economy, which remains unproved.

(iii) **Big-Bill phenomena:** This method hypothesizes that an increase in the relative importance of high dimension currency notes indicates an increase in the size of the shadow economy. It suffers from the assumption of cash being the sole medium of transaction in the shadow economy. Pyle feels that "currency hoardings *per se* are an unpromising indicator" of the size of the shadow economy (Pyle, 1989: 30). O'Higgins did not find this method useful for UK and cites other attempts by Macfee and Feige which were unsuccessful as well (O'Higgins, 1989: 179). O'Higgins concluded that inflation has "substitution" as well as "nominal income" effects on currency hoarding and hence, cannot provide good estimates, a view shared by other researchers.

There are shortcomings common to all methods with the monetary approach. First, that these methods can give an idea how much has been the increase in the size of the shadow economy rather than provide an estimate of its size. Second, these methods do not account for currency irretrievable lost or destroyed. Third, the assumption that all transactions in the shadow economy are paid for in cash has not been proved. Lastly, the choice of the base year is crucial to the estimates.

2. Discrepancy Approach

(i) **Macro-level income-expenditure discrepancy:** GDP can be measured either by aggregating the total expenditure or total income of the country. It is assumed that all that is earned is not reported but spent. The difference between the expenditure measure of the GDP and the income measure of the GDP provides an estimate of the size of the shadow economy. It is important to bear in mind that under the assumption made above the expenditure measure of the GDP should always exceed the income measure of the GDP. In other words, the residuals should be positive. The measurement of income and expenditure suffer from errors due to difference in statistical coverage. The entire residual cannot be attributed to the shadow economy since part of it can be due to random component of measurement error (Mathews and Rastogi, 1985: 21).

(ii) **Micro-level income-expenditure discrepancy:** Another way to estimate the size of the shadow economy is to calculate the discrepancy between incomes and expenditures at the micro-level, *i.e.*, the household level. The assumption here again is that the household does not report all its income but spends the entire income somewhere. The survey of a small random sample of households can be made and inferences about the population can be easily drawn. The main problem in such surveys is the non-response of the participating households. Another shortcoming of this approach lies in the insufficient quality of the income data, especially with respect to the self-employed. This method is very sensitive to assumption about hidden economic activity of the non-respondents (O'Higgins, 1989). Whether the sample is truly representative of the population will have an important bearing on the estimate. Big time evaders would normally not respond and small time evaders may doctor their responses (Pyle, 1989). Much reliance cannot be placed on the responses in the surveys of this kind especially when respondents suspect some kind of link with the revenue authorities.

(iii) **Labour market participation rate discrepancy:** This method of estimating the size of the shadow economy is based on the difference between official labour force participation rate and the actual labour force participation rate determined by survey. Estimate depends on the assumption about labour productivity in the two sectors. Estimate can suffer from sampling errors. It is doubtful whether surveys can establish a true participation rate. Responses in surveys of this nature usually suffer from wariness of respondents to come out with the truth.

3. Causal Approach

(i) One way of estimating the size of the shadow economy is to look at a number of variables that can influence it or explain it. Tanzi (Tanzi, 1982) developed one such model by using a modified currency ratio originally developed by Cagan in the USA. The explanatory variables in this model are tax rate, share of wage and salary in personal income, real per capita income and interest rate on time deposits. If the predictors can explain most of the variations in the currency ratio, the dependent variable, each of the predictors can be cause for a change in the currency ratio. Changes in the currency ratio can provide estimates of the size of the shadow economy. Tanzi's regression equations have R^2 exceeding 94 per cent and all the coefficients are statistically significant and of the expected sign (Tanzi, 1982: 80-83). This model suffers from all the weaknesses of the models following the monetary approach in spite of its refinements (Pyle, 1989: 22-24).

(ii) **Soft-modeling approach:** Frey, Pommerehne and Weck pioneered this approach. The unobservable size of the shadow economy is the dependent variable in this model. A number of predictors, of which data is available or can be obtained, are used in this analysis. Different values of the parameters to be estimated are plugged in based on prior information and result to see which of the analysis give the best result. Having obtained the values of the parameters thus, the size of the shadow economy can be calculated. The estimate is quite sensitive to the model specification and the guesses about the parameters.

4. Direct Approach

This method is based on random audit of tax pay returns as is done in USA under the Taxpayers' Compliance Measurement Programme (TCMP). However, this cannot be used in all countries unless their laws permit it.

This examination of various methods used to estimate the size of the shadow economy clearly brings to the fore their inherent weaknesses, which inspire little confidence. Consequently, there is need for a different approach, a paradigm shift. While a new approach to the problem of estimation outlined below may not find universal acceptability, we firmly believe that all options need to be explored and out-of-box thinking need not be summarily dismissed.

A good model should not only be theoretically sound but also be capable of unambiguous interpretation. It is important that possibility of empirical testing and validation of the model should exist. The number of assumptions and restrictions on the parameters and variables should be few as well as plausible. The fewer the number of assumptions or restrictions, the greater is the reliability of the results.

Tax revenue is a function of administrative expenditure and other things as tax rates, number of taxpayers, tax laws, etc. I am considering a restricted model in which tax revenue is a function of administrative expenditure; the other factors are treated exogenous. Administrative expenditure keeps changing year to year and is under full control of the government. Tax laws are relatively stable. There is little control over the number of taxpayers.

I. MODEL 1: COLLARD CURVE

This formulation is due to Collard (1987). Tax revenue is a function of the administrative expenditure incurred by tax authority. Collard assumed that there will be no revenue when there is no administrative expenditure and, therefore, the curve passes through the origin. The function increases at a decreasing rate. This means that tax revenue increases with administrative expenditure, but at a decreasing rate. In other words, each additional wing of administrative expenditure brings more revenue, but each successive dose brings lesser amount of revenue than the previous one. To be precise, administrative expenditure faces decreasing returns in terms of tax revenue. A function capturing these characteristics is a negative exponential function. The asymptote in this case is the maximum possible tax yield. As administrative expenditure increases, tax revenue increases, at a decreasing rate, and gets nearer to the maximum possible tax yield. The difference between the actual tax calculation and the maximum possible yield can provide estimate of the size of the shadow economy. This model was developed by Collard to obtain a point estimate of the size of the shadow economy (Collard, 1987). The negative exponential relationship can be expressed as:

T = M* [1 – exp (-w*X)]

T = multiplication

exp( ) = e^0

w = ratio of first derivative to the second derivative with respect to X of this equation and

X = administrative expenditure

Collard derived the size of the shadow economy, q:

q = s/t = (1/t) * [exp (w**X) - 1] ** (-1);

q = size of the shadow economy

s = (M – T)/T

t is the average rate on tax on unreported income relevant to that on disclosed income

** = power

He took the basic rate on personal income as the rate applicable on reported income and assumed the next higher rate as the one applicable to unreported income. These two rates were 0.3 and 0.4 at that point of time in the United Kingdom and gave a value of 1.33 for 't'. This model is sensitive to the assumption regarding the tax rates and is also sensitive to the implicit assumption of independence of M and X. Collard used it for a point estimation of the size of the shadow economy and used the data provided by the tax authorities for both average rate of tax as well as marginal rate of tax. However, tax authorities do not provide the basis for calculation of the average and marginal rate. In order to avoid the pitfalls of such assumption and also to have a calculation based on time series, a modified equation was used which is:

$$T_i = M_i (1 - \exp[-w * X_i])$$

where i stands for time period.

It is possible to factor the changes in the GDP over time. Please remember 'M' will change over a period of time due to various factors like tax rates, number of taxpayers etc.

II. MODEL 2: LOGISTIC CURVE

It is possible that revenue — administrative expenditure function tax shapes other than the Collard curve. For example, it can have an intercept. It seems plausible that tax revenue increases at an increasing rate initially, and after some time the increases decline progressively. This can be captured in the logistic curve. The function having these properties can be recognized

$$T_i = M_i / [2 * \exp(a+b*X_i)]$$

T = actual tax revenue

M = maximum possible tax yield

a = intercept on the Y-axis for X = 0

b = the rate at which revenue changes from the initial value to the final value, or, the rate of change coefficient

X = administrative expenditure

i = time period

The restrictions for this model are that M_i is always positive and b is negative. Intuitively, existence of shadow economy would mean that actual tax revenue is always less than the maximum possible tax yield. There is some kind of relationship between the maximum tax yield and the GDP. Taxable income depends on GDP and should vary with changes in the GDP. Given the tax rates, the tax laws and the number of taxpayers, one plausible assumption can be that the maximum possible tax yield is some percentage of the GDP, which can be found out from the actual national statistics.

The Collard curve as well as the logistic curve seems theoretically sound. Very few assumptions are necessary for estimation of these models although non-linear least squares technique may be required for their estimation. These models can further be refined by incorporating non-constant rates of growth of the maximum possible tax yield.

Using these two models, both by non-linear estimation as well as linear estimation, the size of the shadow economy for the United Kingdom was estimated between 5-8 per cent of the GDP in the year 1988-89.

CONCLUSION

Despite significant differences in the size and composition of the shadow economy across countries, regions, levels of development and time periods, the omnipresence of the shadow economy can hardly be doubted. Recent efforts have led to a heightened consciousness of the need to measure the size of shadow economy by accurate and obtainable data and its validation by rigorous mathematical examination. Exclusion of the shadow economy leads to a lopsided view of basic macroeconomic variables, including output, employment and inflation. This has deleterious impact both on policy formulation and policy implementation at all levels. This paper is a modest exploratory effort in moving towards greater precision and analytical rigour in estimating the shadow economy and may lead to suitable policy prescriptions.

NOTES

1. Thomas J. (1992).
2. Schneider, Friedrich and Enste, Dominick H. (2000).
3. Thomas (1999).
4. Feige, Edgar L. (1990).
5. See Frey and Pommerehne, 1982: 3; Alassandrini and Dallago, 1987, Introduction; Cowell, 1985: 11. It is regarded as a serious problem even in developed economies. "Tax evasion is quantitatively a non-negligible problem in advance western style economies" (Cowell, 1985: 1).
6. Tax rate is one of the predictors in the model developed by Tanzi measuring the size of the shadow economy. Tanzi found tax variable highly significant and with the expected positive sign. He concludes that the higher tax rates bring about the greater use of currency presumably through an evasion effect (Tanzi, 1982).

REFERENCES

Alessandrini & Dallago (1987), "Introduction" in Alessandrini & Dallago (ed.), *The Unofficial Economy,* 1987, Gower Publishing Co. Ltd., England.

Annual Reports of the Board of Inland Revenue, *HMSO,* London.

Collard, D.A. (1987), "A Quick and Lazy Measure of the Shadow Economy" Working Paper, University of Bath, UK.

Cowell, F.A. (1985), "The Economics of Tax Evasion: A Survey" Discussion Paper No. 80, London School of Economics, London.

Dilnot & Morris (1982), "What Do We Know About the Black Economy in the United Kingdom" in Tanzy, B. (ed.), *The Underground Economy in the United States and Abroad,* 1982, D.C. Health & Co., Toronto, Canada.

Economic Trends Annual Supplement, 1990, *HMSO,* London.

Feige, Edgar L. (1990), "Defining and Estimating Underground and Informal Economies: The New Institutional Economies Approach," World Development, 18, No. 7, 989-1002.

Feige, E.L. (1987), "The Anatomy of the Underground Economy" in Alessandrini & Dallago (ed.), 1987, op. cit.

Frey, B.S. (1989), "How large (or small) should the underground economy be?" In Feige, E.L. (ed.). *The Underground Economies,* Cambridge University Press, Cambridge, UK.

Frey & Pommerehne (1982), "Measuring the Hidden Economy: Though This Be Madness, There is Method in it" in Tanzy, V. (ed.), 1982, op. cit.

Lewis, A. (1982), *Psychology of Taxation,* Martin Robertson & Co. Ltd., Oxford, UK.

Macafee, K. (1982), "A Glimple of the Hidden Economy in the National Accounts of the United Kingdom" Tanzy, V. (ed.), 1982, op. cit.

Mathew, K. & Rastogi, A. (1985), "Little Mo and the Moonlighters: Another Look at the Black Economy". *Quarterly Economic Bulletin of the Liverpool Group in Macroeconomics*, Vol. 6, No. 2, 1985.

O'Higgins, M. (1989), "Assessing the underground economy in the United Kingdom" in Feige, E.L. (ed.), 1989, op. cit.

Pyle, D.J. (1989), *Tax Evasion and the Black Economy*, Macmillan, London.

Schneider, Friedrich and Enste, Dominick, H. (2000), "Shadow Economies: Size, Causes and Consequences" (2000) — *The Journal of Economic Literature*.

Skolka, J. (1987), "A Few Facts About the Hidden Economy" in Alessandrini & Dallago (ed.), 1987, op. cit.

Smith, S. (1986), *Britain's Shadow Economy*, Oxford University Press, Oxford, UK.

Tanzi, B. (1982), "Underground Economy and Tax Evasion in the United States, Estimations and Implications" in Tanzi, V. (ed.), 1982, op. cit.

Thomas (1999), op. cit.

Thomas, J. (1992), "Informal Economic Activity", Ann Arbor, University of Michigan Press.

Wiles, P. (1987), "The Second Economy, its Definitional Problems" in Alessandrini & Dallago (ed.), 1987, op. cit.

9

FISCAL REFORMS IN INDIA SINCE 1991: A CRITICAL ASSESSMENT

AJIT KUMAR SINGH

INTRODUCTION

The Government of India launched economic reforms in July 1991 with the objective of macro-economic stabilization and acceleration of the rate of growth of the economy. The reform package, which marked a significant departure from the policy regime followed during the past forty years, covered a number of policy dimensions including fiscal policy, trade policy, industrial policy, agricultural policy, foreign exchange management policy, among others. This paper seeks to have a critical look at the fiscal reforms at the Central and State levels and examines the progress particularly in terms of the targets of fiscal deficits.

Containment of fiscal deficit within reasonable limits is an essential condition for macroeconomic stabilization and success of economics reforms. Fiscal deficit is regarded as the best available summary indicator of the macroeconomic impact of the budget (Chelliah, 1996: 55-56). It is generally believed that excessive government borrowing tends to crowd out private investment and adds to public debt. It has other deleterious consequences as well. As Acharya points out: "Such deficits tend to crowd out private investment, increase inflationary potential, weaken the balance of payments, render financial sector reforms more difficult and impose a serious burden on future generations" (Acharya, 2002: 1522).

During the recent discussion of fiscal policy in India

attention has shifted from the traditional concept of budgetary deficit or deficit financing (measured by borrowing of the GoI from RBI) to the larger concept of fiscal deficit, which indicates net borrowing by the government. In the literature several concepts of deficits have come in vogue, *viz.* fiscal deficit, revenue deficit, primary deficit and monetized deficit. Fiscal deficit is the most comprehensive concept and refers to the expenditure financed by borrowing (*i.e.* total expenditure minus total revenue plus non-debt capital receipts). Revenue deficit refers to the difference between current revenues and revenue expenditure. Primary deficit refers to the difference between borrowing and interest payment. Monetised deficit refers to the borrowings from RBI leading to an increase in reserve money. Though attention is generally focused upon fiscal deficit, reduction in revenue deficit and primary deficit is equally important policy objective. Keeping check on monetized deficit is important because of its implications for expansion of money supply and inflation in the economy.

FISCAL DEFICITS IN 1980s

Reduction in fiscal deficit has been an important policy objective of the Government and received much attention in the earlier years of the reform period. In fact, the high fiscal deficits of the eighties are widely believed in academic circles as the root cause of the 1991 economic crisis (Bajpai and Sachs, 1999: 82-83; Acharya, 2002: 1522; Joshi and Little, 1996: 15). A quick look at the trends in fiscal deficits during the eighties would be highly pertinent at this point.

The Government of India followed an expansionist fiscal policy based on increasing domestic and external borrowing during the eighties to boost the economy. The GFD (Gross Fiscal Deficit) of the Central Government, which averaged around 5 per cent of GDP in the beginning of the 1980s shot up sharply to around 8 per cent of GDP in 1990-91 (Table 1). The combined GFD of the Central and the State Governments exceeded 10 per cent of GDP in the second half of the eighties.

The expansionary fiscal policy had the desired impact on the growth rate of the economy, which jumped to around 5.5 per cent during 1980-90, markedly above the Hindu rate of growth of the previous decades. But it also resulted in a

TABLE 1: Trends in Fiscal Deficit of Central and State Governments (as % of GDP): 1981-2004

Year	Central Government			State Governments			Central and State Governments combined		
	Gross Fiscal Deficit	Gross Primary Deficit	Revenue Deficit	Gross Fiscal Deficit	Gross Primary Deficit	Revenue Deficit	Gross Fiscal Deficit	Gross Primary Deficit	Revenue Deficit
1	2	3	4	5	6	7	8	9	10
1980-81	5.75	3.94	1.41	2.57	1.72	-1.03	8.32	5.66	0.38
1981-82	5.11	3.23	0.23	2.40	1.55	-0.81	7.51	4.78	-0.58
1982-83	5.63	3.54	0.69	2.64	1.74	-0.47	8.27	5.28	0.22
1983-84	5.93	3.75	1.16	2.89	2.00	-0.10	8.82	5.75	1.06
1984-85	7.05	4.63	1.71	3.32	2.32	0.37	10.37	6.95	2.08
1985-86	7.80	5.12	2.10	2.68	1.63	-0.23	10.48	6.75	1.87
1986-87	8.40	5.45	2.48	2.96	1.65	-0.05	11.36	7.10	2.43
1987-88	7.61	4.44	2.57	3.16	1.78	0.31	10.77	6.22	2.88
1988-89	7.30	3.93	2.48	2.76	1.35	0.43	10.06	5.28	2.91
1989-90	7.31	3.66	2.44	3.16	1.69	0.75	10.47	5.35	3.19
1990-91	7.85	4.07	3.26	3.30	1.78	0.93	11.15	5.85	4.19
1991-92	5.56	1.49	2.49	2.89	1.22	0.86	8.45	2.71	3.35
1992-93	5.38	1.22	2.49	2.80	1.03	0.68	8.18	2.25	3.17
1993-94	7.01	2.74	3.81	2.40	0.56	0.44	9.41	3.30	4.25
1994-95	5.71	1.35	3.07	2.74	0.82	0.61	8.45	2.17	3.68

TABLE 1 (Contd.)

Year	Central Government			State Governments			Central and State Governments combined		
	Gross Fiscal Deficit	Gross Primary Deficit	Revenue Deficit	Gross Fiscal Deficit	Gross Primary Deficit	Revenue Deficit	Gross Fiscal Deficit	Gross Primary Deficit	Revenue Deficit
1	2	3	4	5	6	7	8	9	10
1995-96	5.10	0.86	2.52	2.66	0.80	0.69	7.76	1.66	3.21
1996-97	4.90	0.53	2.40	2.74	0.86	1.18	7.64	1.39	3.58
1997-98	5.87	1.54	3.06	2.92	0.93	1.08	8.79	2.47	4.14
1998-99	6.43	2.01	3.85	4.21	2.18	2.48	10.64	4.19	6.33
1999-00	5.40	0.74	3.48	4.72	2.39	2.77	9.54	3.82	6.26
2000-01	5.64	0.92	4.05	4.25	1.79	2.54	9.49	3.70	6.59
2001-02	6.13	1.45	4.36	4.64	1.83	2.63	10.32	3.97	6.99
2002-03(RE)	5.89	1.20	4.24	4.16	1.23	1.95	9.51	3.11	6.19
2003-04(BE)	5.60	1.11	4.09	NA	NA	NA	NA	NA	NA

Source: Reserve Bank of India, *Hand Book of Statistics on Indian Economy, 2002.*

persistent deficit in the current account and sharp jump in inflation rates, ultimately leading to the economic crisis of 1991.

TRENDS IN FISCAL DEFICITS IN 1990s

Reduction in fiscal deficit has been an important target variable of every Finance Minister, while presenting the annual budget since Manmohan Singh's budget of 1991-92. Budget targets have, however, gone awry in almost every year. Only in the first two budgets of Manmohan Singh, that is 1991-92 and 1992-93 budgets, there was a sharp reduction in GFD over the previous levels, which was brought about by a severe compression of government expenditure under IMF pressure. However, as soon as these pressures eased, GFD shot up sharply during 1993-94, but was brought down in the next three years. But GFD of the Central Government again went up in the subsequent years and reached the figure of 6.43 per cent during 1998-99 and has remained above 5 per cent of GDP in the last few years (Table 1). Though GFD is considerably lower than the high levels witnessed in the late eighties, the recent trends show inability of the Central Government to bring down fiscal deficit further.

The revenue deficit of the Central Government have, on the other hand, gone up during the reform period and have been hovering around 4 per cent of GDP in the last few years. Revenue deficit, in fact, now accounts for over two-thirds of the GFD. Thus, the government is borrowing to meet its current expenditure against the norms of prudent public finance. Primary deficits have also proved to be sticky.

The combined GFD of the State Governments as per cent of GDP came down from 3.30 per cent in 1990-91 to 2.40 per cent in 1993-94, but went up in the subsequent years, particularly after 1996-97 (Table 1). In last few years it has averaged over 4 per cent of GDP. Equally alarming is the sharp jump in the ratio of combined revenue deficit of all State Governments.

Let us now look at the trends in the combined fiscal deficit of the Centre and the State governments. The combined GFD of the Centre and the States came down from the high levels of the late eighties touching the lowest level of 7.64 per cent of GDP in 1996-97 (Table 1). But it rose sharply thereafter and exceeded the alarming figure of 10 per cent during the last few years. The combined revenue deficit has almost doubled by the end of the nineties as compared to the end of the eighties. The same is true of the combined primary deficit.

To sum up the above trends, our analysis reveals that though some progress in controlling fiscal and revenue deficits was made in the early years of economic reforms, there have been significant slippages since then and we are almost back to the same stage which sparked the crisis of 1991. Both fiscal and revenue deficits have gone up in the last five years or so. The level of primary deficit also remains high. What is more worrisome is the fact that revenue deficit now accounts for over two-thirds of the fiscal deficit.

Let us now examine the underlying factors behind these trends.

Revenue Trends

Whatever fiscal adjustment was brought about was on the expenditure side rather than the revenue side. In fact, during the nineties the ratio of central tax revenue to GDP has witnessed a decline of about 1.5 per cent point — from around 10.5 per cent to around 9.0 per cent (Table 2). The ratio of direct taxes to GDP registered a welcome jump as a result of the tax reforms, which aimed at reduction in tax rates to improve tax compliance and broadening of the tax base. This was, however, more than offset by the decline in the share of indirect taxes following the efforts at reduction of tariffs and nationalisation of excise duties as part of the reform policy.

The decline in the tax-GDP ratio at the Central level is a matter of serious concern as it affects the process of fiscal restructuring and adds to fiscal strain. Non-tax revenues of the Centre have also remained stagnant throughout the nineties. At the state level the tax-GDP ratio has remained more or less constant, but there has been a decline of about 1 per cent point in non-tax receipts (Table 2). Thus, both the Central and the State Governments, for political considerations have failed to mobilize tax and non-tax resources to improve their financial position. This is a most disappointing failure of the Indian public finances of the past decade.

TABLE 2: Trends in Tax and Non-Tax Receipts of Central and State Governments (as % of GDP): 1981-2003

Year	Central Government					State Governments		
	Gross Tax Receipts			Non-Tax Revenue	Capital Receipts	Tax Receipts	Non-Tax Receipts	Aggregate
	Direct	Indirect	Total					
1	2	3	4	5	6	7	8	9
1980-81	2.01	7.09	9.10	2.09	5.48	7.21	4.08	15.07
1981-82	2.10	7.24	9.34	2.05	5.22	7.37	3.52	14.25
1982-83	2.05	7.30	9.35	2.34	6.2	7.48	3.71	14.78
1983-84	1.97	7.45	9.42	1.94	6.56	7.17	3.76	15.01
1984-85	1.87	7.62	9.49	2.36	6.65	7.34	3.77	15.56
1985-86	1.99	8.23	10.22	2.46	6.89	7.78	4.14	16.61
1986-87	1.97	8.48	10.45	2.79	6.88	8.00	4.19	16.3
1987-88	1.88	8.70	10.58	2.54	7.15	8.15	4.23	16.83
1988-89	2.07	8.42	10.49	2.32	7.06	7.82	4.08	15.93
1989-90	2.04	8.54	10.58	2.86	6.15	8.02	3.58	15.71
1990-91	1.94	8.17	10.11	2.11	6.86	7.84	3.85	16.03
1991-92	2.33	7.97	10.30	2.44	5.9	8.05	4.28	16.5
1992-93	2.43	7.55	9.98	2.69	4.84	8.09	4.10	16.21
1993-94	2.36	6.45	8.81	2.56	6.45	8.01	4.28	15.62

TABLE 2 (Contd.)

Year	Central Government					State Governmentsr		
	Gross Tax Receipts			Non-Tax Revenue	Capital Receipts	Tax Receipts	Non-Tax Receipts	Aggregate
	Direct	Indirect	Total					
1	2	3	4	5	6	7	8	9
1994-95	2.67	6.47	9.14	2.34	6.8	7.98	4.13	16.44
1995-96	2.84	6.57	9.41	2.39	4.94	7.86	3.71	15.27
1996-97	2.86	6.60	9.46	2.39	4.52	7.79	3.43	14.37
1997-98	3.19	6.00	9.19	2.52	6.54	8.03	3.21	15.19
1998-99	2.64	5.51	8.15	2.54	7.37	7.29	2.72	14.91
1999-00	2.13	4.48	6.62	2.74	5.97	7.57	3.12	16.04
2000-01	2.32	4.18	6.49	2.65	6.37	8.01	3.29	16.61
2001-02	2.10	3.71	5.82	2.95	7.01	8.20	3.58	17.17
2002-03(RE)	2.46	4.17	6.64	2.94	6.76	8.70	3.72	17.24

Source: Reserve Bank of India, *Hand Book of Statistics on Indian Economy, 2002.*

Expenditure Policies

The burden of fiscal adjustment, in the above circumstances, has fallen on the expenditure side wholly. The Central Government was relatively more successful in restraining the growth of its total expenditure. Thus, the ratio of expenditure to GDP fell perceptibly from around 19 per cent at the beginning of the nineties to around 15 per cent in 1996-97 (Table 3). Since then it has remained in the vicinity of 16 per cent of GDP. However, the quality of expenditure adjustment was not appropriate as whatever compression took place was on the capital side rather than on the revenue side.

TABLE 3: Trends in Revenue and Capital Expenditure of the Central Government (as % to GDP): 1981-2003

Year	Revenue Expenditure	Interest Payments	Subsidies	Defence Expenditure	Capital Expenditure	Capital Outlay	Total Expenditure
1980-81	9.98	1.80	1.40	2.50	5.79	2.13	15.77
1981-82	9.09	1.89	1.15	2.55	5.82	2.48	14.91
1982-83	9.92	2.09	1.20	2.66	6.38	2.47	16.30
1983-84	10.13	2.18	1.32	2.65	6.05	2.38	16.17
1984-85	11.22	2.42	1.64	2.86	6.46	2.73	17.67
1985-86	12.10	2.68	1.71	2.85	6.69	2.73	18.79
1986-87	13.03	2.95	1.74	3.34	7.03	2.95	20.06
1987-88	12.99	3.17	1.68	3.37	6.21	2.61	19.21
1988-89	12.78	3.37	1.83	3.15	5.90	2.42	18.68
1989-90	13.16	3.64	2.15	2.96	5.88	2.42	19.05
1990-91	12.93	3.78	2.14	2.71	5.59	2.13	18.51
1991-92	12.60	4.07	1.88	2.50	4.46	1.74	17.05
1992-93	12.40	4.16	1.60	2.35	4.00	1.82	16.41
1993-94	12.59	4.28	1.48	2.54	3.92	1.54	16.51
1994-95	12.09	4.36	1.28	2.30	3.82	1.47	15.92
1995-96	11.83	4.23	1.13	2.27	3.25	1.19	15.08
1996-97	11.67	4.37	1.20	2.17	3.09	1.04	14.76
1997-98	11.90	4.33	1.29	2.33	3.41	1.16	15.31
1998-99	12.34	4.42	1.41	2.26	3.51	1.02	15.85
1999-00	12.85	4.65	1.26	2.43	2.52	1.24	15.38
2000-01	13.20	4.71	1.27	2.35	2.26	1.17	15.47
2001-02	13.13	4.68	1.35	2.36	2.64	1.15	15.78
2002-03(RE)	13.83	4.68	1.80	2.26	2.52	1.22	16.35

Source: Reserve Bank of India, *Hand Book of Statistics on Indian Economy, 2002.*

The expenditure on interest payment has gone up by almost one percentage point over the last decade — from around 3.8 per cent of GDP to around 4.6 per cent of GDP. Interest payments by the Central Government account for over one-third of revenue expenditure and around 70 per cent of the net tax receipts. Subsidies, however, show a clear decline both as a percentage of GDP and revenue expenditure.

Fiscal slippages at the state level are even more glaring. Total expenditure as well as revenue expenditure of State governments has gone up by almost one percentage point of GDP (Table 4). While expenditure on social services as a proportion of GDP has remained stable that on economic services has declined. Interest payment, on the other hand, shows a sharp jump as also expenditure on general services. The inability to check the growth of revenue expenditure has led to the crowding out of capital expenditure, which shows a sharp decline as a per cent of GDP (Table 4).

TABLE 4: Trends in State Expenditure

Item of Expenditure	Percentage of States' Expenditure to GDP		Growth Rate (Per cent per annum)	
	1990-91	1999-2000	1985-95	1990-2000
Total Revenue Expenditure	12.62	13.68	15.16	13.92
1. General Services	4.03	5.68	17.85	16.84
Of which — interest payment	1.52	2.30	19.99	17.39
2. Social Services	4.92	5.09	13.30	13.82
Education	2.73	2.91	14.44	14.09
Health and Family Welfare	0.81	0.75	12.58	12.71
3. Economic Services	3.67	2.91	14.41	9.75
Agriculture and Allied activities	1.10	0.88	13.33	9.83
Rural Development	0.88	0.69	13.20	9.35
Irrigation	0.60	0.48	11.99	11.53
Power	0.17	0.29	29.33	14.59
Industry and Minerals	0.21	0.12	11.40	8.12
Transport and Communications	0.41	0.29	13.95	9.77
4. Capital Expenditure	2.37	1.81	9.48	10.55
Total Expenditure	14.62	15.50	14.24	13.48

Source: Acharya, 2002.

Possibly the single most important factor which has been responsible for the deterioration of the public finances both at the central and the state level has been the hefty salary hike which was given to the Central Government employees following the recommendations of the Fifth Pay Commission (FPC). Given the political compulsions of the situation the State Governments, one after another, also increased the salaries of their employees as well as those of the aided educational institutions and local bodies. In the last five years the compensation to employees of the Centre, States and UTs more than doubled going up from Rs. 63,710 crore in 1995-96 to Rs. 1,33,381 crore in 1999-2000 (Acharya, 2002: 1531). Over the same period the compensation to employees as per cent of GDP went up from 5.4 to 6.9. Many economists have commented upon the adverse consequences of this on savings and investments in the economy (Acharya, 2002; Lahiri, 2000; Rao, 2002).

Trends in Debt Indicators

To deal with the problem of the ever-growing interest burden, it is imperative to reduce the indebtedness of the Central as well as the State Governments. However, there has been little progress in this regard (Table 5). The domestic liabilities of the Central as well as the State Governments as a proportion of GDP have remained more or less static during the nineties. However, after 1998-99 the ratio shows a sharp rise. There has, however, been a marked improvement as far as external liabilities are concerned.

FISCAL RESPONSIBILITY BILL 2000

With a view to bring down the revenue and fiscal deficit of the Central Government and put a cap on its borrowings, the Government of India introduced the Fiscal Responsibility and Budget Management (FRBM) Bill in the Parliament in December 2000. After much procrastination, the bill was finally adopted in the Parliament in a diluted form in 2003 and came into force on 5 July 2004 as an Act.

The objective of the FRBM bill was: "To provide for the responsibility of the Central Government to ensure inter-generational equity in fiscal management and long-term

TABLE 5: Selected Debt Indicators of Central and State Governments (as % to GDP)

Year	Domestic Liabilities of Centre	External Liabilities of Centre	Total Liabilities of Centre (2+3)	Total Liabilities of States	Combined Domestic Liabilities of Centre & States	Combined Total Liabilities of Centre & States
1980-81	33.60	7.80	41.40	16.60	38.40	46.40
1981-82	33.00	7.30	40.30	16.40	38.10	45.90
1982-83	37.70	7.20	44.90	17.30	42.50	50.00
1983-84	36.50	6.90	43.40	17.30	41.50	48.40
1984-85	39.20	6.70	45.90	18.10	44.90	51.80
1985-86	42.60	6.50	49.10	19.10	48.20	55.20
1986-87	46.60	6.50	53.10	19.40	52.40	59.30
1987-88	48.50	6.50	55.00	19.70	54.30	61.00
1988-89	48.20	6.10	54.30	19.10	54.10	60.40
1989-90	49.20	5.80	55.00	19.30	55.40	61.40
1990-91	49.80	5.50	55.30	19.40	56.20	61.70
1991-92	48.60	5.70	54.30	19.30	55.20	60.90
1992-93	48.10	5.70	53.80	19.00	54.90	60.50
1993-94	50.10	5.50	55.60	18.60	57.00	62.50
1994-95	48.30	5.00	53.30	18.30	55.20	60.10
1995-96	47.00	4.30	51.30	18.00	54.00	58.00
1996-97	45.60	4.00	49.60	17.90	52.80	56.50
1997-98	47.70	3.70	51.40	18.60	55.20	58.60
1998-99	47.30	3.20	50.50	19.40	55.50	59.50
1999-00	49.69	3.01	52.71	21.69	59.16	62.20
2000-01	52.39	3.13	55.53	23.67	62.82	66.00
2001-02	56.39	3.11	59.51	25.66	67.94	71.10
2002-03(RE)	60.91	2.33	63.24	27.66	72.80	75.30

Source: Reserve Bank of India, *Hand Book of Statistics on Indian Economy, 2002.*

macroeconomic stability by achieving sufficient revenue surplus, eliminating fiscal deficit and removing fiscal impediments in the effective conduct of monetary policy and prudential debt management consistent with fiscal sustainability through limits on the Central Government borrowings, debt and deficits, greater transparency in fiscal operation of the Central Government and conducting fiscal policy in a medium-term framework and for matters connected therewith or incidental thereto."

The major targets of the FRMB Act included elimination of revenue deficit and reduction of fiscal deficit to 2 per cent of GDP by end of fiscal year 2008-09, and restricting the total liabilities of the Central Government to 50 per cent of the estimated GDP at the end of a period of ten years.

FRBM bill has been welcomed as a well intentioned step to clean up public finances and put them on a sustainable footing and for providing credible commitments for fiscal discipline and for creating a more predictable policy scenario (Chandrashekhar and Ghosh, 2004; Karnik, 2002). It is seen as a bulwark against the populist policies of the government (Mishra, 2001). On the other hand, FRBM bill has also been faulted on many accounts. It has been observed that by restricting borrowing from the Reserve Bank of India, it forces the government to borrow at much higher rates from the market. It is also felt that by ignoring the changes in the macroeconomic scenario it makes the legislation excessively rigid and ties the hands of the government to respond to changing needs of the times (Chandrashekhar and Ghosh, 2004). Concerns have also been expressed that by limiting fiscal deficit to 2 per cent of GDP FRBM Act restricts the public investment to a low level. It is also feared that in order to attain the target of zero revenue deficit the government may reduce its social expenditure (Karnik, 2002). At more fundamental level the question has been asked whether the management of fiscal deficit really needs legislation by Parliament limiting borrowing by the centre statutorily (EPW, 2000). It amounts to asking parliament to abdicate its regular budgetary function. The crucial question remains whether the Act will work or future governments will find ways to get away with violations of its provisions one way or the other (Karnik, 2002).

In the last few years several State governments have passed FRBM Acts setting targets for revenue and fiscal deficits and size of debt in line with the Central Act. However, the real impact of these Acts still remains to be seen.

EFC RECOMMENDATIONS FOR FISCAL RESTRUCTURING

In view of the persistence of fiscal deficits the Eleventh Finance Commission (EFC) was specifically asked under para 4 of its ToR to "review the state of the finance of the Union and the States and suggest ways and means by which the governments, collectively and severally, may bring about a restructuring of the public finances so as to restore budgetary balance and maintain macroeconomic stability." EFC suggested a restructuring programme, which envisaged the following fiscal targets in relation to GDP to be realized by 2004-05:

- A reduction of 5.77 per cent point in the revenue deficit, which should come down to zero in case of States and 1 per cent in case of the Centre.
- Fiscal deficit to be brought down by 3.34 percentage point to 4.50 in case of Centre and 2.50 in case of States.
- An increase of revenue receipt of 2.58 per cent in case of States and 1.74 per cent in case of the Centre.
- Expenditure restructuring by reducing revenue expenditure by 2.37 per cent points and an increase of 2.94 per cent point in capital expenditure.

Detailed suggestions were given by the EFC for enhancing revenue — GDP ratio and bringing down revenue expenditure.

Incentivisation of Central Transfers

Subsequently the EFC was also asked by the Government of India to "draw a monitorable fiscal reforms programme aimed at reduction of revenue deficit of the state and recommend the manner in which the grants to States to cover the assessed deficit in their Non-Plan Revenue account may be linked to progress in implementing the programme." In its Supplementary Report the EFC majority view has recommended a monitorable fiscal reform programmes for all States. According to the suggested scheme 15 per cent of the revenue deficit grants meant for 15 States and a matching contribution by Central Government were be credited into an incentive fund from which fiscal performance based grants were to be made available to all 25 States.

The GoI has accepted the recommendation and taken follow up measures to implement them. The States have been asked to frame their Medium Term Fiscal Reforms Programme. The performance is to be measured on the basis of a single monitorable fiscal objective, that is, improvement in the revenue deficit by at least 5 per cent of its revenues.

The incentive-based transfer scheme has been criticised as being violative of the principle of sharing of resources between the States and the Centre as envisaged in the Constitution on the one hand, while some feel that the amount of funds available for incentive payments may not be enough to incentivise the transfers (Rao, 2002: 3267).

Unfinished Agenda of Fiscal Reforms

Many important steps have been taken in the past decade to gear up the fiscal policy to meet the challenges of the economic reforms. Tax rates have been reduced, tax structure rationalized, tax base widened and tax administration modernised. Efforts have also been made to restructure public expenditure and curb its growth, though with relatively less success. However, as our critical review of fiscal trends during the last decade shows the targets with respect to reduction of fiscal and revenue deficits have not been met. There have been important slippages on the fiscal front especially at the State level, though the Central Government has also not set a good example of fiscal prudence either. The current level of combined fiscal deficits of the Centre and the States continues to be at an unsustainable level of around 10 per cent, with serious implications for the health of public finances as well as savings, investment and economic growth. Restructuring of the public finances along the lines suggested by the EFC continues to present the major challenge for the Central and the States Governments in the years to come.

The major components of the unfinished agenda of fiscal reforms are briefly mentioned below:

Determined efforts have to be made to bring down the level of fiscal and revenue deficits to sustainable levels. The fiscal responsibility acts need to be enacted by the Central and the State Governments at the earliest and the specified targets strictly adhered to. Bringing down of fiscal deficits would require firm action both on the revenue raising and expenditure sides.

The need to contain the growth of unproductive revenue expenditure remains high. Downsizing of the government to reduce salary burden, curtailing wasteful expenditure and reviewing the schemes which have outlived their utility remains high in this context. Improvement in the performance of the public sector enterprises along with a programme of disinvestment are critical to the goal of reducing revenue deficits and reduce pressure on the government finances. Reform of the power sector has to be high on the reform agenda. This is undoubtedly the single most important area connected to the programme of fiscal reform and economic growth at the State level.

Public expenditure has to be restructured by reducing revenue expenditure and increasing capital expenditure particularly on economic and social infrastructure, which is essential to increase investment and accelerate economic growth. Thus, total expenditure as a ratio of GDP is not likely to go down.

In view of the above it becomes imperative to increase the ratio of government revenues, both tax and non-tax, to GDP has to be increased, for which there is a definite scope. Since the tariff rates have to be brought down further in line with the rates prevailing in other countries, while commodity taxes need to be further rationalized and harmonized, additional tax revenues can only be generated by raising the collection of direct taxes. In case of income tax there is a need to bring down the rates at the lower levels of income and introduce progressivity to a greater extent, while keeping the ceiling rates within reasonable limits. However, there is ample scope of expanding the base of income tax substantially and improve tax administration to realize more revenue. There is fairly widespread tax evasion in the case of informal sector and professionals like doctors, lawyers, etc. Presumptive tax needs to be imposed on a much wider scale to bring so far untaxed people in the tax net. Punishment for tax evasion needs to be made more stringent to improve tax compliance.

Services, which now contribute more than half of GDP,

provide a large untapped area for raising more revenue. Some initiatives have been taken in the past in this direction, but the process has to be carried forward with speed. Taxation of services also raises important issues regarding the sharing of tax base or tax revenues with the States, which need to be settled in a judicious manner.

In case of State Governments also a reluctance to raise more resources through taxation has been noticed. The State tax-SDP ratio shows wide variations across States and has remained static in most of the cases. State Governments have to show greater initiative to raise more resources and reform their tax system. Rationalisation of rates, broadening of the tax base, ensuring more effective compliance, revamping of tax administration machinery are some important areas where effective action is required. There is a good scope for raising more revenues by taxing the agricultural sector particularly through reform of the land revenue system. Introduction of national level VAT on goods and services is another area of fiscal challenge which has to be adequately addressed in the coming years.

The developments of the past decade have put severe strains on the Centre-State financial relations. The change over to the global revenue sharing system, following the recommendations of the EFC, by which 29.5 per cent revenue of the Centre will be shared with the states, is expected to increase buoyancy of revenue transfers to states, though dispute about the adequacy of the present ratio of sharing continue. Nevertheless, the fact remains that the level of financial transfers from the Centre to the states as per cent of GDP has gone down over the previous decade putting further strains on state finances. The need for tax harmonization between states has also reduced their ability to raise more resources by changing the tax rates. The introduction of uniform rates of VAT across states is also expected to constrict the ability of states to raise more resources. Sharing of revenue from taxes on services is also a ticklish issue to be addressed in future. Similarly the system of plan transfers based on 30 per cent grant and 70 per cent loan formula has also remained a matter of dispute and also introduces an element of built in increase in the indebtedness of states. Another area with important long term implications for state finances is that of the newly introduced system of incentive based transfers, which is likely to benefit the richer and better performing states more and thus lead to increase in inter-state disparities over the long run. These changes have reduced the fiscal autonomy of the State Governments to a considerable extent and have important implications for Centre-State financial relations and the working of the federal system in the country. Perhaps it is time now to constitute a Commission, which should go into these questions and amend the Constitution to bring about a better balance in the Centre-State financial relations after a thorough debate on its recommendations.

REFERENCES

Acharya, Shankar (2002), "Macro-Economic Management in the Nineties", *Economic and Political Weekly*, Vol. 37, No. 16, April 20.

Bajpai, Nirupam and J.D. Sachs (1999), "Fiscal Policy in India's Economic Reforms", in Sachs, Jeffery, D., Ashutosh Varshney and Nirupam Bajpai (eds.), *India in the Era of Economic Reforms*, Oxford University Press, New Delhi.

Chandrasekhar, C.P. & Jayati Ghosh (2004), "Fiscal Responsibility and Democratic Accountability," *Macroscan*, July 26th.

Chelliah, Raja, J. (1996), *Towards Sustainable Growth : Essays in Fiscal and Financial Sector Reforms in India*, Oxford University Press, Delhi.

EPW Editorial (2000), "Fiscal Responsibility: Why an Act?", *Economic and Political Weekly*, April 8.

Joshi, Vijay and I.M.D. Little (1996), *India's Economic Reforms, 1991-2001*, Oxford University Press, Delhi.

Karnik, Ajit (2002), "Fiscal Responsibility and Budget Management Bill: Offering Credible Commitments," *Economic and Political Weekly*, January 19.

Lahiri, Ashok K. (2000), "Sub-National Public Finance in India", *Economic and Political Weekly*, Vol. 35, No. 18, April 29.

Mishra, Veena (2001), Fiscal Deficits and Fiscal Responsibility Act, *Economic and Political Weekly*, Vol. 36, No. 8.

Rao, M. Govinda (2002), "State Finances in India : Issues and Challenges", *Economic and Political Weekly*, Vol. 37, August 3.

CONTRIBUTORS

Rakesh Mohan, Secretary, Economic Affairs, Govt. of India, New Delhi & Former Deputy Governor, Reserve Bank of India.

Ameer Batcha, Faculty Member, Bankers' Training College, Mumbai & General Manager, RBI, Mumbai.

Arun Kumar Misra, Economist, Canara Bank, HO, Bangalore.

A.K. Ramanathan, Professor of Economics, IIT, Mumbai.

Debesh Roy, Asst. General Manager, NABARD, Lucknow.

P. Satish, Chief General Manager, NABARD, Mumbai.

Manoranjan Sharma, Chief Economist, Canara Bank, Head Office, Bangalore.

Ashima Goyal, Professor, Indira Gandhi Institute of Development Research (IGIDR), Goregaon, Mumbai.

Amitabh Kumar, IRS, Director-General, Competition Commission, Government of India, Paryavaran Bhavan, New Delhi.

Ajit Kumar Singh, Director, Giri Institute of Development Studies, Aliganj, Sector O, Lucknow.